With the
29th Regiment
in the Peninsula

With the
29th Regiment in the Peninsula
& the 60th Rifles in Canada
1807-1832

Charles Leslie

*With the 29th Regiment in the Peninsula
& the 60th Rifles in Canada, 1807-1832*
by Charles Leslie

Leonaur is an imprint of Oakpast Ltd

Material original to this edition and presentation of the text in this form copyright © 2012 Oakpast Ltd

First published in 1887 under the title
Military Journal of Colonel Leslie, K.H., of Balquhain Whilst Serving With the 29th Regt. in the Peninsula, and the 60th Rifles in Canada, &c., 1807-1832

ISBN: 978-0-85706-974-0 (hardcover)
ISBN: 978-0-85706-975-7 (softcover)

http://www.leonaur.com

Publisher's Notes

The views expressed in this book are not necessarily those of the publisher.

Contents

Preface	7
1807-8	9
1809	84
1810-11	165
1812-1813	207
1816-1832	252
Appendices	285
Notes For Portugal	287
Notes For Spain	292
Resume of Spanish Notes	304
Notes For Halifax	306
Anecdotes of Colonel Leslie	309

Preface

This military journal appears to begin and end rather abruptly, because only those parts are given which refer to subjects of public interest. It is hoped it may prove both amusing and instructive. The notes *at the end* were not left ready for press by Colonel Leslie; it has therefore been necessary to add them separately.

Part 1
1807-8

In February, 1807, I received orders to join the depot of my regiment in the Isle of Wight. I took my passage in one of the Aberdeen smacks, and, after a stormy voyage, I arrived in London, 1st March.

On the 13th March I reached Southampton. Next morning, the 14th, I went to Cowes and Newport. On the following day, the 15th, I reported myself to Colonel Barlow, the commandant of the army depot, at Parkhurst Barracks, which was the general rendezvous for all the officers and recruits who were under orders to join their respective corps on foreign service.

Owing to this circumstance there was at times an immense assemblage of officers at Parkhurst Barracks. Many of these officers proved to be very disorderly in their habits. This chiefly arose from a wrong system then pursued of allowing officers who had got into scrapes in their own corps to exchange into other regiments, instead of bringing them to trial in their own, in order to save its credit. These persons always found respectable officers belonging to regiments quartered in unhealthy stations who were willing to give them a large sum to exchange. Consequently, a young man, on joining the depot, required to act with great prudence and circumspection, and to be guarded in his choice of acquaintances and associates. Fortunately for me, I found there two very respectable young men, also belonging to the 29th Regiment—a Mr. Duguid and another gentleman. We formed a little mess, and dined together.

Two or three weeks after my arrival, although I had never done any duty, and had not even attained the length of this goose-step in the way of drill, I was ordered on detachment to Niton with a party of the New South Wales Corps, under the command of Captain Cumming. This hero, I found, had tried his luck in several corps, but had never remained long in any. It appeared that he knew little or nothing of his real professional duties. He aspired to be a great martinet, especially in petty barrack detail. Nothing would satisfy him but that he must have the soldiers' rooms washed and scrubbed out every morning. He issued an order that man, woman, and child, and every article of bedding, furniture, &c., should be turned out into the barrack-yard every morning at daybreak. This was a sharp order for any corps, but it fell particularly hard on the New South Walesers, inasmuch as every man of them had a wife, and many had two, three, or more children—they having been expressly permitted, as married men, to volunteer from other corps to go to that colony.

After the second morning the men began to grumble, and on the third, a cold, bleak day, they swore it was all nonsense to be so humbugged. On the fourth day they positively refused to obey the captain's orders. They put on their accoutrements, knapsacks, &c., and paraded with their arms in marching order, and determined to march back to the depot. I then knew nothing of military affairs, but common-sense told me that all was wrong here. I ventured to interfere, first expostulating with the captain, and then, by a short harangue to the mutineers, I brought both parties to reason, and the soldiers returned to their duty. After ruralising two or three weeks in this romantic part of the island, to my great satisfaction I was released from my post, and I returned to Newport in April.

Soon afterwards the 56th Regiment, under command of Colonel Keating, arrived, and was quartered at Newport preparatory to their embarking for India. My cousin, Charles Macdonell, was a captain in this regiment. I had never seen him. Happening to go into a shop where he chanced to be, I observed an officer staring at me. He then exclaimed, "Oh! you must be my cousin, you so much resemble some of the Leslie family I have seen!"

I pleaded guilty, and was delighted to make his acquaintance, as he was a most worthy gentleman.

One day I observed a dashingly dressed, gentlemanlike young

man brought into barracks handcuffed under a military escort. A court-martial was immediately ordered to assemble, and the young man was accused of desertion, and was found guilty. I was present in court. The *Hue and Cry* was produced, in which he was advertised under a dozen different characters. He was sentenced to be flogged, and he received *five hundred lashes*. His story was a singular one. He was the natural son of a noble lord. He was brought up luxuriously, but having a bent for dissipation and gambling, he spent his all. By way of raising the wind, he enlisted with various recruiting parties, the bounty to recruits being at that period very high. He no sooner pocketed his bounty than he deserted, and by his dexterity in assuming different characters, for a length of time he evaded detection. However, one evening he was recognised lounging in the saloons at Drury Lane, and was taken as a deserter, and sent a prisoner to the depot in the Isle of Wight. He was lodged in the guard-room, and retained the dress which he wore when he was taken. He availed himself of this circumstance to effect his escape, which he did in the following manner. Soon after daybreak on the morning following his arrival, he pretended to be taken with an urgent necessity of nature. A sentinel, as is customary, was sent to conduct him to the privy. Having plenty of money, he put a few guineas into the sentinel's hand—in short, bribed him, not only to allow him to escape, but to desert with him. He made the best of his way to Hyde with all expedition, gave out that his rascally servant had robbed him and deserted with all his money, and that he was determined to pursue him. He got a well-manned boat, and proceeded to Portsmouth. On landing he gave the boatmen money, and told them to go and refresh themselves, while he went to the general to get an order for parties to search for his servant. He then went to a Jew's shop, sold his fashionable toggery, and purchased others of a different sort. After this he took a place in the first coach to London, fairly escaped, and commenced a new career. Soon afterwards he was again discovered, brought back a prisoner to the Isle of Wight, and was tried and convicted as I have described.

It was announced to us in May, 1807, that the 29th Regiment was to return home from North America, and consequently that we were to remain at the depot till its arrival. My cousin, Captain Charles Macdonell, of the 56th Regiment, introduced me to Colonel Keating, who very kindly offered to get me promoted to a lieutenancy in his regiment. I felt very grateful to him, but I declined his obliging offer, because I had always a desire to serve in any campaign that might take place on the continent of Europe.

On the 26th July, 1807, Captain Nestor arrived at the depot with some invalids of the 29th Regiment, which had arrived at Spithead, and was waiting there for orders. Lieutenant Gregory and I left the depot next day, the 27th, with the captain, to join the regiment; but on our arrival at Portsmouth we found that it had sailed for the Downs some hours before. We were therefore obliged to proceed by coach to London next morning. On the following day we set out for Deal. On our arrival at Canterbury we found that the coach went no farther. We were transferred to a sort of two-horse carriage of the most wretched description, and we did not reach Deal until late at night—so bad were the public conveyances at that time.

On the 30th July I went on board the headquarter ship and reported myself to the commanding officer, Brevet Lieutenant-Colonel White. All were then in full expectation that the regiment would be employed in the expedition then assembling in the Downs, and which shortly afterwards proceeded to Copenhagen, and took that capital. But to our great disappointment, a few hours afterwards the 29th Regiment received orders to disembark, and occupy the barracks at Deal. We afterwards learned that the reason why we were ordered to remain was that the authorities at the Horse Guards supposed the regiment could not be in a fit state for immediate service, owing to its having been so long in North America. Never was there a greater mistake. All the general officers who beheld its disembarkation declared that it was one of the finest corps they had ever seen.

One evening in September, 1807, while we were sitting at mess, we heard a sharp firing of musketry. We went into the barrack-yard, and several shots flew over our heads. We went to the barrack-gate, which opened towards the sea, there being only the public road betwixt the gate and the beach. There we found that a large smuggling boat had run on shore, having passed through the fleet then lying at anchor. The smugglers had been observed, and were pursued by the boats of the men-of-war, who fired on them. The moment the smugglers landed they drew up and most daringly returned the fire. While both parties were thus engaged, we observed the wives and children of the smugglers, assisted by their friends, emptying the boat of its cargo of brandy casks and boxes of lace, and hurrying off with them, regardless of the firing, which was still maintained with great energy; nor did it entirely cease until the smugglers actually brought down a couple of horses, yoked them to the boat, and started off with it at a hard-gallop to the country. As we had then no authority or orders to interfere, we could only be silent spectators of this extraordinary scene. The melancholy part remains to be told. On the part of the Royal Navy one man was killed, and two or three were severely wounded. It was said that the smugglers lost several men, but as they were carried off by their friends the number could not be ascertained. After the affair was over the custom-house officers applied for military assistance. Our light company was immediately turned out, and assisted in searching houses on the outskirts of the town. Some fifty kegs of brandy were got, but the greater part had been sent into the country. It seemed very odd that none of the revenue people appeared to seize the goods when landing, or even to prevent the smugglers from carrying them off.

On the 7th November, 1807, the 29th Regiment received a route to march to Bradborn, where there was one of those low wooden temporary barracks, situated on a swampy common between Hythe and Ashford, in Kent. In passing through Dover, Lord Forbes, who then commanded there, very kindly invited all the officers to breakfast, but owing to my having command of the baggage-guard, I could not partake of his hospitality. This was a tremendously long day's march, being upwards of thirty miles.

At Bradborn we received intelligence that the expedition to Copenhagen had proved eminently successful, and that the city had been taken, and the Danish fleet secured. Rumours began to circulate that a force was to be assembled to be employed on some secret service, and a few days afterwards a route arrived ordering the regiment to march for Portsmouth. On the 28th November, 1807, the 29th Regiment commenced its march. Passing through Tenterden, we reached Cranbrooke. Next day being Sunday, we halted. During the day there was a considerable fall of snow. On Monday we reached Tunbridge Wells. They told me at the hotel in the morning that I had slept with my head in one county and my heels in another. On the 1st December we reached East Grinstead; on the 2nd, Cuckfield; on the 3rd, Horsham; on the 4th, Petworth. Next day we halted, and availed ourselves of this opportunity to inspect the splendid mansion of the Earl of Egremont, situated in a richly-wooded park contiguous to the town. On the 6th we marched through Midhurst to Petersfield, where General Gordon Forbes, the colonel of the 29th Regiment, inspected us. He afterwards entertained all the officers at a splendid dinner, and informed us that we were to embark next day to be employed on a secret expedition, but that we were not to divulge this to our men. This was glorious news for us. The chance of seeing active service inspired all us youngsters with visions of military glory.

We marched from Petersfield at an early hour on the morning of the 7th December, 1807. On reaching the small town of Cosham, about four miles from Portsmouth, the Honourable Lieutenant-Colonel Lake, who had recently been appointed to the 29th, joined, and took command of the regiment. He ordered us to halt, and invited all the officers to breakfast, which he had previously ordered. He likewise treated all the men to a substantial repast.

The regiment then proceeded to Portsmouth, and, without halting, marched directly to the point, where we found flat-bottomed boats all ready to carry us on board the transports. This was the first notice that the men had of their embarkation for foreign service. They were all instantly in great spirits, and they entered the boats with as great coolness and regularity as if they had only been going to cross a ferry. They embarked amidst the cheers of an immense multitude and the sounds of martial music, to which they cheerfully responded. It was, however, very distressing to hear the wailings of many poor women and children, who were thus suddenly separated from their husbands and fathers, and left destitute on the beach. A certain number belonging to each company were afterwards permitted to embark.

We now learned that a force, under the command of Sir Brent Spencer, was to be employed on a secret service, and that the transports were ordered to be provisioned for six months—but our destination remained a profound mystery. No one could divine what was the object of the expedition, or to what part of the world it was likely to go. We only knew that we were to sail under sealed orders with the first fair wind after the 10th December, 1807.

The force employed in this expedition consisted of the 29th, 50th, 32nd, and 82nd Regiments, with four battalions of the German Legion, and some batteries of artillery, all under the command of Lieutenant-General Sir Brent Spencer, and Major-Generals Sir Miles Nightingale and Sir Robert Macfarlane commanding brigades. Afterwards the 6th, 9th, 91st, and a detachment of the 95th Rifles, under the command of Lieutenant-General Bowes, joined.

The 29th Regiment embarked in four transports. The headquarter ship, under Lieutenant-Colonel Lake, took four companies; the second, under Captain Richard Egerton, took two companies; the third, under Captain Nestor, two companies; and the fourth, the *John* transport, under Captain Gauntlett, took one company and the weakly men—this being also the hospital ship. In this latter ship I embarked. We had the pleasure and advantage of having on board with us the regimental surgeon, the eminent Mr. Guthrie; also Lieutenant Humphrey, a clever, amusing Irishman, and Ensign Alexander Young, who played Scotch reels on the violin with great vigour, to our amusement. This gentleman had been a captain in the Aberdeenshire Militia, and had volunteered to serve in the regular army.

The convoy was detained by contrary winds after the day fixed for sailing. The wind being from the west proved that our destination lay in that direction, and not to the eastward. During this delay an officer from the regiment was sent on shore every day to receive orders from the office of the adjutant-general of the expedition. On one occasion, it being my turn to perform this duty, I had to take a copy of a code of private signals established for the expedition, and the officers commanding each transport received three letters, each sealed, marked private, and numbered I, II, III.

On the 20th December, 1807, the wind having chopped round to the eastward, the convoy, consisting of about three hundred sail, got under weigh, and passed through the Needles. On the 22nd we were fairly in the Bay of Biscay. Next day the wind failed. It became a dead calm, and the sea was as smooth as glass, so that we lowered our boats and exchanged visits with the other transports.

During the night the wind began to rise, coming from the southwest, directly in our teeth. I happened to be on the midnight watch. The night was pitchy dark; suddenly I observed a round red light, and called the attention of the mate to it. He said, "It is the Commodore's light, but how on earth can it be so near us, for just before dark I saw him a long way ahead?"

While in this wonderment, the light suddenly enlarged, and moved two or three times quickly up and down, and then vanished, leaving us in still greater amazement. It was a meteor, which proved to be a bad omen. The wind increased in violence. All sail was shortened. It was evident that a gale of wind had commenced. The gale was so bad on the 25th—Christmas day—that we could only get a small quantity of meat cooked, and we were obliged to eat our food seated like Turks on sails on the cabin floor. This tremendous storm continued for some time with unabated fury. The fleet was much dispersed, and we were buffeted about for three days without being able to make an inch of headway. On the 28th December, the commodore hoisted a blue and yellow checked flag. This puzzled our ship-captain, and also our commander. No one could make anything of it. When I I saw that they all gave it up, I suggested that they had better look into the code of private signals, and they would find that it meant to repair to the rendezvous No. I. They did so, and I was right. The sealed order No. I. being opened, it was found that the fleet was directed to rendezvous off Lisbon. We were, if possible, more anxious than ever to get on, but we were doomed to disappointment. The hurricane still raged. On the 31st December only two vessels remained in sight. Our vessel, which was by no means of large size, was straining very much. No fire could be lighted, and no progress could be made. We were therefore obliged to lay too. The ship-captain represented all the difficulties to the commanding officer, and recommended that we should bear up for Falmouth. This was accordingly done, and on the morning of the 1st January, 1808, we found ourselves scudding back to England under almost bare poles, much against our inclination. We were driven past Falmouth, and then tried for Plymouth, but as the storm still blew furiously, no pilot could reach us. We therefore proceeded to Portsmouth, and arrived at the Motherbank on the 5th January, 1808.

Two or three days afterwards we received orders to go to Falmouth. We sailed again from Portsmouth as soon as the wind became fair, which it did on the 18th January—Queen Charlotte's birthday. We reached Falmouth on the 23rd. We found that a considerable part of the convoy had reassembled there; but amongst many of the transports missing, there was one belonging to the 29th Regiment, under Captain Nestor. After a lapse of some days, we learned that the missing ships had reached the fleet then blockading Lisbon.

It now transpired that our original destination had been to take possession of Lisbon; but owing to our delay, the French army had succeeded in occupying that capital, so that our primary object was frustrated.

While we were lying at Falmouth waiting orders, time passed heavily—being cooped up in a transport in harbour is very tantalising. Many officers who could afford it lived at hotels on shore, but the state of my finances did not admit of such indulgence. We were anchored on a mass of oyster-beds, embedded on copper-banks, and consequently impregnated with that poisonous metal. There was a great temptation to indulge in the poisonous delicacies.

On the 18th February, 1808, all the officers had gone on shore except myself, who was left in charge of the ship. On hearing the bugle sound for orders on board the headquarter ship, I sent the orderly-sergeant on board, and he shortly afterwards returned and brought me the orderly-book. On opening it I was most agreeably surprised to find I had been promoted to a lieutenancy without purchase, and had been gazetted on the 10th February, with several others under me. This was an important step for me, who had neither money nor political friend to rely on. I lost no time in announcing this rise in the military profession to my father, as an evidence that I had not only got a commission, but that I was also getting on.

Our destination still remained a mystery. Orders, however, at length arrived for our departure: but except the general and the naval commander, no one knew whither. Our former excitement and expectation of soon entering on some particular service were revived. We were glad to depart, particularly as the whole country was wrapped in a wintery mantle of snow.

The fleet sailed from Falmouth with a fair wind on the 23rd February, 1808. In two or three days we were nearly across the Bay of Biscay, which, although as usual very rough, was comparatively smooth to what it was two month before. During one of the nights there was a vessel not far from us firing signal-guns of distress; but the sea was so rough that no boat could venture to go to her assistance.

Fortunately the weather moderated after daybreak, and the vessels nearest the one in distress succeeded in rescuing the troops and crew on board; and well they did so, for the ship went down head-foremost soon after being abandoned. A heroic action deserves to be recorded; two ladies, officers' wives, on board the distressed vessel sat on deck during the whole night, cutting up flannel petticoats, and made them into cartridge bags.

We kept a southerly course, and on the morning of the 28th February, 1808, we made the Rock of Lisbon; and in the evening we passed outside the English fleet blockading the port, the French being then in possession of the country. We continued running down the coast of Portugal, and late on the 1st March, 1808, we made Cape St. Vincent. Here the wind became light, so that we made but little way for some days. Then we found that our course was taking an easterly direction. The ship-captain informed us that we were off Cadiz, and that as there were no orders to stop there, we must be going up the straits. His surmise proved correct. Next day we were off Trafalgar, of glorious memory, and at daylight on the morning of the 12th March we beheld the pillars of Hercules. There lay the verdant highlands of Spain on the left hand, and the bold blue hills of Africa on the right.

The channel gradually closed, and we were about to enter the gut, when we observed another large convoy bearing down upon us from the southward. This was a fleet of merchantmen, also from England. It was a grand and magnificent sight to see five or six hundred vessels, all under the British flag, passing in proud defiance within gunshot of the hostile shore.

All eyes were eagerly gazing to catch the first glimpse of the celebrated Rock of Gibraltar. On approaching the headland, one more distant, of stupendous magnificence, began to open upon us. All stood mute for a while, and then everyone called out, "That is Gibraltar!"

There it stood before us in all its grandeur. But before we had time to get a good view of it with our telescopes, a loud booming of heavy artillery came over the water on our ears, from the left hand, and we observed large shot plunging or ricocheting on the water at no great distance from us. Our glasses were instantly turned in that direction. We had just passed the old Moorish town of Tariffa, having an island in front of it, on the Spanish coast, when we observed a squadron of Spanish gunboats which had been concealed behind this island. These gunboats were very annoying to our trade, and even to ships of war. They concealed themselves behind the island of Tariffa, and in coves and creeks, and when there was no wind they dashed out and attacked the vessels which were becalmed, with little risk to themselves, as they were mere specks on the water. The Spanish gunboats were pushing along the shore, and blazing away at us. On reaching Cape Cabrito point the fleet was obliged to hug the Spanish shore, in order to enter the Bay of Gibraltar, and to avoid being carried past it by the current. The Spaniards took advantage of this to open their batteries on us, while another squadron of gunboats coming from Algeçiras attempted to intercept us. A heavy fire was kept up for a time, but they hit only two or three of the transports, and the headquarters ship of the 50th Regiment, commanded by Colonel George Walker, which suffered considerably, several soldiers being killed and wounded; the mate of the vessel was also shot dead. The Spaniards, no doubt, might have done us considerable damage had not a detachment of our own gunboats come out from Gibraltar to protect us. The British gunboats formed line between us and the enemy, and the wind and tide being in our favour, we passed rapidly on. We soon entered the bay, when a magnificent view of Gibraltar appeared before us as a splendid panorama.

We came to anchor on the 12th March, 1808, at the new mole, near the dockyard, and on the 14th all the English portion of the expedition disembarked, and the four battalions of the German Legion proceeded on to Sicily under Major-General Macfarlane.

I found it a great relief to be once more on *terra firma* after such a long confinement, having been on board ship since the 7th December, without having slept even one night on shore during the whole winter. Our duty had been also rather severe, owing to there being only three subalterns on board, one for each watch. We had each to be four long hours on deck every night while at sea—that is to say, for example, I went on watch the first night at eight o'clock in the evening, and remained until twelve o'clock at night; next night I went on at midnight, and remained till four o'clock in the morning; and on the following night I was called up at four o'clock, and remained till eight o'clock in the morning. No matter how stormy, how wet, or how dark it might be, turn out of your warm berth you must, creep upon deck, and then shiver for hours, having nothing on earth to do.

We had left England some ten days before buried in snow, and here we were in the Garden of Eden. The transition was very remarkable. The almond and other fruit trees were in full bloom, and the orange-groves dazzling with ripe fruit and snow-white blossoms.

What our destination was to be was still a mystery. We were not amalgamated with the other troops of the garrison; indeed, our force had so overcrowded the place that there was not sufficient accommodation for all. Two companies of each regiment were ordered on board the transports, and were relieved every fortnight; all, however, took their turn in the various garrison duties.

I lost no time in exploring the wonders of this remarkable place, and in making myself acquainted with all the details of its exterior defences. One day, shortly after our arrival, I passed out at the land-port gate to the neutral ground, in order, if possible, to inspect the Spanish lines and works, which were erected across the low peninsula. In my eagerness I got closer up to them than prudence warranted, when I observed a Spanish soldier coming rapidly out towards me. This rather puzzled me. It was too late to retreat, and I had no firearms. So I thought it best to put on a bold face, and await his coming close. I was greatly relieved when he held up a couple of dead kids, evidently offering them for sale. We came to a parley. I had acquired a few words of Spanish from my grammar. I was giving him to understand that I did not want the kids, when the officer on duty came out, took off his hat, and saluted me. I returned his salute, and he wished me *"buenas dias,"* and then inquired for news.

I said we had not heard from England for some time, and that I was in a hurry. So I made him a bow, and shook hands, and got clear off, well pleased to be out of the scrape, as what I had done was contrary to the garrison regulations. I thought the Spaniards were very civil enemies.

Amongst the numerous vessels of war then stationed at Gibraltar was the *Red Wing,* a well-manned, fast-sailing sloop of war. Her gallant commander, Captain Usher, was a most daring and enterprising officer. He was continually cruising along the Spanish coast, dashing at the enemy's ships and convoys going from one port to another. He always succeeded in making captures in defiance of the Spanish cruisers and batteries. We used to watch him when he quitted the bay. He used to stand over close to the Spanish shore, when the Spaniards would pay him the compliment of saluting him with heavy guns from the batteries as he dashed along. We could often see the splashes of the shots as they struck the sea, some dropping short, others going over him.

No place is more worthy of the traveller's notice than Gibraltar, and to a military man it is particularly interesting from its natural and artificial strength. In approaching it by sea its formidable and picturesque appearance is very striking. The stupendous height of the rock rising abruptly from the flat sandy plain on the north, or Spanish, side, the cragged peaks of the upper ridge, the length of rock extending towards the south, and ending in the lower rocky ground of Europa Point, present a panorama which cannot be rivalled. The town presents a gay appearance, situated as it is on a declivity on the north-west corner of the rock. It is built like an amphitheatre, ranges of building towering one above the other, all the houses being painted various colours. It is surmounted by an ancient Moorish castle. Long lines of fortifications run along the seafront. The various quays and moles are crowded with shipping of every size and description, British and foreign. The general bluish-grey appearance of the stem rock is enlivened by the rich verdure of the evergreens, and various sorts of fruit-trees embellish the neat gardens attached to the various houses, some of which are built on ledges seeming to overhang the precipitous rock, and others are situated on gentle slopes. Such is the external appearance of Gibraltar.

Nor is it less remarkable within. The diversified nature of the fortifications, their immense extent and impregnable strength, strike every observer. The north front of the rock towards Spain presents an almost perpendicular face. This is pierced with galleries, one above the other, cut out of the solid rock, having portholes for cannon. These tiers of guns look like the broadside of a man-of-war. On the top of the rock, where it is tolerably level, there are mortar batteries and magazines, high in air. All these batteries command the neutral ground. Each gun has its range marked, so that a column approaching, or being in any particular spot, can be hit with certainty. Beneath this commence the regular fortifications of the land-port and water-port, on the north-west angle, and which are continued southwards along the whole sea-front, facing the west, to Europa Point, about two or three miles. From the water-port a long battery, mounted with heavy guns, runs out into the bay in a northerly direction, flanking the neutral ground, and, being on a level with it, sweeping it completely by a cross fire. These formidable works are called by the appropriate name of the Devil's Tongue. This, however, is but a meagre outline of the numerous artificial and natural defences. Viewed as a whole, the rock inspires awe and admiration. The immense storehouses, the vast magazines, the piles of shot and shell lying in every direction, the grand reservoir for water, the order and regularity with which everything is arranged, prove that every preparation is made and held in readiness for a resolute defence.

There are many peculiarities in the town which strike a stranger—such as the various styles of building; but nothing strikes one more than the motley appearance of the inhabitants. These are composed of all nations from every quarter of the globe. All are dressed in the fashion of their several countries. One sees numbers of Arabs and Turks, in their rich loose dresses and morocco slippers; dark Moors, in their white camel-hair cloaks; multitudes of Jews, in their small sealskin caps, blue cassocks, and with bare legs; Greeks, in their splendid costumes; Genoese women, in red cloaks with black spots; Spanish beauties, in their native attire, *saya* and *mantilla*, pacing gracefully along; English and French, in every variety of fashion; military uniforms of every shade, without uniformity, from the kilted Highlander to the dark-green rifleman. In fact, the public square at any time of the day represents the most perfect *bal costumé* that can be imagined. It must be allowed, however, that behind this fancy scene there are some drawbacks. The streets are narrow, and in general by no means clean. A horrid smell of garlic pervades them during the dinner hour.

I was much gratified by having seen Gibraltar. It is a place which every military man ought to visit at least once in his lifetime. But we left it without regret. Owing to its being the time of war, all communication with the country was closed, so that after the first novelty wore off, the garrison became a kind of prison. Boating in the bay was a favourite amusement with some, but it was frequently attended with no small risk from the sudden eddies or gusts of wind. Beyond our military circle we found little or no society. It was not thought proper at that time for the military to associate much with the civilians; nor were the English inhabitants, except those holding public situations, generally admitted to the parties at government house, or to the garrison balls. Our greatest resource was the garrison public library, which contained a valuable collection of all the best works on every subject, and the reading-room, where were newspapers from every country in the world. It is a very handsome public building, which also contains the garrison assembly-rooms, and it was in contemplation to erect billiard-rooms and a tennis-court.

Our expedition still lingered at Gibraltar, now seemingly without any definite object. But we got hints that it was in contemplation that we should make a dash at the fortress of Centa on the opposite coast of Africa, and carry that stronghold of the Spaniards by a *coup de main*.

About the 8th May, 1808, we were surprised to hear the batteries of Algeçiras firing a salute. Shortly afterwards the intelligence was promulgated that there had been a tumult at Madrid on the 2nd May, that the Spaniards had risen against the French, and there had been desperate fighting in the streets. The Spanish people were jealous of French interference in their affairs, and resented the occupation of their country. Being animated by just indignation and high national spirit, they nobly rose to resist and to avenge themselves on their oppressors. Although at Madrid the gallant people had been overpowered by superior numbers, and many had been massacred, yet the spirit of revenge and patriotism rapidly spread over the land. The signals of resistance blazed on the most conspicuous mountains. The banner of freedom waved over every town. The terrible war-cry, *"Guerra! Guerra! a cuchello!"* resounded through the remotest valleys, and was eagerly responded to from the surrounding hills.

The English fleet was then blockading the combined fleets of France and Spain in the harbour of Cadiz. The new turn of affairs seemed to afford a fit opportunity of endeavouring to disunite them, and to secure the one as allies and the other as captives. With a view of promoting the success of this enterprise, the services of our expedition were called into play.

On the 14th May, 1808, sudden orders were given for our immediate embarkation, and so complete were all our arrangements, that in less than four hours every man and all the baggage and provisions were on board the transports, ready to sail the moment the wind should become fair.

On the evening of the 16th May, as the wind appeared to be coming fair, our headquarter ship had unmoored, and shortened cable as a preparation to be ready to start, but it seemed that she had taken in too much cable, as she dragged her anchor, and before it was observed, she had drifted within range of the Spanish batteries at Algeçiras. They opened a sharp fire upon her; she, however, escaped with little damage, only one large shot having hit her, going through the quarter gallery.

The wind having come fair from the eastward, the whole of the convoy got under weigh at daybreak on the 17th May. In passing from the bay into the straits, many of the transports got rather close to the Spanish shore. The Spaniards, not being yet aware whether our movements were of a friendly or hostile nature, saluted us from their numerous batteries with showers of round shot. Fortunately their practice was not very accurate. Although we were so close that we could see the artillerymen in the embrasures leading their guns and pointing them at us, yet they did us no great damage.

We arrived off Cadiz next day, the 18th May, and joined the blockading fleet under Lord Collingwood and Admiral Purvis. We stood off and on for a day or two, and were then ordered to anchor close inshore. From our position we could clearly see every ship of the enemy's fleet, because, from their lying in the upper harbour, there was only the low, narrow strip of land which unites

Cadiz to the mainland between us and them. The combined fleet consisted of five or six French ships of the line, with some frigates, under the command of Admiral Rossilly, six Spanish sail of the line, and some frigates.

Being anchored pretty much inshore, many of the inhabitants came out to welcome us, shouting, *"Viva, viva, los Ingleses!"* and expressing most earnest wishes to unite with England in driving the French from their town and country. Hundreds of fishing boats now resumed their former occupation. Their sharp, angular lateen sails gave them the resemblance of an encampment on the ocean.

The English admiral and general, taking advantage of this favourable disposition on the part of the people, sent a flag of truce to the governor, the Marquis of Solano, offering our friendly assistance and services. But he declined all overtures, asserting that he had no orders from his government to treat with us. Hence it was universally believed that he was in the French interest. The inhabitants began to get impatient; they urged him to admit the English, and to attack the French fleet, which was cooped up in the inner harbour. He, however, resisted all applications. The people became indignant; a large assemblage of them proceeded to his palace, and called loudly on him to come forth. On his appearing at a balcony, they saluted him with cries of "Peace with England, and war with France!" In reply, he pointed to the English fleet: "There," said he, "my friends, there are your enemies," and he abruptly retired, amidst the groans and execrations of the multitudes. They then dispersed for a time, but only to renew the attempt with increased vigour of combination. The governor, notwithstanding what had occurred, had the imprudence to attend the theatre in the evening, but instead of being received with the customary demonstrations of respect, the audience remained seated in a sullen and foreboding silence. When he sat down, he was assailed with loud cries of "Traitor, traitor!" which was continued during the performance. The unfortunate marquis retired as soon as he could decently get away; and on entering his house, he exclaimed to his wife, "Dearest Mary, I am a lost man!"

Early next morning the mob, infuriated by his obstinacy, rose *en masse*, and proceeding to his residence, in a tumultuous manner demanded to see him. No one appearing, and their request remaining unheeded, they, with the assistance of cannon, forced an entrance; but he and his family had fled. The populace ransacked the residence, made a bonfire of the splendid furniture, and left the place in flames. It appeared that, alter sending his family to a place of safety, the marquis had made his escape by the flat roofs of the neighbouring houses. The city was now in a terrible commotion—a decided revolution had commenced. The French had retired on board their fleet, and put themselves into the best position for defence that circumstances would permit. Meantime the mob was searching in vain all the houses in the district to find the marquis; and amongst other places the house of Mr Peter Strange, an Irish merchant, who had married a lady of Irish parentage, but born and bred at Cadiz. This remarkable woman here most strikingly evinced the possession of a more than ordinary share of the generosity, address, and courage of her countrywomen. She had actually concealed the unfortunate governor, but, with great tact and presence of mind, she had managed to mislead the enraged populace, and to dissuade them from a search of the premises.

On their retreat, however, they were met by a carpenter, who exclaimed, "Have you not found the traitor?"

A thousand voices shouted, "No, no."

"Then," said he, "I will."

And accordingly he placed himself at the head of the infuriated rabble, thirsting for the blood of their devoted victim, and he reconducted them to the house of the noble and devoted heroine. On an entry being forced, he immediately led them to a certain chamber, and, pointing to a particular panel, "There," said he, "there he must be; for I but a short time ago fitted up a place of concealment behind that spot."

Mrs. Strange now exerted all the eloquence that anxiety for the preservation of a fellow-creature inspired her with to combat this statement, and induce them again to retreat. But her efforts were in vain; they had now more than suspicion to act upon, and became furious for their prey. Some of the foremost, therefore, rushed towards the panel. The noble woman instantly threw herself before them, placed herself firmly against the wainscot, and, stretching out her arms, boldly faced the assailants, and presented her own body as a bulwark of defence to the lair of the baited governor.

The headlong career of the exasperated mob was not, however, to be thus checked; they pressed on—a bayonet was thrust through the arms of the devoted lady; and thus, literally pinned to the wainscot, she continued her endeavours, by struggling and supplications, to compel them to desist. Her magnanimous efforts, her sufferings, were, alas! in vain. They dragged her from the spot, and discovered the unhappy marquis. All instantly pounced upon him like tigers; a rope was put round his neck, and they dragged him towards the market-place for summary execution. This disgrace was, however, spared him; for the maddened insurgents, after hurrying him along for a short distance, commenced striking at him with their *cuchellos*, or *stilettos*; and, ere he got half-way to the market-place, he fell pierced with as many wounds as were the number of hands that reached him.

Thus perished the Marquis of Solano, viceroy of Andalusia, captain-general of the province, and governor of Cadiz, a victim to popular vengeance.

When quartered, some years after this event, at Cadiz, I frequently met the noble-minded heroine of this tragic occurrence, both in private society and at the ambassador's parties; and often have I seen the scar—the truly honourable scar—just above the elbow, the effect and evidence of the wound which she so nobly received in the effort to preserve the life of one bound to her by no ties but the common bonds of humanity. And prouder might she honestly be of that so unusual ornament than of the most gorgeous armlet, rich in barbaric pearl and gold, that ever graced an empress.

On the death of the Marquis of Solano, governor of Cadiz, the command was assumed by Don Thomas de Morla.

As an instance how much every class of these noble people felt the degraded state to which their country was reduced by misgovernment, the following incident may be mentioned. A number of boats came daily from the shore to the English fleet, laden with provisions, fruit, &c., for which a ready market was found on board our vessels. One of these boats was lying alongside of our ship, containing a man and two a Spanish smart boys, who acted as his navigators, while he carried on the mercantile department. All on a sudden an alarm was given that the boat was sinking. As I was on watch at the time, I ordered the old man and all his stock to he brought on deck. This was no sooner done than the young rogues pushed off the frail bark, hoisted sail and decamped. We then perceived that the alarm was all a trick. In fact, the youngsters having got tired of waiting, pulled out a plug in the bottom of the boat, and admitted water enough to frighten the old gentleman. However, here he was left on board, and it being then still doubtful whether we were the friends or enemies of his country, the poor fellow was in the utmost despair, not knowing whether he and his property would be respected. Observing his state of mind, I said nothing to him, but I ordered two boards to be placed on a couple of barrels set on end near the quarter-deck. On these boards he arranged all his fruit, bread, eggs, &c., like a stall at a fair. I then placed the old trader behind his stall, and with cash in hand we all began to purchase from him, paying him *d'argent comptant*. The amazement and delight which he expressed were beyond description when he found that not only was his stock fast disappearing, but that he was equally rapidly pocketing ready coin.

The soldiers entered into the spirit of the thing, and bought up every article which he had. When I told him that he should be sent on shore by the first boat that came off in the morning, his joy was complete. He made himself quite at home, and became very amusing, singing a variety of songs and dancing *fandangos* and *boleros*. On entering into conversation with him, we found that he was a very intelligent man. With much feeling he described the state to which his country was reduced by having been betrayed by traitors into the hands of the French, and words could not express his indignation at the trick by which his sovereign had been kidnapped. He concluded by saying, *"Oh, signor, somos bueno gente, pero mal gobernado!"*—"We are a good people, but badly governed!" And he spoke the truth.

After the death of the Marquis of Solano, the people turned their fury against the French, who, seeing the state of affairs, prudently retired on board their vessels. The new governor, Don Thomas de Morla, and the magistrates of Cadiz, in compliance with the public wish, immediately entered into friendly negotiations with our admiral, Lord Collingwood, and our general, Sir Brent Spencer. The Spaniards separated their fleet from the

French, and stationed themselves at the entrance of the inner harbour, so as to cut off all retreat. They then summoned the French to surrender, which they refused to do, but offered to enter into a capitulation with the English. Having the French now completely in their power, the Spaniards rejected all terms, and demanded unconditional surrender, and even declined the assistance of Lord Collingwood and the English fleet. They took the guns, which had been pointed against us, from the sea-walls, and placed them in batteries all round the upper part of the bay, and the fleet and gunboats got ready for action on the lower side. The French were thus hemmed in on all sides.

We were held in readiness to land, having three days' provisions cooked, and our arms and knapsacks prepared to step into flat boats lying alongside of us. Notwithstanding these formidable preparations, the French admiral, Rossilly, gallantly determined not to yield without a trial of strength in defence of his honour.

While matters were in this state, and we were eagerly looking out for the expected signal to disembark, on the 10th June, soon after midday, to our great surprise, a thousand piece of heavy artillery opened fire at once. The two fleets were warmly engaged, while the mortars and gun batteries round the bay poured a concentrated fire on the unfortunate French fleet. It was a magnificent spectacle. We now beheld the two fleets, which our navy had so long anxiously watched, actually engaged in sinking, burning, and destroying one another. As there was only a low strip of land intervening between us and them, we had a full view of the combat. Hard fighting continued without intermission until eight o'clock in the evening, and was renewed occasionally on the two following days, when the French, after suffering a most severe loss, and eight hundred men, finally surrendered.

No sooner were the French vessels taken possession of than the port was opened to us, and we were received with acclamations of joy by all ranks, and our fleet was thus released from a tedious and irksome duty.

General Morla, governor of Cadiz, having received information of the French forces under General Avril, requested General Spencer's assistance. Our expedition immediately received orders to proceed to make a movement against the French army collecting at Tavira and Castro Marino, at the mouth of the Guadiana, in the province of Algarve, with a view of crossing the river and entering Spain at Ayamonte. This force, under General Avril, had been despatched by Junot to suppress any attempt at insurrection in the south, and to move on Cadiz to join Dupont.

We left Cadiz on the 12th June, 1808, and arrived on the 14th at the mouth of the Guadiana, which here forms the frontier separating Spain from Portugal. The object of our expedition was to make a demonstration against the French, and to cover and protect the Spanish insurrection for freedom, which had just commenced at Ayamonte, that it might not be obstructed or put down by the French forces in Portugal in that neighbourhood.

As our troops were in want of fresh provisions, the Spanish governor, anxious to oblige his new allies, promised to procure them for us. Accordingly, the general commanding permitted each ship to send a boat on shore. I had the good fortune to be the officer sent in charge of the one from our ship. But not being aware that the month of the Guadiana consisted of several branches, and that the enemy was in immediate possession of the Portuguese branch, we entered the main channel. On passing a battery which commanded the entrance, we were challenged. But taking no notice we pushed on and soon entered a branch on the Spanish side, by which we reached Ayamonte. I then learned the escape I had just made of being taken prisoner, as the battery we had passed was occupied by the enemy. The other boats had entered by a channel in the Spanish territory. We being the first English who had landed in Spain since the breaking out of the patriotic cause, were received with the most enthusiastic demonstrations of joy by the inhabitants. The governor invited all the officers to an entertainment in the evening, and had provided for us billets in all the best houses. The Spanish officers, both of the army and navy, almost crushed us in their fraternal embraces, and insisted on carrying us from house to house, and introducing us to all the pretty ladies in the place. These dark beauties gave us the most cordial reception, and sang patriotic songs and warlike hymns, accompanied on the guitar or piano. Some of the naval officers, who had been in England, repeatedly sang *God Save the King* and *Rule Britannia*. Their admiration of England's prowess seemed unaffected.

In many houses we observed busts of Mr. Pitt. Everyone extolled him as the greatest man in Europe, and they acknowledged that his policy was the wisest that could have been pursued, and that his causing the Spanish ships of war bearing treasure from South America to be intercepted showed his great foresight, although viewed by them at the time as a breach of international law, because they admitted that the whole of the money was destined as a subsidy for France to be employed by Napoleon against themselves. The governor's supper went off with great harmony. Mutual toasts were given, and bumpers were drunk to the perpetual union of the two nations. We took our departure next morning amidst many regrets at our short acquaintance.

Ayamonte being but a small town, and the market being but scantily supplied, the number of patriots from the neighbourhood then in the town made everything extremely scarce, so that we were able to procure only a few vegetables, fruit, bread, &c. The town was crowded with armed peasantry of all ages, from seventeen to sixty, eager to enrol themselves under the patriotic banner. There is no finer peasantry in the world, they being a hardy race, of robust frames, sober and active habits, high minded, and of generous dispositions. They were armed with any weapons that they could lay hands on: a few muskets, more fowling-pieces, some pikes or poles with old bayonets stuck at the end, and many pitchforks. There was as little uniformity in dress as in arms. Yet, had these brave and resolute people been properly directed under good officers—had all persons in authority been as well-disposed in their country's cause, a formidable army might have been organized. Unfortunately, from the want of experience and skill of the officers in command, and the pusillanimity or traitorous conduct of many members of the various provisional governments, and of the nobility, who, in order to save themselves and their property, too often betrayed the cause of the people by either publicly joining or secretly favouring that of the invaders, the saddest disasters occurred.

The dispersion of these new levies, and of whole armies, which afterwards took place, attests the fact that the superior orders, notwithstanding their boasted nice sense of honour and pompous gravity of character, proved equally destitute of abilities as of moral courage. The inhabitants of towns likewise degenerated after the first burst of patriotism. With a few brilliant exceptions, such as Saragossa and others, they succumbed to whatever authority was in power—friend or foe. Indeed, many of this class are a lazy, indolent set of beings, idly lounging in the streets, basking in the sun by day, wrapped up in their cloaks, smoking cigars, and gambling in the evening. These seem to be their great enjoyments. Puffed up with a false pride, they disdain to work. Few of the master artisans are natives. The principal tailors are Germans, watchmakers generally French, innkeepers Italians; and there were many Irish ready for all work. Consequently, numbers of this improvident race fall into dissolute habits, become quarrelsome companions, and, being of warm tempers, and all armed with *cuchellos*, constantly stuck in their sashes, assassinations were frequent even at noonday. These evils would appear to have originated in the immense wealth formerly imported from South America, and the facility with which fortunes were made there. The natives could thus afford to supply all their wants by importations from foreign countries without any exertion on their own part. Hence trade and commerce came to be neglected; nor were there manufacturers to employ the people.

The demonstration we had made had the desired effect. General Avril was compelled to make a hasty retreat towards Lisbon. The people immediately rose in the province of Algarve on learning the arrival of the British force at Ayamonte. General Maurin, who commanded in that province, unable to resist the hostility of the people even with a force of nearly two thousand men, retreated to Mertola, abandoning his baggage, which fell into the hands of the patriots.

Our expedition was reinforced by the arrival of some additional corps. We cruised for a few days along the coast to Cape St. Vincent, and were recalled to Cadiz, when the intelligence arrived that a large French force under Dupont had entered the Sierra Morena to invade Andalusia. The whole of our troops were disembarked on 3rd July at Port St. Mary's, on the opposite side of the town of Cadiz.

We had the honour of being the first British troops who landed in the Peninsula. The Spaniards received us apparently with many marks of friendship and gladness, shouting *"Viva, viva los Ingleses! Rompez los Franceses!"* But even at that early period of the war, the higher orders seemed to entertain a jealousy of our assistance and undervalued our services. At this season St. Mary's, a remarkably neat town, was particularly gay, being much resorted to by the fashionables of Cadiz as a summer retreat and bathing quarter, and having a superb amphitheatre for bullfights. We saw, consequently, a great deal of society. There were numerous *tertulias*—music and dancing parties. I had the honour of frequently attending those of her Highness Donna M. de Saavedra. This lady was of royal blood, and her husband was at that period president of the grand *junta* of Seville; in fact, the head of the then Spanish government. She had two very accomplished and charming daughters. Thus, though then only a young subaltern, I had opportunities of learning, and actually knew, more of what was going on in the country than many of my seniors.

The unfortunate wife of that fortunate sycophant and minion of the queen, Don Manuel Godoy, had taken refuge here after her husband's escape from the popular rage at Madrid. She being a member of the royal family, our guards had orders to pay her the honours due to her rank on all occasions of her passing. It must have been galling to her feelings to hear the scurrilous songs sung in the streets, recording her husband's misdeeds. So much had the queen been infatuated with this man, and so extraordinary was the confidence or insensibility of her royal consort, that many courtiers, wishing to open his eyes, would slip notes under his cover before dinner, disclosing facts, which he on finding would read, and then laughingly toss them to her majesty for her edification.

From the extreme heat of the weather, we could do little else after early parade than pore over our Spanish grammars. Morning calls were not much the fashion, for in this climate the people rise early to enjoy the cool of the morning.

The ladies first walk to church; and after breakfast, which consists of a cup of chocolate and a morsel of bread, washed down with a glass of cold water, remain at home; lounging generally in loose *deshabille,* or seated in the Moorish fashion on mats, working, or playing the guitar, until the dinner hour, which is usually about two o'clock. Immediately after this, man, woman, and child take a *siesta* for a couple of hours. The ladies then adorn themselves for the amusements of the evening, which consist in promenading, attending the theatre, *tertulias*, &c. As the day declines, one sees the elegant forms of the pretty *signoratas* slowly, but gracefully, pacing along, with erect carriage, to their favourite public walk, they being always in advance of their mammas or the old *duenna*, who follow at a short distance behind.

They still adhere to their national dress, which is certainly unique, and most becoming, being well calculated to display the symmetry of their persons to advantage; and the fair *gaditanas* flatter themselves that they excel in dress, figure, and fortunes all the rest of their countrywomen. Their pretty little feet, in tight silk hose and the neatest slippers in the world, show advantageously under the black *saya*, always put on previously to going out over their undress. It is of satin or silk, ornamented with flounces of network, composed of black jet beads and silk tufts or tassels; the lower hem all round is loaded with small shot, to keep it close to the figure. The bodice, which is likewise richly trimmed with network at the shoulders and cuffs, where there are gold buttons, is closely fitted on. Their fine, dark hair is tastefully dressed and adorned with choice flowers, having a high comb inlaid with gold devices. Over this is thrown the graceful white lace *mantilla*, so placed in the comb as to leave the face and forehead bare. The flowing ends are crossed in front of the chest, and held close by the left arm. In the right hand is held their constant companion, the fan, which they handle with a dexterity peculiar to themselves, playfully tossing it open, or shutting it with great rapidity, or, at times, courting the gentle breeze by fanning themselves; at others, it supplants the parasol, being employed to keep off the sun. When closed, if they look at you, and shake it, held upwards, it means "How do you do." If held pointing downwards, "Come here; I want to speak to you." When in a rage they flirt it open, and close it in a hasty manner, to show their indignation; in fact, they have a complete fan language. They are unquestionably noble-looking women, possessing, exclusive of elegant persons and deportment, most commanding countenances, to which their dark sparkling eyes give a fine expression. But although the Spanish ladies are of forms feminine and features delicate, there is something masculine in their minds. Endowed with undaunted spirit and great natural abilities, graced with manner and address, enlivened with vivacity, ready wit, and extraordinary musical talents, were their minds cultivated with due care to more serious and useful attainments than they generally are, they might be esteemed the most perfect of their sex. But the system of their education is in most cases very deficient. They become more eager to make a display of their charms by showy appearance and ornamental accomplishments than to attend to the duties of domestic life.

The patriots having assumed a red cockade, with the cipher FVII worked upon them, woe to any man who ventured to appear without one. The ladies took a pride in presenting us with this national emblem, embroidered with their own fair hands, as we had been ordered to put them above our black ones.

We found this a very agreeable cantonment. The place was well supplied with all the necessaries, and with numerous luxuries, of life, at a reasonable rate. Being so near Xeres, we got excellent wines, and also a pleasant beverage, something like cider, named *agraz*, made from unripe grapes.

We were kept in constant readiness to take the field, and were actually under orders to march in aid of Generals Reding and Castanos, when information arrived that they having surrounded Dupont's army at Baylen, in the Sierra Morena, the latter had capitulated.

Dupont and his army having become captives, there was no further occasion for our services in this quarter; and more important operations being in contemplation on the shores of Portugal, the whole of the troops were re-embarked on the 19th July, and we sailed next day. We were detained off Cape St. Vincent some days by contrary winds. On the 31st we joined the fleet cruising off Lisbon, and kept standing off and on with them.

On the 3rd August we received orders to make the best of our way to Mondego Bay, to join the expedition which had arrived from England under Sir Arthur Wellesley.

After a pleasant run, we came to anchor in Mondego Bay on the evening of the 6th August. There we received orders to disembark next morning. All was now bustle on board. Animation shone in every countenance. Our anxious hopes of being employed in active service were now about to be realised. Everyone was employed in selecting the few articles requisite for a campaign, and getting their heavy baggage properly secured. This was effected with no small trouble. A tremendous swell caused the ship to roll in the most violent manner, and everything was slipping and flying about.

We got into flat boats soon after midday, but the process of disembarkation became a tedious and dangerous operation. Owing to the swell and dreadful surf, only a few boats could approach the beach, where Portuguese fishermen were employed in wading to meet them and conduct them to the shore. During this we had to remain for hours tossing and rolling about till our time came. Several boats were upset, and one containing a part of our grenadiers lost arms and everything, and the men narrowly escaped with their lives.

It was late when we reached the army encamped on the heights above the small town of Lavos. It was so dark that we had some difficulty in finding our tents; and in regard to food, nothing whatever could be got, so we had to content ourselves with a morsel of ship biscuit and a glass of rum from our haversacks. We then wrapped ourselves in our cloaks, and lay down on the *benty* grass, eagerly seeking repose after our fatigues.

Vain hope! The orderly sergeant disturbed our incipient slumbers by warning us that the army was to be under arms at two o'clock in the morning. Accordingly, half-an-hour before that time, one of those regular tormentors of military life, another orderly sergeant, made his appearance to give us a hint that it was time to be up. Our toilet was soon made: a comb for the head, the corner of a towel for the face, and a brush for the cloak did all that was required.

On the 8th August, without a bugle sounding or the beat of a drum, which might have given notice to the enemy, the whole army was soon under arms.

There we stood steady and motionless until an hour after sunrise. We now began to feel that we were seriously entering upon the active duties and habits of a soldier's life, and we were convinced that although a vigilant alertness is at all times necessary, it becomes indispensable when in front of a victorious and experienced enemy.

There is something most solemn and impressive in beholding at the still hour of morn so many thousands of brave and determined men remaining in such silence. There is something in this more than the bare routine of duty of ordinary military life. Under such circumstances the youthful warrior feels as if called into a new existence, that he is about to open his professional career, and to take part in events of the most animating kind. This contributes to inspire a martial ardour and exalted sentiments, with an eager hope of distinguishing himself in the path of honour, leading to his own advancement, and to the good and glory of his country. Fatigues and dangers are held as nought. The greater the hardships and privations, the more imminent the risk, the more determined is his resolution to encounter them. Although our small army was at the moment but little experienced in the practical art of war, particularly on the grand scale on which it was about to commence; the world did not produce a finer body of men. Every corps was in the highest state of discipline, every heart possessed undaunted courage, ready to dare anything, as the result of the glorious campaign most fully proved. The regiment to which I had the good fortune to belong was at this period one of the finest in his Majesty's service, not only in point of members, but from the excellent system established in the corps. It had attained a high pitch of perfection with regard to discipline, training, and internal economy, and these qualifications were put to the test during several years' constant service in the field in presence of the enemy, and were maintained on all occasions, as will be shown in the sequel.

From our division having landed the last, we found that every animal in the neighbourhood had been purchased, so that it was impossible to get horses or mules to carry our tents and baggage. Our officers were therefore obliged to carry their own haversacks, containing a few shirts, stockings, shaving articles, &c., with their cloaks slung on their shoulder on one side and a canteen of rum on the other. The people received us with open arms. The appearance of our brave fellows, and such a well-appointed army, seemed to inspire them with great confidence.

The French army was supposed to consist of about 20,000 men, and, after deducting garrisons, there might be about 15,000 to meet as in the field.

Our army began its first march in the Peninsula on the 10th August, 1808, at 4 p.m.

But my hopes of glory were nearly being frustrated. After

marching about six miles, to my dismay I received orders to return with a party of the most weakly men, to strike the tents which had been left standing, and to have them packed and delivered over to the commissariat, with further instructions that if I could not get this done by next morning, I was to embark again with my whole party on board the transport. Knowing that it was not my turn for detachment duty, I remonstrated most strongly, but I was told that there was now no time to settle such questions, and that I must instantly proceed. I lost no time in returning. I had the tents struck and packed them. I impressed every country car I could lay hands on, and had them loaded and handed over to the commissary. I instantly recommenced my march to overtake the army, which by a forced march I accomplished that evening. I considered myself most fortunate in getting so well rid of an inglorious duty, which might have deprived me of the chance of making a first campaign and of sharing in its triumphs The Hon. Lieutenant-Colonel Lake expressed himself highly pleased with the successful exertions I had made to rejoin the army. I found the army encamped in a wood, but as our division had no tents, they were in bivouac, or huts made of the branches of trees. From my not being expected, there were no preparations made for me. It was now too late to have a hut erected for me, and not being able to find my cloak, which in the hurry of moving I had left with an officer's servant, I was obliged to lay myself down at the foot of a tree, without any covering whatever. Corporal Chambers observing me in this situation, very attentively took off his jacket and begged leave to throw it over me, which, although but a scanty covering, enabled me to recover from the fatigues of the day by a sound nap.

 The next morning, the 11th August, 1808, we marched for Leiria, a small country town having a large Moorish castle situated on a rocky eminence in it we bivouacked in an olive-grove situated on a range of heights in the rear of the town, which with its ancient towers and steeples formed a most romantic object in our front. We were now in the land of the vine and the olive, which form the principal productions of the country. The general features of Portugal are neither plain nor mountainous, but rather a succession of undulating wooded heights, with plains intervening, with often large barren wastes, so that the country in most parts, except in the vicinity of towns and villages, seems as if it were only partially cultivated. The principal crop is Indian corn, with smaller patches of wheat and barley. The extensive vineyards and numerous olive-groves which cover the richest portions of the land, the orange-groves, orchards, and gardens affording every species of European fruit, give a varied and interesting aspect to the country peculiar to itself. But however beautiful this may be, it was very inconvenient to us, as we had positive orders not to cut any olive or fruit trees; and there being no woods of common forest trees in that particular part of the country, we had no means of constructing huts, and having no tents, we were deprived of all covering except the canopy of heaven.

Every protection being offered to the Portuguese bringing in supplies to the camp, we got bread, wine, and vegetables at a reasonable rate. By this means, and our rations of beef, &c., we contrived to make a tolerable mess.

At this place an unfortunate French commissary was captured. Not being aware that we were in the vicinity, he came into the town to obtain provisions. He was surprised by our men, and was brought in triumph into the camp.

The Portuguese army, 5,000 strong, under the command of General Bernardin de Freire, arrived at Leiria on 12th Aug., 1808. But Sir Arthur Wellesley, not having it in his power to supply them with provisions, General Freire declined to act with us. He remained at Leiria, and gave us only about 1000 infantry, about 400 irregulars, and some squadrons of cavalry.

About midnight there was an alert, the alarm being given that the enemy was advancing. Our brigade was immediately under arms, and the outposts were ordered to be reinforced. For this purpose two companies of the regiment, to one of which I belonged, were sent as advanced piquet. We were posted in an olive wood, with a strong chain of sentries in front. However, nothing extraordinary occurred, except that a few men of the Lisbon Polish Guard, who had made their escape from the French army, came over to us. We were relieved in the following evening at a late hour.

Next morning, on the 13th, we marched and bivouacked at Caviero, near Batalha, from which the enemy's advanced posts had retired only a few hours previously. We had hitherto seen but little of the Portuguese people, and still less of their army, but about 200 of their cavalry joined us here.

The following day we marched towards Alcobaco, but soon after commencing the march the column was halted. All the baggage and women were ordered to remain in the rear. The peasants had given information that an advance body of 2000 French were at a short distance in our front. When we had made the necessary preparations we pushed on, and after a few miles of hasty march, we passed a bivouac which the enemy had quitted only an hour before.

We were soon afterwards formed in contiguous column of brigade in a good position, while the cavalry and light troops were feeling the way in front. The enemy, however, did not choose to wait for us. We dashed after them, and pushed them through Alcobaco in such haste that they left the bullocks which they had killed, but had not had time to serve out to the troops, and also some wagon-loads of stores. As we hurriedly passed through the streets of the town, the inhabitants hailed us with the greatest demonstrations of joy, calling out, *"Viva! viva!"* and the ladies strewed flowers upon us from the balconies. We were halted at a short distance beyond the town, and from our position we could trace the retreat of the enemy for a considerable distance by the clouds of dust which they raised.

We found the heat very oppressive, and the only shelter I could find was under the shadow of a large spreading fig-tree. Alcobaco is a remarkably pretty town, having a royal palace and one of the most magnificent convents in Europe, all the monks being of noble families. They most hospitably entertained all the general officers. So friendly were the people disposed towards us, that on sending our servants into the town to procure wine, they returned not only with the canteens full of excellent wine, but they also brought the money back, the inhabitants refusing to take anything from them. The country in the vicinity is very picturesque and well cultivated.

On the 15th we proceeded to Caldas. In the latter part of the road we descended into a plain of deep sandy soil. There was on either hand a dark pine forest, which had a gloomy appearance. After passing through the town we bivouacked in a most luxuriant vineyard. It was painful to be under the necessity of occupying such a position, and to devastate for a time that which had taken so much industry to cultivate. Caldas is a very neat place. Many of the houses are built in the Italian style. It is a most fashionable watering place, and possesses hot wells and public baths, of which we availed ourselves, and found them most refreshing after our late fatigues. The principal bath-room is a handsome building, and the bath is about 60 feet long by 20 broad and 3 feet deep. It has dressing-rooms on each side. I entered the bath suddenly, and without due precaution, and the water was so warm that it made my pores bleed.

Soon after six o'clock in the evening of the 15th, the alarm was given that our outposts were engaged. Our brigade instantly turned out and marched off to support them. When we had got about two miles, we met General Sir Brent Spencer returning. He explained to us that a party of our 95th Rifle Corps had pushed on too far, and had got into contact with the French outposts, but that they had succeeded in driving the enemy from the long aqueduct and the old Moorish castle of Obidos, of which they retained possession. The 95th Regiment lost a lieutenant and some men in this affair. We retraced our steps, and remained accoutred the whole night.

Next day the army remained perfectly tranquil. Two of our men, who were caught in town against orders, were tried by drum-head court martial, and punished, Colonel Lake at the time telling them that they should not have the honour of meeting the enemy, an event which was hourly expected.

Some thousands of Portuguese troops, under General Friere, joined us here. They were in a very indifferent state, and it could hardly have been otherwise, it having been the French policy to disorganise the whole army.

On the evening of the 16th August I went on advanced post duty. The outlying piquet consisted of fifty men, under Major R. Egerton, Lieutenant Stanus, and myself. It was posted in an open wood, with the chain of sentinels along the outer edge. Stanus and I had to patrol each hour alternately during the whole night.

Soon after daybreak on the 17th August all the piquets were called in. We joined the army, which had already commenced its march towards Obidos, five miles distant. We reached the plain in front of the town and castle about eight o'clock. Here the whole army was formed in mass, each brigade in contiguous columns of battalions at half distance. While waiting in this order, I saw an officer dressed in a plain blue frock-coat, a small low cocked hat, and mounted on a white horse, quite alone, without any attendant, coming up from the rear. He rode up to a flank, seeming to cast a scrutinising glance over the whole. He exchanged a few words with General Spencer, and then passed on to the front. I then discovered that this was Sir Arthur Wellesley, our commander-in-chief.

While we were in this position a careless observer would not, perhaps, have noticed anything particular. He would have seen the arms piled, and the men occupied as they usually are on all occasions of a morning halt—some sitting on their knapsacks, others stretched on the grass, many with a morsel of cold meat on a ration biscuit for a plate in one hand, with a clasp-knife in the other, all doing justice to the contents of their haversacks, and not a few with their heads thrown hack and canteens at their mouths, eagerly gulping down his Majesty's grog, or the wine of the country, while others, whiffing their pipes, were jestingly promising their comrades better billets and softer beds for the next night, or repeating the valorous war-cry of the Portuguese.

But to a person of reflecting mind there was more in this condensed formation than a casual halt required. A close observer would have noticed the silence and anxious looks of the several general officers of brigades, the repeated departure and arrival of staff-officers and *aides-de-camp*, and he would have known that the enemy was not far distant, and that an important event was on the eve of taking place. These reflections were the more impressive owing to our gallant little band of British Islanders being placed in a most peculiar position by the then present state of the Continent. By the despotic and selfish policy of Napoleon, the ban of Europe was pronounced against us, and not even a single ship in the utmost distress had a friendly port whither it could run for refuge, from the cold regions of the North Sea to the milder clime of the Mediterranean. In despite of this proscription, we had audaciously forced our way, and were now assembled in martial array in a foreign land, ready to hurl defiance at the arms of France, which held Europe as a camp armed at all points to resist us. Whilst musing in this strain I felt the importance of our situation. My breast swelled with honourable ambition, proud to be one of the select number of British soldiers who were first to meet the enemy in the Peninsula. Although hitherto we had been precluded from opportunities of acquiring the habits and usages of war on a large scale, yet we felt undaunted, and we were all willing and ready to dare anything against the foe, however much more experienced he might be in the art of war.

Many officers, on observing our significant preparations, were led to form various conjectures, because the enemy hitherto had always retired before us as we advanced towards them. Our gallant Colonel Lake, knowing that I kept a journal, and had a map of the country, asked me how long I thought it would be before we reached Lisbon. I replied that if the enemy continued to retire before us as they had done, we would be there in three or four days. Some Portuguese peasants coming up, I inquired if they knew where the French were. They one and all told me that the enemy was only about one league off, and that they thought they would wait for us. Our surmises were soon cleared up. In a moment the scene became most animated. An order was given for all the women and baggage to go to the rear, and for all the troops to stand to their arms.

The final dispositions for attacking the enemy having been made, the army was put in motion. The only audible order I heard given was by Sir Brent Spencer, who shouted out, "Bring up four hundred of those ragamuffins here, and let them march off to the right." He meant our allies, the Portuguese, who, poor fellows, had little or no uniform, but were merely in white jackets, large broad-brimmed hats turned up at one side, some having feathers, and others none, so that they cut rather a grotesque appearance. We now had every prospect of having what the army had so long and so ardently looked for—an opportunity of meeting the enemy.

The army having broken up from the encampment at Caldas at daylight on the morning of the 17th August, 1808, was assembled in contiguous column on the plain of Obidos, where the final arrangements having been made for the attack, the army was put in motion. Soon after passing through Obidos the columns struck off into different routes to reach the ordered points of attack. That under General Ferguson went to the left, and General Hill's to the right. The centre column proceeded on the main road. The third brigade, consisting of the 29th and 82nd Regiments, under General Nightingale, was in front, and the 29th the leading regiment.

We continued to march direct for the enemy, whom we discovered apparently in three columns, posted on an elevated plain beyond the village of Mamed, having the commanding heights of Rolica at a short distance in their rear. We made a momentary halt; the men were ordered to prime and load; we moved forward through the village of Mamed; after crossing a bridge, formed line and advanced, expecting to engage every moment. When we arrived at the position where we first saw the French posted, we found they had retreated. Their right was filing to the rear, masked by a cloud of skirmishers, posted on some rising ground covered with brushwood at the foot of the mountains, and warmly engaged with General Fane's riflemen. Their left had retired through the village of Columbeira, and occupied the heights of Rolica or Zambugeira, which ran in rear of and commanded that village.

Our artillery took up a position near a windmill on an eminence to the left of the village, which commanded the aforesaid rising ground, and opened a well-directed fire on the enemy.

The 82nd Regiment being ordered to another point of the attack, the 29th broke into open column, and advanced in column of sections through the village of Columbeira, led by the gallant Colonel Lake. They were now much galled by the enemy's sharpshooters from the heights, particularly from a high pinnacle commanding the village, and by a cannonade of round shot on the left. It being observed that the regiment was so much exposed, the left wing was ordered not to follow the right through the village, but to move round it to the left, and hence it did not reach the entrance of the pass until a considerable time after the right wing. The light company of the 29th was also detached with those of the 5th and 82nd Regiments to make a demonstration on a pass farther to the right. On leaving the village the right wing turned to the left through some vineyards, and advanced along the foot of the heights in order to gain the pass, exposed to a flank fire the whole way, from which we suffered considerably.

We now entered the pass, which was extremely steep, narrow,

and craggy, being the dried-up bed of a mountain torrent, so that at some places only two or three men could get up at a time. The enemy kept up a tremendous fire at point-blank upon us, to which not a shot was returned; but we kept eagerly pushing on as fast as circumstances would admit. About half-way up there was a small olive-grove, in which we halted to form, and the men were ordered to take off their haversacks, greatcoats, &c., which was done under a continual shower of bullets. The pass turned again very difficult; we could only advance by files, but no disorder took place, the men showing a laudable anxiety to push forward.

The farther we advanced the more the ravine receded into the centre of the enemy, and numbers were now falling from the continued fire on all sides.

Colonel Lake's horse was shot about this time, upon which Major Way dismounted, and gave up his horse to the colonel.

After clearing the narrow defile, we entered some open ground, thinly wooded, under shelter of which the officers lost no time in forming the men; the whole then pushed forward, and at last gained the wished-for heights; but we were now obliged, under a heavy fire, to take ground to the right, previous to forming in line, in order to give room for the rear to form as they came up, there not being at this time above three or four companies in line, and these much reduced from casualties. When the enemy, who appeared to have been lying down behind a broken earthen fence, which ran rather in an oblique direction along our front, suddenly rose up and opened their fire, their officers seemed to endeavour to restrain them, and apparently urged them on to the charge, as we observed them knocking down the men's firelocks with their swords, but they did not advance.

Colonel Lake called out, "Don't fire, men; don't fire; wait a little, we shall soon charge," (meaning when more companies should come up), adding, "the bayonet is the true weapon for a British soldier," which were his dying words, for, as he moved towards the left to superintend the line being prolonged, he was marked and killed by a skirmisher (as will be shown), and his horse galloped into the French lines.

The right (in consequence of his death), not receiving any orders to advance, opened their fire, and a desperate engagement ensued. Some of the enemy in front of the extreme right, either as a ruse or in earnest, called out that they were poor Swiss, and did not wish to fight against the English; some were actually shaking hands, and a parley ensued, during which the enemy's troops, who had been posted on the side of the ravine, finding we had forced it, and that they were likely to be cut off, began to retire, and coming in the rear of our right dashed through, carrying with them one major, who was dismounted, as before stated, five officers, and about twenty-five privates.

Owing to this accident, and the enemy continuing a tremendous fire from all sides, being left without support or a superior officer to command, and our numbers decreasing very fast, Brevet-Major Egerton seeing the impossibility of making an effectual resistance, ordered us to fall, back upon our left wing, which was still in the rear. We accordingly retired and got under cover of the wood.

On observing this the enemy set up a shout, and then, but not till then, advanced upon us, as if with a view to charge; some individuals on both sides got mixed, and had personal encounters with the bayonet; they, however, did not venture to press us, nor to follow us into the woody ground, where we formed on the left wing, which had now come up, being also joined by the 9th Regiment (which was sent to support the 29th when it was found that they were so seriously engaged). The whole now rapidly pushed forward and cleared the front of the enemy, who, after an ineffectual resistance, were driven from their position.

The 29th were then halted, and on mustering the regiment, there were found one lieutenant-colonel and one lieutenant killed, two captains severely wounded, one major and seven officers and 25 men prisoners, and 177 rank and file lying on the field killed and wounded—making a total of 214, exclusive of several officers who were hit, but were not returned as wounded. The whole of those taken prisoners belonged to the 3rd or 4th right companies, and not any from the left wing. There were but three officers remaining in the right wing, of whom I was one.

That Colonel Lake was killed by a sharpshooter was ascertained by the officers who were taken prisoners. There were two brothers named Bellegarde, forming part of the escort which conducted them to the rear. These brothers were eagerly disputing which of them had the honour of killing the colonel, one declaring that he was lying under a bush close to Colonel Lake, and deliberately shot him while he was giving orders and forming the line. The horse, as stated, sprang forward into the French line, where he was taken, and was afterwards returned to the regiment in the most handsome manner by General Laborde, when we were doing duty in Lisbon with the French army, previous to their embarkation, in consequence of the Convention of Cintra.

To show that the regiment was not in disorder when we arrived at the top, I may state that after clearing the wood where we had re-formed, and were advancing in column of sections, a ball knocked off the steel of a sergeant's halbert, who was leading the section in front of me, which came flying backwards and struck Major Way, who, being dismounted, was walking alongside. Soon afterwards, when we were forming line, I saw his sword broken by a ball, whilst in the act of waving it and cheering the men. When he was taken prisoner, as before related, General Laborde gave him permission to retain the hilt of his sword, in which a part of the blade was still remaining; however, the escort (who behaved very brutally to him) afterwards made him throw it away.

We afterwards understood that it was not intended the 29th should have so soon attacked the strong pass, nor penetrate so far as we did, but were merely in the first instance to have occupied the village of Columbeira, and make a demonstration on the enemy's centre, whilst General Ferguson on the left, and General Hill on the right, should attack and turn his flanks. By some mistake, however, the order was misunderstood, and our gallant colonel pushed on. This account of the battle of Rolica, the correctness of which can be established by the testimony of several officers, I deem sufficient to prove:

1. That the 9th Regiment did not force a separate pass.
2. That the 29th Regiment did not arrive in disorder at the top.
3. That the French did not break through the midst of the regiment, slaying the colonel and making sixty prisoners, as was asserted by Colonel Napier in his *History of the Peninsular War*.

With regard to General Breunier's assertion, that he, with only two companies, broke the 29th Regiment, I have to observe that it may no doubt be true that he sent two companies from his own left, but it ought at the same time to have been stated that those companies could only have come in support of troops already defending the debouch of the pass, and that neither they nor others broke through the centre of the regiment; because, at the time stated, it is sufficiently proved that there were not formed more than the remains of three or four weak companies, reduced by the dreadful fire they had been exposed to, so that he would have had no great achievement to boast of, even if correct.

While we were engaged in this desperate conflict, the enemy's balls which passed through our ranks or over our heads fell amongst the 9th Regiment, which was moving up in our rear to support us. They, not being aware that we were so immediately in their front, because the wood concealed us from their view, some of their leading companies opened their fire upon us, nor could this be stopped until they had occasioned serious casualties in our ranks. They, however, soon afterwards rushed up and formed upon our left. We all dashed boldly on. The enemy gave way at all points. They again attempted to make a stand at Zambugeira. We continued to pursue them, but as our cavalry was not up to follow the pursuit, we were at last ordered to halt, and the enemy continued their retreat on the road to Torres Vedras. We took up a good position. The army re-formed in order of battle, and we received orders to remain accoutred, and ready to fall in at a moment's warning. Strong piquets were posted in the front and rear, and every precaution that was necessary in the circumstances was taken.

The baggage did not come up till late in the evening. My servant had been severely wounded by a ball through his arm, so I had no one to do anything for me, and no means of cooking. I was fain to content myself with a morsel of cold beef and a ration biscuit which I found in my haversack, wrapped myself up in my cloak, and lay down on the open heath, and slept soundly until before daybreak, when we stood to our arms. The number of officers' servants who were hit in this action was very remarkable, there being no less than fifteen amongst the killed and wounded. Indeed, so close had been the hand-to-hand fighting, that Private Millbank, servant of Captain Davie of the company to which I belonged, was found lying opposite to a Frenchman, both killed by bayonet wounds. Two soldiers of my company had been schoolfellows with me in the same Latin class at the Grammar School of Aberdeen. One of them, Connon, lost his leg in this battle, and the other, Boyle, was afterwards killed in another engagement. One of the men who had been punished the previous day, scorning to remain in the rear while his corps was engaged, gallantly broke away from the hospital sergeant, joined his company, and fought most daringly against the enemy. He escaped unhurt, while his lamented colonel, who, not twenty-four hours before, had told him that he should not have that honour, was now lying a bloody corpse on the field of battle. When we were moving on to the attack, Captain Harding, of the quartermaster-general's department, was riding with Lieutenant-Colonel Bradford, one of the deputy adjutant-generals, leading the column and looking out for the enemy. The captain observed a party of *tirailleurs* posted behind a bank, in the act of preparing to fire. He immediately stooped down, saying, "Take care, Bradford; they are going to fire." The colonel, instead of stooping, raised himself erect to look out where they were. At the same instant the enemy fired a volley, and six balls pierced the gallant colonel's breast, while Harding escaped unhurt.

On the morning of the 18th we stood to our arms about two o'clock, and as the enemy had entirely disappeared from our front, we received orders to march. I was on the baggage guard. After having proceeded some miles, I was engaged in observing whether all the mules of our brigade were keeping well together, when a bullet went whizzing past my head. This shot came from the left flank, and must have been fired either by some party of the enemy hovering on that flank, or by some of the peasantry. We learned that we were not following the enemy, but were merely on the road to the coast to cover the disembarkment of expected reinforcements. In the evening we bivouacked at Lourinha, a small dirty village.

On the next day, the 19th, we proceeded to Vimieiro, a small country town situated about a couple miles from the coast, in order, as we understood, to cover the disembarkment of a reinforcement of troops under Generals Anstruther and Ackland. The army was posted on a circular chain of heights, which runs betwixt the town and the sea, and then stretches eastward into the country. The town is situated on a rising ground in front, having a flat low space between it and the foot of the heights, on which were placed the parks of artillery, commissary stores, bullock-carts, oxen, &c. The whole had an imposing and picturesque effect, particularly at night, when illuminated with the glare of the camp-fires on the heights, and those of the artillery and stores, surrounded by groups of soldiers and peasants, drivers, and others, in the low grounds, and the advanced guard beyond the town.

Hitherto we had slept without any cover, because the woods we had passed through were principally olive-groves, which we had positive orders not to cut down. But there being a fir-wood in this vicinity, many of the officers got huts erected.

About eleven o'clock on the night of the 20th August the alarm was given that the enemy was advancing. All the inlying piquets were ordered under arms, and a brigade was ordered to occupy some heights on our left, and the rest of the army lay down by their arms. Nothing, however, occurred, and we got a quiet nap. We were on the alert an hour before daybreak on the 21st, and the expected reinforcement under General Anstruther marched into the camp about six o'clock a.m., after which we were dismissed. I ordered my servant to have breakfast ready about eight o'clock, and then threw myself down to get another nap. I was aroused about eight o'clock by the bugles sounding the alarm, the drums beating to arms, and the general cry of "Stand to your arms." This we accordingly did. I had just time to devour a morsel of bread, and swallow a tin of bad tea, while the men were falling in. We then observed a column of the enemy's cavalry on the top of some heights about a mile in our front, and moving to the left.

Our brigade, consisting of the 29th and 82nd Regiments, under General Nightingale, were ordered to support the force under General Ferguson, who was posted on the heights to the left of the town, and towards which the enemy's column was pointing. Our men were directed to leave their knapsacks in the camp under charge of the quarter guard.

On reaching the foot of the heights the road was found to be so steep and heavy that two companies of the 29th Regiment were ordered to assist in dragging the guns up in addition to the artillery horses. After gaining the ascent, the 29th, being the leading regiment, moved along the edge of the heights, which sloped abruptly to the valley below. After advancing some distance we were deployed into line. From this point we had a grand view of the country to our right below. We could distinctly observe every movement made either by our own right wing, which was posted partly in the town and along a rising ground to a wood on the extreme right, or those made by the enemy, then forming preparatory to their grand attack, while the light troops and riflemen were warmly engaged.

It was a most inspiring sight to see the enemy advancing to attack. They were formed in two lines, the second supporting the front one. They moved with great rapidity and admirable regularity, pushing on in the most gallant and daring manner, apparently making a dash to force our centre. It had been thought that the first attack would have been made on the left, where we were, and every preparation had been made accordingly. Sir Arthur Wellesley and General Spencer were riding through our ranks, but on their observing that the centre was attacked with such vivacity, their attention was turned to that point, particularly when it was found that a column of the enemy emerging from a wood was attempting to penetrate down the valley which separated our heights from the town and our right wing. General Spencer exclaimed, "Can nothing be done to save the centre?" He immediately ordered the grenadier and another company of the 29th Regiment, whose right rested on the verge of the height commanding this valley, to retire to the rear, and brought up two or three pieces of artillery, which opened a well-directed fire. This, with the imposing attitude of our right companies, effectually checked the column of the enemy, who would have been exposed to a flank fire had they persisted in advancing. They went to the right about, and retired in haste. While watching with intense interest the progress of the enemy's attack on our centre, we observed a party of the 43rd Light Infantry stealing out of the village and moving behind a wall to gain the right flank of the enemy's lines, on which they opened a fire at the moment when the enemy came in contact with our troops in position. The French had been allowed to come close, then our gallant fellows, suddenly springing up, rapidly poured on them two or three volleys with great precision, and rushing on, charged with the bayonet. We soon had the satisfaction of seeing the enemy broken and retreating in the utmost haste and disorder, closely pursued by our small force of cavalry, under Colonel Taylor, who made a brilliant charge, in which he fell. About this part of the action I first observed Sir Harry Burrard making his appearance. He had just disembarked, and assumed the command.

Scarcely was this victorious achievement and repulse of the enemy accomplished by the right wing, when we on the left wing were attacked with great vigour. The enemy attempted to turn the extreme left of our lines, so that the 29th Regiment, being on the right, had at first little to do. But the light companies of the 29th, 82nd, and 40th Regiments were warmly engaged in skirmishing close in our front. Our men were ordered to lie flat down on the ground, yet we lost a considerable number. We found it rather difficult to keep the men still, as they were impatient to get forward, particularly as they were under a galling fire, and were not allowed to return a shot. We at length received orders to advance against a column of the enemy. Their artillery opened a very sharp fire upon us, but as our line was descending, they did little execution, although every shot passed close over our heads. On our approaching the enemy we were not allowed to fire, but we marched steadily on, ready to charge. They began to waver, retired some distance, and fired about. But on our continuing to push on, they rapidly retreated before we could close with them, and abandoned all their guns.

We were then halted, and as the enemy appeared to have gone completely off, our men were allowed to stand at ease. While resting in this manner we suddenly observed a column of the enemy, which, it seems, had remained concealed in a village on the opposite heights, make a dash down as if they meant to attack us, while a body of cavalry at the same time appeared on our right flank, threatening to turn and attack us in that flank. We were instantly ordered to form four deep, which formation afforded the advantage of showing a front to meet the enemy in line, and at the same time of sufficient strength to resist cavalry. On the enemy approaching the low ground a destructive fire was opened upon him by the 71st Regiment, and the light companies of the 29th and 8th Regiments, which had been lying there concealed by the willow beds and bushes, unknown to us, much less to this column of the enemy, who, after returning an irregular fire, broke and fled in the utmost disorder up the hill again to the village. Our artillery opened a well-directed fire upon them, and we beheld the poor fellows scampering off in all directions to avoid the shot and shells continually falling amongst them. They made an attempt to rally in the village again, but our guns made it too hot for them, so they continued their flight right over the hill, and disappeared from our view. The cavalry, which had threatened us, on observing the discomfiture of their infantry, rapidly retired. This was the last expiring effort on the part of the French that day. We afterwards observed the shattered remains of their various columns concentrating again at a point nearly two miles off. We now learned that our right wing had been equally successful, and had defeated the enemy. From the description of this battle it will be observed that, from the nature of the ground, it consisted of two distinct actions, both fought nearly at the same time, and about a mile or two apart.

While we were still halted on the field of battle, I saw Sir Arthur Wellesley shake hands with General Ferguson, saying, "Ferguson, we have had a glorious day. Your brigade—the 40th, 71st, and 91st Regiments—has done wonders. Now I am ready." We all, of course, expected that we would instantly move on to follow up our victory, and prevent the defeated foe from rallying. All were disappointed that we remained inactive. Even the private soldiers were making remarks, saying that they wondered that the general did not go on, and that they were never in better humour for a brush or in better trim. The knapsacks had been left in camp, and we were in proper light order for a pursuit, and had marched only a short distance, while the French had been marching the whole of the previous night, and were heavily laden, every man being dressed in long white linen frocks—their shakos, pouches, &c., covered with the same material—and their uniform coats being strapped outside their knapsacks. Moreover, several men of each company had to carry large mess-tins, and others cooking-kettles.

After resting some time on our arms, we marched back to our bivouac, with bands playing and colours flying. It was amusing to see many of the French soldiers who had been taken prisoners, or who had come over to us, marching along with our men, with shouldered arms and fixed bayonets, apparently in the greatest good humour, and all expressing anxious wishes to be sent to England. Two genteel-looking young men who were among the prisoners told me that they were conscripts torn from their homes, and that when their regiment gave way they threw themselves down, pretending to be wounded, in order that they might fall into our hands.

Fatigue parties having been left to bury the dead, many of our men had possessed themselves of the French white linen frocks; and it was grotesque enough to see Highland soldiers strolling about the bivouac in these dresses. The field of battle after the action presented a curious feature from so many lying killed and wounded. There were quantities of letters and papers strewed about in all directions. I picked up a bill for several hundred *francs* payable in Paris, from which it appeared that the poor fellow who had owned it had gone as a substitute, and had received this bill in part payment. Many of the letters were from parents and friends, but not a word of politics was to be found in any of them.

We afterwards understood that the reason we had not followed the defeated enemy was owing to orders from Sir Harry Burrard. Sir Arthur Wellesley had intended that, as the enemy had fled in an easterly direction, part of our army should have marched by their right to the south-west, and thus gain the pass of Torres Vedras before the French, so as to cut off their retreat, while he with the left wing should continue to follow up the enemy, but Sir Harry Burrard said we had done enough for one day, and that it might be imprudent to push on too hastily. We were all convinced that had Sir Arthur Wellesley been allowed to execute his plan the most splendid advantages would have resulted.

In this battle the 60th Riflemen, who were all Germans, showed great tact in taking advantage of the ground, and dexterity in the use of their arms. General Fane, who commanded the light troops, observing one of these men successfully hit one or two French officers who were gallantly exposing themselves in front leading on their men, exclaimed in the excitement of the moment, "Well done, my fine fellow! I will give you half a doubloon for every other one you bring down." The man coolly loaded again, fired, and hit another, then looking at the general, he said gravely, "By Gott, I vill make my vortune."

We stood to arms next morning, the 22nd August, as usual from before daybreak until an hour after sunrise. After this, I, with some other officers, went to bathe. We passed through a ravine leading through the heights on which we were encamped, towards the sea. Through this ravine runs the small rivulet Vimieiro, on whose banks are some ancient Roman baths. On our return we strolled into the park of artillery, to look at the French guns which had been captured on the preceding day. We were remarking on the uncouth appearance of their material—the heavy carriages of the guns, the long, narrow, coffin-looking *tumbrils*, the miserably made harness with rope traces, the large collars and broad wooden hems, and the small, punchy, rough, heavy-heeled horses—and wondering how with such clumsy gear they had kept up such a dreadful fire on us, when we suddenly observed several men and officers running past us as if they were mad, shouting out, "Stand to your arms! stand to your arms! The French are advancing."

We, of course, started off to our camp in double time. There we found all the troops getting under arms. The whole were soon formed up, ready to meet any foe. We hastened to occupy the same positions on the heights which we had done during the battle the day before, and were all eagerly looking out for the enemy, but none could be discovered. After some delay we received orders to march back to our bivouac. It proved to have been a false alarm. This arose from a party of French cavalry having approached our advanced guard bearing a flag of truce, and escorting General Kellerman, who was sent by Marshal Junot to propose an armistice.

In the afternoon it was announced that Lieutenant-General Sir Hew Darymple had arrived, and was now the commander-in-chief of the army, so that within twenty-four hours we had three different commanders. It began to be whispered in camp that the French wished to make terms with us. Being anxious to learn if there was any truth in these reports, I went into Vimieiro, and, sure enough, while standing in the street near the headquarters, I heard a staff-officer, who had just come out, exclaim to some of his friends, "Well, it is all over; we shall have no more fighting."

The army did not much relish this news, all being flushed with the recent victories. The officers were excited with the hopes of reaping more laurels, and gaining promotion; and the soldiers looked forward to the prospect of getting more booty. Many of them, particularly the light troops, had acquired rich prizes taken from the enemy. Indeed, every Frenchman who was killed or taken prisoner had a good supply of plunder either in money or plate, taken from the Portuguese. They had not spared even the sacred vessels used in the churches, remains of which were found in their knapsacks bruised or broken up. All ranks and degrees of our army anticipated, moreover, a considerable amount of prize-money, from the immense treasures which it was well known that the French had amassed by the contributions exacted from the Portuguese.

Several delays occurred in the negotiation of the proposed armistice, and it was thought that the French wished to gain time. On the 23rd August we marched to Ramalhal. We bivouacked on some sterile heights, covered with heath and struggling clumps of pine-trees, which, being of little value, we were allowed to cut down, and to hut ourselves in a proper manner for the first time. The men's huts were laid out in streets like a regular encampment, and those of the officers in a line along the rear, but these, frail *wigwam* abodes not being waterproof, we got completely drenched during the night by a thunder and heavy rains. Our only resource was to get up and stand in our cloaks round large fires.

On the 28th August we marched to Torres Vedras, and were encamped on some heights on the north of the town. Torres Vedras (glass towers) is a small old town, with an ancient Moorish castle, situated on a round height in the middle of a romantic valley, surrounded with hills, ornamented with wood. A rivulet meanders through this vale, and passes close under the town, where there is a bridge. This was the line of demarcation between us and the enemy, who occupied the heights on the other side of the place.

I proceeded towards the town with several other officers with the view of purchasing some of the good things of this life. On arriving at the bridge we were stopped, and were prevented from entering the town by a sentinel. He was a Scotchman, one of the gallant 92nd Highlanders. No art or persuasion would induce him to let us pass. We were returning grumbling and growling, when we happened to meet the quartermaster of the 92nd Regiment. On learning our dilemma, he assured us that he would manage that we should get over the bridge. So wheeling about we followed him up to the sentry, who again peremptorily ordered us to halt. The following dialogue then took place:

Quartermaster—"Oh! how is this, Donald?"

Sentry—"Ye maunna pass! I hae orders to lat naebody gang by!"

Quartermaster—"But I am the quartermaster of your regiment, and I must get over to get things required for the corps."

Sentry—"Oh, weel, sir, I canna help it; I maun obey my orders—nae person to pass the brig."

There was no disputing with the sturdy Highlander. However, seeing his quartermaster rather puzzled, the sentry gave a significant glance to some stepping-stones lower down the river, and slyly whispered to him:

"I ha'e nae orders to stop fouk gaein' that gait."

Accordingly we took the hint, made the best of our way across the stones into the town, where we found but little to recompense us for our trouble. Most of the houses and shops were closed, and few people were to be met with in the streets. It appeared that the inhabitants, seeing two hostile armies on either side of them, feared that the place might become the scene of a bloody struggle. Such, however, was not to be the case. We learned from a staff-officer the reason why the sentry on the bridge had orders to allow no one to pass. In consequence of the armistice, Torres Vedras was by mutual agreement not to be occupied by the troops of either party, but to be held as a neutral place.

Wishing to procure a Portuguese grammar, I was looking out for a bookseller's shop. At last I descried something like one. The place appeared to be filled up with a counter and shelves all round, filled, apparently, with books all bound in parchment. On entering I observed an officer in the uniform of the quartermaster-general. He had his back to the door, and was reading a paper. I waited for some time, thinking that the shopman had gone into a back room, and would soon appear. The officer, however, on turning and observing me, very politely begged to know if I wished for anything. On my explaining that I thought it was a bookseller's shop he laughed and said it was a lawyer's office, which he intended to convert into the quartermaster-general's office, and was waiting for his clerks and paper. This was Lord ——.

On the 31st August we moved to Sobral do Monte Graeea, a small neat town. Having gone into the town, I observed a battalion of the Portuguese Police Guards, who had made their escape through the French army from Lisbon, march into the public square. They formed line, and on my going in front to look at them, the commanding officer opened ranks, and ordered a general salute. On observing that there was no general or other superior officer on the ground, I enquired at a Portuguese *fidalgo* standing near me why they had saluted. He, to my no small surprise, informed me that the honour was meant for me and some other officers, as being English.

The French rear-guard was still close in our front. One of their piquets, not having received proper orders in regard to the armistice, took post in advance rather too close to one of ours. Our piquet rather hastily drove back the French one, but fortunately without loss on either side.

On the 2nd September we marched towards Bucelles, but on learning that the French rear-guard had not yet evacuated the place, we were halted on the heights above the town. While we were waiting in this position, we were rather surprised at hearing what appeared to be a sharp firing, and we were led to imagine that some misunderstanding had taken place with our advance guard. However, we soon learned that it was only the Portuguese inhabitants, who, as soon as the French had marched off, began firing pistols and letting off rockets, in rejoicing for the event, and to celebrate our entry into the town. We soon afterwards moved on, and passed through the place amidst the cheers and warm congratulations of the inhabitants. We continued our route to St. Antonio de Tozal, near which we bivouacked.

St. Antonio de Tozal is a very beautiful village, adjacent to which is the country palace of the Patriarch of Lisbon, situated in pretty grounds, with very fine and extensive gardens. There is also in the vicinity a Moorish aqueduct. This place affords a most desirable summer retreat for the citizens of Lisbon, and we were informed that in former times many English people who came to Lisbon for their health resided here.

The ground on which we were bivouacked was open, and had not even a tree for shelter. However, in rear of our regiment there were fortunately some windmills. My captain, Davy, and myself took possession of one of them, and a capital quarter it made. This was the first time I had slept under any sort of cover since we had taken the field. Being in a fine part of the country, we were plentifully supplied with all sorts of provisions and wine, so that we lived remarkably well. A soldier brought us one day a very fine turkey, which he offered for sale at the low price of eighteen pence. As his character was not particularly good, I had my doubts about his having come by the turkey honestly. He swore that he had bought it at a village not far off, so away I marched him, turkey and all. On entering the village we found all the people in great commotion, and a crowd assembled round an old dame, who with loud vociferations was detailing how she had been plundered, and lamenting the loss of her darling bird, the careful mother of a numerous young progeny. To her surprise, and to the delight of all the villagers, the valued bird was restored safe and sound. All were astonished at getting redress in so satisfactory a manner. The soldier looked very blue; so strictly were the orders against plundering enforced that he was tried, convicted, and punished before sunset that evening.

During the respite we had from war's alarms, the untoward Convention of Cintra was in progress, and we were rather impatient to know the result. One day all the officers of our regiment who had been taken prisoner at the battle of Rolica returned into camp, having been released in consequence of the convention having been amicably concluded. Civilities began to pass between the two armies. One day I saw a French dragoon riding through our camp as if he had been in his own. He had come with a present of fine tea to some of our generals. On examining his arms, I found that his carbine was of English manufacture, and was marked "Tower."

Our officers who had been prisoners told us some of their adventures during their captivity. When they were taken prisoners a French soldier made a thrust at Lieutenant Langton with his bayonet, which fortunately hit the buff sword-belt. He was about to repeat the thrust when a French officer knocked up the bayonet with his sword, and thus saved Langton's life. When our officers were conducted to General Delaborde, he very courteously said, "Gentlemen, now that you are prisoners, we are no longer enemies." Major Way, who retained the hilt of his sword in his hand, only a few inches of the blade remaining, the remainder having been broken off by a musket-shot, requested the general's permission to retain the hilt, which was very politely granted. The prisoners were ordered to proceed to Lisbon. Among the escort who attended them were two brothers named Bellegarde, one a *sous-officier* and the other a private. Both laid claim to having had the honour of shooting our gallant Colonel Lake. The *sous-officier* insisted that it was he who did it, and that he was lying behind a bush, and when the colonel was in front of his men superintending the forming of our line, he had a fair opportunity, and shot him through the body; and when the colonel fell, his horse, Black Jack, sprang forward into the French lines. Some of the escort afterwards made Major Way throw away the hilt of his sword, which annoyed him very much.

The French, to intimidate the Portuguese, gave out everywhere that they had defeated the English, and they paraded the prisoners in great triumph through Lisbon. Marshal Junot, dreading that the Portuguese would learn the truth from the prisoners, ordered them to be confined on board the Russian fleet, then lying in the Tagus, so as to prevent all communication. However, on his return to Lisbon, after having been defeated at Vimieiro, the marshal was very civil to them, and invited then to dinner every day, taking care to send carriages for them, and to send them back in the same manner in the evening. He lived at free quarters in gorgeous style in the splendid palace of Baron Quentilles. Every luxury was there to be found. On one occasion one of our officers remarked to another:

"What a capital dinner this is. It wants only a glass of English porter for our cheese to make it perfect."

This was overheard by a servant, who to their surprise said:

"Porter, porter! Would you like some?" and he quickly brought them some excellent brown stout.

With our officers also came back Lieutenant Wills of the Engineers, who had been taken prisoner at the battle of Vimiero in a most absurd way. He was acting on the staff of General Anstruther, and about the time the French infantry were giving way, he was directed by the general to go to the Portuguese cavalry, then on the right, and tell them to advance. He instantly rode off; but being very short-sighted, on observing a body of cavalry a little in advance of the right, he dashed up to the commanding officer and delivered the order to advance in French, which language was then used as the medium of communication with the Portuguese army. The French officer coolly replied, *"Ah, oui, monsieur, mais en attendant vous etes mon prisonnier,"* while at the same time our poor lieutenant descried several pistols pointed at his head by the French soldiers. To his utter dismay he found out that he had gone up to a body of the enemy, in whose hands he remained a prisoner.

About this time the 79th Regiment, which had recently arrived, marched into our bivouac. I went with some officers one morning to look at them. Their colonel, old Sir Allan Cameron, whose son commanded the regiment, came with them. He had a marquee on the right of the line. On perceiving us he came out of his tent, and addressing himself to us, said:

"Weel, gentlemen, are ye come to see my breechless boys? Gang up to them, they'll bear inspection. Allan'll wheel them for ye."

They were really a remarkably fine corps, and their worthy colonel was very proud of them. After the parade was over he mixed with the officers and men, and having just got letters from Scotland, he had something to tell to every one of them, he called them all by their names, Donald, or Ranald, or Roderick, and he looked like a venerable patriarch in the midst of his tribe.

The whole of our force was marched into the gardens or park at Campo Grande. We had orders to rest on our arms, and no one was allowed to go outside the iron railings. Sentinels were posted at all the gates to prevent any of the military from going out, or any of the people from getting in. We waited there with great patience. Evening came, and still no orders to move on or to get into quarters. Being reluctant to eat a tough beefsteak in the open air when there were such savoury smells streaming from the various restaurants and saloons, under pretence of wishing to get some necessary articles for the men, we got an officer of the guard to pass us out. We soon had a capital dinner at a *casa de pasta,* or eating-house. When it was getting late I took a stroll up the street, observing the numerous houses, all well lighted up, and listening to the sounds of singing and music proceeding from them. Soon I heard a voice in broken English say:

"How you do, sir? You please come up. Come, sir!"

I looked up and saw a gentleman at a window waving his hand to me. So, ready for an adventure, up I went. I was cordially received by some gentlemen who had come out from Lisbon to see us. They insisted on my staying to supper with them. There I saw for the first time an excellent fish called *save,* something in the taste like a salmon, only the flesh is of a white rose colour. We had plenty of delicious wine. The gentlemen played the guitar, sang and danced. They expressed their regret that they had no ladies with them, as their families were afraid to venture out in such warlike limes. They would not allow me to return to the gardens to bivouac in the cold air, but gave me a mattress and a cloak, and assured me that one of them would call me up the moment the troops began to stir in the gardens in front, which was done accordingly. I quietly stepped in as the corps was getting under arms about three o'clock in the morning.

Our brigade, the 29th and 50th Regiments, marched, on the morning of the 12th September, into Lisbon, and took post in the Campo St. Anna, a large friendly square in the upper part of the town, in which is situated the *placa de torres,* or amphitheatre, for the bullfights. We had positive orders that no one should quit the square, or even enter into the houses, so that we could not accept the pressing invitations of the inhabitants who requested us to come in and take refreshments. They, however, very kindly brought out chairs and sofas for us to sit on or lie down upon. Many opened their *porte-cocheres,* that we might get underneath and be sheltered from the sun. At night I stepped into the amphitheatre, and took a nap in one of the boxes.

The French occupied all the lower part of the town, and were encamped in all the large public squares. They had loaded cannon pointed down each street leading from them. Constant patrols were kept going to see that all was quiet, the French patrolling up to our posts, and we down to theirs. To the astonishment of the Portuguese, these patrols were constantly meeting and passing one another, neither cutting the throats of the other. The truth was that, in conformity with the Convention of Cintra, the French were now beginning to embark, and as their numbers diminished on shore they were afraid that the people might attack them, so they were eager for us to come and protect them.

On the morning of the 13th September, I and another subaltern were ordered with a piquet of seventy men, under the command of Captain Clunes, of the 50th Regiment, to proceed to relieve a

French post. As the staff-officer who was to conduct us had not arrived at the hour appointed, Clunes, who was a cool soldier of commanding appearance, being six feet six inches in height, and stout in proportion, said:

"It is of no consequence; having been quartered here before I know the way perfectly."

So off we set. After passing through some streets we came to a large one leading to the Rocio Square. The French sentry, on seeing us advance, instantly challenged, *"Qui vive?"*

Observing that the captain took no notice, I said to him:

"Sir, the sentry has challenged, and is presenting to fire at us."

"Let him fire," said he; "my orders are to proceed. If the staff have neglected to inform the French, or to make arrangements, it is not my fault."

I then saw a French officer run up to the sentry and make him recover his arms, at the same time calling to the guard to turn out. We continued right on, and entered the square. We turned down the left side, the centre being occupied with tents. The guard presented arms, and we passed on carrying ours without a word being exchanged between us; but they looked rather surprised. All the other posts did the same as we passed. When we came to a French magazine of stores on a wharf by the river side, we relieved the French guard with all the honours. The Portuguese were quite amazed when they saw us on such friendly terms with the French officers, and more particularly when they saw our men laughing and shaking hands with the French soldiers when they met at the well to get water.

I was much amused on observing a proclamation of Marshal Junot's posted on the walls, announcing that he had defeated the English, and that the 29th and 9th Regiments had been cut to pieces.

I saw a French drummer boy, about fourteen years of age, politely assisting two old ladies down rather a steep slope from a high pathway. I said to him:

"You boy, are a very smart little fellow."

"Oh!" said he, "I am young now, but I hope soon to have the honour of bearing arms."

I then asked him if he had been with the army engaged against us. He replied, "I beat the charge at Vimieiro."

"Well, my friend," said I, "and did you also beat the retreat?"

"Ah!" said he, "you were double our number."

Curiously enough I found that the two old ladies were Irish, and they told me that they had been long resident in Lisbon.

We ordered dinner at a hotel in the vicinity, and we made up for past abstemiousness by indulgence in all the luxuries which the place afforded. Indeed, to sit down on chairs at a table with a clean cloth and a capital dinner before us was what we had not enjoyed for some months. On calling for the bill, we were amazed at the amount, it being no less than five thousand *mil reis*! Not being accustomed to the Portuguese mode of calculation, we were rather puzzled. Our gallant captain, however, to our satisfaction, assured us that we were not ruined, as each thousand *reis* was only about five shillings, so that our feast was a cheap affair after all.

During our wine Captain Clunes related to us the following anecdote:

Several years before he was coming from Minorca in a ship of war, on board of which Junot, the present commander of the French army in Portugal, also was, he having been taken prisoner. In a conversation on the subject of grenadiers, Junot, alluding to the British grenadiers, said to Clunes, who was captain of the grenadier company of the 50th Regiment:

"Your men are only called grenadiers because they are great, large men, and are often awkward fellows. Ours are all choice men, selected for their meritorious service and distinguished bravery in the field."

"That may be," replied Clunes, "but I wish for nothing better than a chance of meeting the best of yours some day in the field with our men such as they are."

That chance happened. They met on a fair field at Vimieiro. Our fellows charged the men of merit as they came on them, charging bayonets, and dashing forward on the advancing foe. The issue is well known. These choice veterans of France wavered, scarcely venturing to stand the British shock. They turned and fled, leaving their front rank to be mowed down by our sturdy fellows. The captain added that in the *melee* which took place he never drew his sword, but with a shillelagh, which he always carried, he knocked about him right and left, and warded off with it many thrusts made at himself.

We were relieved next morning, the 14th of September, and we rejoined our regiments in the Campo St. Anna. The whole afterwards marched out to Picoas, about a mile north-east of Lisbon, where we found the whole army encamped on some heights commanding the town. The army was now under canvas. The following day, the 15th September, was that on which, as agreed upon by the Convention of Cintra, the French flag was to be hauled down, and the Portuguese to be hoisted, once more to wave free on the towers of Lisbon—in fine, that the French dominion was to cease, and the castle and all other military posts were to be delivered up to the English army.

A grand guard was formed, consisting of the grenadiers of the 29th, 40th, 50th, and 79th Regiments, with a party of the 95th Rifle Corps and some pieces of artillery, all under the orders of General Cameron. They marched off at six o'clock a.m., for the purpose of taking possession of the citadel. The gallant veteran headed the guard mounted on a favourite black charger, on which it had been his fortunate lot proudly to enter several captured fortified places, the last of which was Copenhagen. The 29th Regiment, with colours flying and band playing, marched off at the same time, and proceeded to the Placo de Rocio, or grand square of Lisbon, which they occupied, relieving all the French posts in that quarter. It was curious to observe the countenances and conduct of the immense concourse of people as we passed through the streets. At first all looked anxious, as if something fearful was going to happen. So great had been the system of terror practised on them by the French, that they seemed to be afraid to give free vent to their joy at our entrance to deliver them from their oppressors. Some, bolder than the others, creeped near us, whispering softly, *"Viva! viva!"* others began to call out louder. We then answered with loud shouts, *"Viva!"* This acted as an electric shock. In a moment handkerchiefs were waved from every balcony and window by many fair hands, and showers of flowers came falling on our heads. The dense masses took up the cry. All hats waved on high; loud shouts of *"Viva!"* were prolonged on every side. All faces gleamed with joy, and in their excitement the people began kissing one another. At midday the French flag was struck at the citadel, the forts, and the shipping, and the Portuguese flag was instantly displayed in its stead. The Portuguese flag was saluted by our artillery firing royal salutes at different points, and also by our ships of war which had entered the Tagus.

Three companies of the 29th Regiment were ordered to cover the embarkation of the French army. We marched from the Rocio to the small square in front of the naval arsenal, and were drawn up in line opposite the grand entrance gateway, through which the French had to pass to get to the boats waiting at the wharf to convey them to the transports. Several columns defiled past us with music playing. After entering the dockyard they piled arms, each corps waiting till its turn came to embark. Many of their officers came out again, and stood talking together. The populace, who had been in great agitation all the morning, on observing the French fast decreasing in numbers, and that we were now masters of Lisbon, became emboldened, and very audacious, reviling the French troops as they marched past, and shouting at the officers standing at the gate, calling them the most opprobrious names. I heard a noise in rear of our line. On looking round, I observed about a dozen of French soldiers, officers' servants, carrying hat-boxes, bundles, cloaks, &c. They were running for their lives, chased by a furious mob. Before I could get up to protect them a Portuguese lad drew one of the unfortunate men's swords from its scabbard at his side, and stabbed him to the heart, before he had time to throw down the luggage he had in his hands, so as to be able to protect himself. We, however, got all the others safe. Soon afterwards several artillery ammunition wagons, drawn by four horses each, came down the large, wide street, from the right, at full gallop. The mob having attacked them by firing pistols and pelting them with stones, we rushed out and drove back the outrageous assailants. But many of the poor drivers were seriously wounded, and one or two were felled to the ground. Sir John Hope, the general of the day, went up to the French officers standing outside, and explained to them how awkwardly we were situated to keep peace between them and an excited mob. He said to them in his gentle manner:

"I should he sorry to impose any restraint upon you, but may I request of you as a personal favour that you would retire inside the arsenal?"

This they all did immediately. But all the men and officers were much enraged, and were almost on the point of rushing out to punish the mob in spite of us.

One of the French officers said to me:

"This is badly arranged. I was captain of the main-guard in the Rocio Square, and had only forty-five men, but not a man in Lisbon dared venture to say 'boo' to me. Look at the cowardly rascals, now that they are under your protection, how they insult us."

Another officer told me that, being on duty the previous night, he could not return to his lodgings when the guards were withdrawn, and that consequently all his baggage was still there; and he said he would be much obliged if I could do anything for him. I immediately got leave from Major Way to send a corporal and a file of men of the 29th Regiment as an escort to protect him. But on his looking up the street and seeing the threatening attitude of the mob, he said with tears in his eyes:

"*Ah! monsieur, vous avez trop peu de gens,*" and he declined to go with them.

Another officer, called St. Albans, was more fortunate. He spoke English extremely well, and had been acquainted with our officers when they were prisoners on hoard the Russian fleet. To one of these officers he gave a description of his baggage, which he had left in his lodgings. The officer took a section of our men and brought all the luggage safe into the dockyard. The moment it was put down the French officer hastened to open a particular box. Finding its contents all safe, he said with a joyous face:

"This is all right. I do not care about the others."

The truth was, that he had there two large bags of doubloons, which plunder he had acquired when commanding at St. Ubes. No fishing-boat was allowed to go out of the harbour without a written pass from him, and for this he charged a doubloon each.

Long trains of wagons under French escorts also passed into the arsenal, loaded with something termed stores, baggage, &c. I saw some carts containing what appeared to be bars of metal about eighteen inches long and two broad. These, I understood, were of silver, being plundered plate melted down. They were detained, by us and given over to the Portuguese treasury.

In the after part of the day I was sent in command of a detachment consisting of a strong party of the 29th Regiment, and a party of the German hussars. My orders were to escort and protect the French fatigue parties employed in conveying the sick and wounded men from the different hospitals to the wharves for embarkation. This was a service of rather a difficult nature. The mob was very audacious, frequently pelting us, both foe and friend, with dirt and stones, and often threatening to use violence, notwithstanding that one portion of the cavalry were in advance to clear the way, and another covered the rear, while the infantry marched in files on each side. The whole formed an extensive procession, as each sick litter required four men as bearers. I was under the necessity of making at times demonstrations of using force to keep the mob at a distance. I had to make several trips, owing to the hospitals being in different parts of the city. In the evening, when all the sick were safely conveyed to the boats, the French fatigue parties all assembled at the Estrella Convent, which had been the principal general hospital. They put on their accoutrements, primed, loaded, and fixed bayonets. One of the *sous-officiers* asked me how I wished them formed. I told him to form them in column of subdivision at quarter distance, and to keep well together during the march. When we were about to move off, the director-general of hospitals came to thank me for the trouble I had taken, and for affording our protection to the sick. He requested my permission to give my men a glass of wine. I opened the ranks, and faced them inwards. He began and gave each man to right and left as the steward went down a small jug of wine, and excellent port it was.

I then disposed my party to conduct the French fatigue parties to the wharf. The Portuguese seemed quite lost in amazement when they beheld a British officer marching at the head of an armed body of Frenchmen. We formed rather a formidable appearance, and no one ventured to molest us, so we escorted them to the boats in safety. I observed numbers of poor fellows lying on the wharf, who had been fired at by the Portuguese from windows, or hit with stones as they passed. Indeed, it was not safe for any Frenchman to appear, unless guarded by the English, The French soldiers' wives, however, made a good fight of it through the crowd. I heard some of them tell the mob:

"You shall pay for these outrages; our victorious armies will return again, and we will wash our hands in Portuguese blood," at the same time suiting their actions to their words.

Several of the French officers felt so grateful for the protection which we had afforded them, that they made presents of their horses to some of our officers. Our regiment was most anxious to recover Black Jack, our gallant colonel's charger. A communication was made to General Delaborde that any sum he chose to name would be paid for him if he would part with him. The general, in the handsomest manner possible, sent the horse back to us as a present to the regiment, and said that he was happy to have it in his power to gratify a corps which had displayed such determined gallantry against him.

After the urgent duties of this eventful day were all over, we had expected some respite. We, however, received orders to remain in the square in front of the arsenal all night, with instructions that no person was to quit it, or to go into a house. A proprietor of a large house begged us to take shelter in his *porte-cochere,* and for our accommodation he placed on the ground several fine new mattresses, which, he said, the French officers had left in his house. On these we took our rest by turns, as we relieved one another of duty every two hours. Next morning a message came from a French general, begging that these mattresses might he given up to him, as they were his property. We afterwards learned that they were all made of the finest cotton, which he had taken somewhere, and had it made up in this form to get it away. This, however, was a small matter compared with the plunder of church plate, of the palaces, libraries, and royal museum, and of the public arsenals. The Portuguese were indignant, with some reason, at the Convention of Cintra, when they saw that the French were allowed to quit Portugal in so peaceful a manner with all their plunder.

The Russian admiral Siniavin, with his fleet of nine sail of the line and some frigates, surrendered to Sir Charles Cotton. The ships were to be sent to England to be detained during the war, and the men were to be sent to their own country. The troops were disembarked, and had their arms restored to them; and, after they had been refitted with all necessaries, they were embarked, and sailed for Catalonia.

We were relieved on the 16th September by the 50th Regiment, and we marched out to our camp, glad to get a quiet night after so much fatigue. Our repose was not, however, of long duration. Next morning, 17th Sept., we marched into Lisbon and relieved the 79th Regiment in the Black Horse Square. But as the French were now nearly all embarked, our duties were less arduous, and we could sit and dine in the capital cafes which surround this elegant square, the Exchange of Lisbon. We had only to protect some French stores now given over to our commissariat, and to guard against any disturbance arising on the part of the people to avenge themselves on such of their countrymen as had been found to have taken part with their enemies, the French. On the following day, the 18th, we were relieved, and proceeded to the camp, there being no further occasion for this daily duty, as a garrison had been established in the citadel, and took all the guards and other duties deemed necessary in the citadel.

The French being now fairly cleared out of Portugal, and the gloom and dread caused by the tyrannous invader being dispelled, the people gave themselves up to unbounded joy and festivity. The city was illuminated for several nights, and the theatres were opened for free admission. A grand public ball was given at the opera-house, and all the English officers were invited.

From my having been for some days continually employed in the most harassing duty, without time or opportunity of even changing my clothes, with my feet frequently wet, and obliged to take the little sleep I got lying on the damp ground, I got a bad cold, and felt very unwell; and next day, for the first time in my life, I was obliged to report myself sick, and to be placed on the sick list. One of the gentlemen who had treated me to a supper at Campo Grande brought his family out to see our camp, and to pay me a visit. Finding that I was unwell, they most kindly invited me to remove to their house in town, where every attention would be shown to me. However, perhaps through a mistaken *esprit de corps*, being unwilling to leave my regiment while it was still in the field, I declined their friendly offer, and much reason I had to regret it. I got daily worse, and I was declared to have got typhus fever, which had attacked many of our stoutest men and some of our officers. There being no hospital yet prepared, we were obliged to remain in tents, sick as we were, lying on some straw on the ground. At length, on the 24th September, the encampment at Picons was broken up, and the troops marched to another position some miles from Lisbon, where the force was very much increased by reinforcements which had arrived some time before, under Sir John Moore. I, with seven other officers, and about one hundred and fifty men of our regiment, all ill of fever, was removed into a gentleman's country house, which had been fitted up as an hospital, under the charge of our able surgeon, Dr. Guthrie, to whose great skill and attention I may, under providence, attribute my recovery. After my life having been despaired of for many days, my case took a favourable turn; but being left in a most debilitated condition, my progress towards recovery was tediously slow. In the meantime, many of our brave fellows who had escaped the dangers of war had fallen under the cruel hand of disease. What is most remarkable is, that those who succumbed appeared to be the most robust men in the regiment. During my long convalescence, which lasted for several weeks, I was much indebted to the hospital surgeon's wife, Mrs. Gundley, who had been our housekeeper during our long abode on board the transport ship during the previous winter. She used to make me light chicken-broth and sago nicely prepared.

I was lying one morning on a sofa placed between two windows, while Dr. Guthrie was sitting writing at a table near the centre of the room. On a sudden I heard a crash of glass near my head, and at the same moment I saw the doctor start up from his chair, exclaiming:

"Bless me, Langton, what the deuce are you about? You have cut my legs."

He evidently imagined that Langton, who shortly before had been standing near him, had played him some practical joke, which he was fond of doing. I soon let him into the secret of what had happened to him. He had been hit by a musket-ball. On examination, we found that a ball had entered through the window, passed close to my head, grazed against one of the legs of the chair on which the doctor was sitting, and hit him on the calf of both legs, cutting through the pantaloons and upper leather of the boot, and slightly wounding his right leg, but cutting only the pantaloons of the left one. We congratulated each other on our narrow escape.

Had the ball not hit the leg of the chair first, it would have gone through both the doctor's legs. On looking out from the window we could discover no one.

After the fever left me, I still continued weak, and not being able to take exercise, I amused myself by continuing my journal, which had been interrupted for some time.

We found the Portuguese in a most wretched state, without leaders or government of any kind. The king and most of the nobility had fled, abandoning the country to the tender mercies of a rapacious foe. Bonaparte, having successfully cheated Spain out of her liberty, had determined to acquire Portugal in like manner. The French army entered Portugal in 1807, accompanied by a Spanish force, under the guise of friendship. They hoped to surprise the king in his capital, and to secure him and his fleet also. Indeed, so rapid had been their march, that, I am assured, they arrived at Lisbon, officers and soldiers, without baggage of any kind, many even without shoes on their feet—in fact, in such disorder that they might have been cut to pieces in their passage through the country, had any active, determined leader mustered even a small force for that purpose.

The Portuguese, hoping for the best, had received the invaders in a friendly manner, and cheerfully supplied all their immediate wants. Many gentlemen told me that besides inviting French officers to take quarters in their houses, they even presented them with shirts and other articles. But scarcely had eight days elapsed, when the French, finding that no resistance was offered, and that the Portuguese were lulled into security, one night suddenly surrounded all the various barracks in which the Portuguese regiments were quartered, with troops and artillery ready to open fire upon them. The alternative was offered either to give up their arms or be cut to pieces. Under such circumstances resistance was in vain. The Portuguese afterwards had the choice either to be disbanded, all the officers losing their commissions, or to march to France, all the officers getting a step of promotion. About 12,000 of the troops accepted the latter terms, but many afterwards made their escape on their road to France.

The next step which the French took was to disarm all the inhabitants. A proclamation was issued prohibiting anyone to carry or possess arms, and a place was appointed where all arms were to be delivered up. All opposition having been carefully guarded against, the usual French plundering system began. Heavy contributions in money were imposed under penalty of martial law. All the shops were visited, and most of the articles which they contained were confiscated, under the pretence that they were English goods, particularly all cloth and cotton, which were taken to clothe the French army, to the ruin of the merchants. Hence commerce and trade of every kind was at a stand, more especially as the English fleet blockading the port would not allow any vessel to enter. Most of those who held office or public employments were dismissed, and a few only were replaced by persons favourable to the French interests. From all these causes thousands were reduced to beggary, and many to absolute want. Contributions of grain having been afterwards demanded, and no fishing-boats being allowed to go to sea, from the dread lest they should communicate with our fleet, the poor people were indeed in a state of absolute want and starvation.

Strong detachments of troops were encamped in all the large public squares, from which loaded cannon were pointed down every street, while piquets and patrols traversed the streets continually in all directions. The shops were ordered to be closed every evening at nightfall, and no inhabitant was permitted to appear in the streets after the retreat was beat. The citizens could scarcely venture to walk at any time without danger to their lives. They were liable to be challenged every instant by the numerous sentinels, who instantly fired when they did not receive an immediate or a proper answer. Many were killed in this manner, but no redress could be got from Junot. Indeed, in such dread were the French held that the people in passing the sentries would take off their hats, saying to them "With your permission," and thus pass on bareheaded.

The French exactions were not confined to Lisbon. Every province and town suffered in like manner. The church plate was everywhere seized; the altars and monuments were broken up to see whether treasure bad been concealed in them; the churches were often made quarters for the troops, and sometimes even used us stables. A movable column, under General Loison, was employed to collect forced contributions and to amass plunder. The most brutal excesses, too shocking to be mentioned, were committed under the orders of this savage commander, when he pillaged the convents and churches at Evora. He was employed in the same disgraceful mission in Portugal, and was in the act of receiving a portion of an exorbitant contribution when the unexpected news of our disembarkation in Portugal was announced. The cash was hurriedly raked from the tables into bags, and five of the principal inhabitants were seized as hostages and security for the portion remaining uncollected. The drums beat to arms, and the robber marched off in great haste, taking with him the very silk hangings which adorned the saloons of the mansion in which he had lived.

Lisbon swarmed with mendicants of every class and description. I have often been astonished at being stopped by remarkably well-dressed people, who, taking off their hats with a polite bow, begged *"Alma cozino por amor de Dios."* To such a pitch of distress did the French reduce these people, and with such awe had their severity inspired them, that even on our triumphal entry into Lisbon as conquerors to free them from this odious bondage of their oppressors, they could scarcely venture to give vent to their joy by an open public demonstration. Their *"Vivas"* were at first but whispered in subdued tones, until they saw that we were able and willing to protect them.

Marshal Junot, for his unopposed inroad into Portugal, styled a conquest, had the pompous title of Duke of Avrantes conferred on him by his Corsican master. By force of arms he ruled with the most arbitrary sway, in civil as well as in military affairs, more absolute than any king. There was a *junta*, or council of state, consisting of Portuguese of rank and ability, but it existed only in name. Junot made use of them only as the means of communicating his will and demands to the nation, and to execute his iniquitous measures for the ruin of their country. He was wont to attend their sittings, and to treat them with the most supercilious insolence. If anyone attempted to remonstrate against an unreasonable demand or project, he used to reply:

"It must be. *Notre Empereur est tres just ma is an meme temps ties severe."*

At another time, if a serious discussion was going on, he would stand at the window, and then call one of the members, a venerable marquis, or an old *conde*, and, pointing to some girl passing in the street, say:

"Come, tell me, who is that pretty *signora?*" or he would make some absurd jest.

He occupied the splendid palace of Baron Quintelle, where he lived in the most magnificent style. He especially endeavoured to ingratiate himself with the ladies by giving brilliant *fetes,* hoping by their influence to succeed in prevailing on the magnates of the land to adopt opinions favourable to the French interest. On one occasion a superb ball was given in the opera-house. It was hinted to the noble and wealthy that it would add much to the splendour of the festive supper-board if they would send their plate for the night. The good, simple souls obeyed the bidding. The supper was eaten, and, it would appear, much of the plate also. From that night to this more than one-half never returned to the owners. The opera was kept open, and so fond of pleasure was the Marshal, that he even brought ladies with him in his coach when he came to fight us at Vimieiro.

When the Spanish nation rose in May, 1808, and declared war against their oppressors, the French, Junot became very apprehensive that a like proceeding would take place in Portugal. He enforced with great rigour every stringent precautionary measure against an outbreak. He was sadly puzzled how to dispose of the Spanish army which came with him as allies to Lisbon. He dreaded that they would stir up the Portuguese to resistance against him, or that they would give him the slip and march back to join their brethren in Spain. He determined to outwit them. With seeming-liberality, he assured them that he would send them back by sea to their own country. Ships were assigned for this purpose, and a certain day was fixed for the embarkation of the Spaniards. When the day came they were marched down to the Black Horse Square. Under various pretences they were detained there waiting. During this time large bodies of French troops, with guns, were brought down and rapidly formed in their rear, while the Spaniards were enclosed by the sea-like river in their front. They were then, to their utter astonishment and grief, ordered to pile their arms, and were told that they must embark as prisoners, and if they did not comply with the order immediately, they would be cut to pieces. The Portuguese army was reduced to seven regiments of infantry and three of cavalry, and of these a large proportion was sent off to France under the command of the Marquis of Alorna. The Portuguese, having no leaders, could offer no resistance to their oppressors, but they longed to take vengeance on the authors of their degradation. Our army expelled the invaders, and the people received us as their deliverers. The French were compelled to retire, and the scenes which I have described when they embarked at Lisbon display the deep-rooted hatred of the Portuguese.

We found the Portuguese, as individuals, a good-natured, kind-hearted people, in many instances showing great hospitality and attention to the officers billeted on them. They observe the most strict forms of politeness to one another. Even the meanest persons meeting in the street take off their hats and bow, and frequently embrace one another. But taken as a whole, they appeared to us rather a helpless race, displaying no energy, and possessing no daring or enterprising spirit. Had they followed the example of Spain, and formed *guerillas* between Lisbon and the frontiers, they might have forced the French to retire, and have freed their capital and country of their presence, without having left it to us, strangers, to do it for them. For *guerilla* operations the country, intersected by numerous passes, is particularly favourable, and the French rear could easily have been threatened, and all reinforcements and communication with the main army in Spain cut off.

When we had accomplished our glorious work, and had restored to the Portuguese their own government and laws, they seemed but little sensible of the great benefits we had conferred upon them. Some even asserted that they could have driven the enemy out without our aid. They actually appropriated to themselves all the honour of having done so, and had the impudence to publish a view of the battle of Vimieiro, in which the Portuguese horse and foot were hewing and hacking the French to pieces, while not an English uniform was even represented.

Lisbon has a very magnificent appearance in beholding it from the water. On entering it one finds the portion which was rebuilt after the dreadful earthquake laid out in handsome streets and two spacious squares. But in other parts of the city the streets are generally narrow, and all are disgustingly dirty. There being no public sewers, all the filth is thrown into the centre of the streets, and there accumulated in a high ridge throughout the whole length. Packs of half-starved looking dogs lie basking in the sun in retired corners, or go prowling about picking up what they can find in the dunghills. The houses in general are constructed of stone, and each is entered by a large gateway leading to a court within, round which are stables, coach-house, offices, &c., as the lower story is seldom inhabited.

To get admittance into almost any house, however well you may be acquainted, is an affair of no small difficulty, owing to the numerous precautions taken to keep out unwelcome visitors. These precautions strike a stranger as if the Portuguese viewed one another with great suspicion and distrust. In all those houses having gateways, before the wicket is opened to admit anyone, they are narrowly examined and cross-questioned through a small square hole covered with an iron grating; in others you are questioned through a hole in the floor above the entrance. On ascending the staircase and reaching the first floor, you are again scrutinised through a strong grating.

Portugal being now completely liberated from the French yoke, the British government determined on sending a force to the north of Spain to act in conjunction with the Spanish armies. It was notified to Sir Hew Dalrymple, commanding the forces in Portugal, that he was to send a corps of 20,000 infantry, two regiments of German light cavalry, and a certain number of brigades of artillery, to join 10,000 troops under Sir David Baird, who would land at Corunna, and that the whole was to be under the command of Sir John Moore, as Commander-in-Chief, he having received his appointment on the 6th October, 1808.

The army destined for service in Spain, under the command of Sir John Moore, commenced in October to march towards the Spanish frontier, in separate columns and by different routes. The cavalry, four brigades of artillery, and four regiments of infantry, under Lieutenant-General Sir John Hope, proceeded the south road, through Alentejo, Badajos, Merida, Truxillo, Talavera de la Reyna, and the Escurial. Three brigades, under Lieutenant-General Fraser, marched by Abrantes and Almeida. Two brigades went by the north road, under Major-General Beresford, by Coimbra and Almeida. Sir John Moore, with his headquarters, set out on the 27th October, 1808.

But the 29th Regiment, owing to the severe loss it had sustained in the actions in which it had been engaged, and many wounded and sick still remaining in hospital, was, to our great mortification, ordered to remain in Portugal, and to be stationed in Lisbon. They consequently marched into the citadel.

The hospital establishment at Picons, where I still remained, was not broken up when the regiment moved into Lisbon. However, after a protracted convalescence, I was at length sufficiently recovered to be able to be removed into the city, and I was carried to a billet in the vicinity of the castle where the regiment was, about the 7th 1808. November. This was a miserable quarter of the city. The streets were steep, narrow, and filthy. The dwellings were but second-class small houses. The *entresol* being the only spare part of the house to which I was taken, was assigned to me. It consisted of one room and a small bedroom, miserably furnished, and a sort of kitchen quite unfurnished. The upper part of the house was occupied by the proprietor, a retired tradesman, and his niece, with one servant girl.

I had intended to endeavour to get my billet exchanged for a more cheerful abode, but in a day or two I was attacked with fever and ague, which put removal out of the question. No sooner had the tertian left me, after a couple of weeks' suffering, than I was seized with dysentery. In the meantime, while I laboured under this accumulation of illnesses, the 29th Regiment, having recruited its strength by the recovery of numbers of sick and wounded, and having also received a draft of recruits from England, got orders to proceed to join the army in Spain. Accordingly, it left Lisbon about the 12th December, 1808. The sick, the women and baggage were ordered to move to the grand depot of the army established at Belem.

I remained for some time in Lisbon. My hosts were the first Portuguese family I had been quartered with; but owing to my illness we had for some time little or no intercourse. After I was able to move out a little, the old gentleman and I got occasionally into conversation, and at length he invited me to come up in an evening to chat with him. This I was glad to do. as it afforded me an opportunity of acquiring a knowledge of the Portuguese language.

My accomplished friend, Lieutenant Croker, had made me promise that I should dine with him on Christmas day, promising me English fare. The 25th December came. I, though still far from well, kept my appointment at the hour mentioned. On arriving I found a note to say that my friend had unexpectedly been ordered on some duty, but he hoped to be back by half-past seven. I waited until eight o'clock, and there being no signs of his appearance, I called for his servant. The Portuguese landlady seemed to evade my question. At length she let me into the secret that he was lying mortally drunk. Seeing all hope of roast-beef and plum-pudding vanish, I returned home, ashamed to acknowledge that I had been done out of my dinner.

My quarters being chill and dreary, I applied at the district office to have my billet changed. The secretary, who spoke French very fluently, told me to write to the minister of police. I begged that he would have the goodness to write down what I ought to say. He declared that he could not spell a word of French. We both looked puzzled; but, taking a pen, I requested that he would dictate, and to his surprise, I, who could then only chatter a few sentences, wrote accurately what he told me. I had learned French grammatically, but, unlike him, I had never had practical opportunities of speaking it, and he had learned it by hearing it spoken. A little before this time we heard of the escape of the Marquis de la Romana and his army of 10,000 men. In January, 1807, Bonaparte had induced the Spanish government to place at his disposal 14,000 of their best troops to form a corps of observation on the frontiers of Hanover, and close the mouths of the Weser and the Elbe against the English. These troops were placed under the orders of Romana. They marched through France, and were placed under the supreme command of Bernadotte. After the peace of Tilsit, in July, 1807, war having broken out between England and Denmark, and Bonaparte designing to invade Sweden, the Spanish troops were ordered to the Danish Islands, with a view to their forming the vanguard of Bernadotte's army. They landed in March, April, and May, 1808, in Zeeland, Jutland., and

Fünen. When the Spaniards rose against the French, the English government were anxious to withdraw this Spanish corps from the French army. But this was an affair of no small difficulty, as the Spaniards were surrounded by the French, who distrusted them, and no communications from Spain were allowed to reach them. In order to inform Romana of the actual state of affairs in Spain, and to induce him to return to his country with this army, the English government employed the Rev. James Robertson, a Catholic clergyman, and monk of the Scotch monastery at Ratisbon, to open communications with Romana, and to offer him the services of an English fleet to convey him and his army to Spain. After many narrow escapes, Mr. Robertson succeeded in getting an interview with Romana, who willingly seconded the plans of the English government. His measures were successful. He eluded the vigilance of Bernadotte, and escaped from the islands with the greater part of his force, which immediately set sail for Spain, and disembarked at Santander on the 9th October. Romana himself went to London to make some arrangements with the English ministry, and did not land in Spain till after the battle of Espinosa, 11th November, 1808. Mr. Robertson gave great satisfaction to the English government by the manner in which he conducted his delicate and difficult mission, and he got a grant of a pension of £300 a year. I afterwards met him frequently at my father's house at Fetternear, when he used to recount to us his adventures and hairbreadth escapes. He told us that at that time his portrait was in the possession of the police of every city and town of the continent of Europe.

Before finishing my account of our first campaign, I may add a short description of our mode of living in the field. Neither officers nor men had tents, and having been but rarely halted in the vicinity of common woods, we had seldom opportunities of hutting ourselves, as it was most strictly prohibited to cut any olive or other fruit trees. We were therefore in general obliged to sleep in the open air. Our only choice of place was to secure, when it was practicable, a large walnut or other tree with spreading branches, under the shelter of which to take up our temporary abode. Our beds for the night were easily made up. Mine consisted of a mat made of sedge, about the size of a hearthrug, spread on the ground, on which, wrapped in a large cloak, with a leather cap for a nightcap, I slept like a top.

When we were bivouacked in the vicinity of a pine or other common wood, we erected huts, which were constructed in the following manner:

Two upright posts, about seven feet high, with forked ends, were planted in the ground about fifteen feet asunder. On these was placed a ridge-pole, or roof-tree, against which other poles were placed on each side in a slanting position, so as to form the frame of a roof. The whole was then covered with pine branches, or heath, broom, or straw. One end was closed up with poles placed nearly close together, and stuffed in the joints with grass or moss. The other end, which was left open for the entrance, had for a door a movable screen of wicker-work. Where we could find a tree, we always built the huts a little to the north-east of it, so as to have as much shade as possible. Indeed, on a few occasions when under canvas we had huts also, as we found them so much cooler than the tents during the day; but at night, or during rain, the tents, as being waterproof, had the preference.

Tables and chairs not being portable commodities, we had none; but we supplied the place of both by a most primitive contrivance. We dug two parallel trenches about four feet apart, and five feet long. Two persons could sit on each side with their feet in the trenches, while the intermediate space formed the table. When a light was required, we stuck a bayonet into this verdant festive-board, and placed a candle in the socket. This made a capital military candlestick. Around it we quaffed wine, whiffed cigars, sang songs and narrated adventures.

On first starting we had a very scrambling mode of getting anything to eat, but a little experience soon made us *ait fait* in providing what was needful. Three or four officers usually clubbed together and formed a mess. One undertook to cater, another to superintend the erection of a but, or to see that the tents were pitched in proper positions, and a third had charge of some other department. Our breakfast generally consisted of chocolate, which was excellent all over the Peninsula, and very portable and easily prepared, with ration bread and a morsel of cold meat, with honey sometimes, but butter there was none to be had. However, we found that the chocolate was very heating and excited thirst, and that tea was much preferable, as being more refreshing, and a great restorative after fatigue. Our standard dishes for dinner were a certain portion of ration beef made into soup, with rice, turnips, carrots, onions, and tomatoes. These being long stewed, the soup was nutritious and the beef was always tender. Another portion of our ration beef was made into steaks, fried with onions; sometimes we had the addition of the tongue or the heart of an ox, which the military butcher had the privilege of selling. At other times, when they could be got, we indulged in such luxuries as hares, partridges, or fowls. These we managed to roast by the contrivance of fixing up three ramrods in the form of a triangle, and suspending the game or fowl by a worsted thread, to which the cook now and then gave a twirl.

When dinner was served up, the camp-kettle was placed in the middle as our soup tureen; another camp-kettle, with boiled beef, was placed at the top; and a third, with beefsteaks, was placed at the bottom of our table; and the vegetables, when we could get them, were placed at each side. Our round wooden canteens supplied the place of decanters, and were often filled with some of the excellent wine of the country, which we cooled by covering the canteens with wet cloths, and hanging them on a tree.

No wheeled carriages were permitted to be employed in the conveyance of baggage, as they would have not only impeded the march, but, being liable to break down, would have caused much property to have been lost. Horses and mules were the only means of transport allowed in the line of march, they being capable of proceeding at all times rapidly and over any roads, however precipitous in mountainous districts. Mules were found far preferable to horses for continued hard work. They were less delicate, and less liable to sore backs; they require less care, and can live upon less and coarser food; they can endure more fatigue, and are more sure-footed in rocky paths.

To campaign with tolerable comfort the following equipment was found requisite, and would answer for one, two, or three persons, according to their rank and means. Two good mules; two pack saddles, with wooden frames and hooks attached; two stout portmanteaus, with strong straps and iron loops; two panniers, covered with hide, fitted up as canteens, with straps and loops; one small marquee or pavilion tent; two walking-stick camp-stools; one waterproof bag palliasse, to hold straw and form a bed; two blankets, one pillow, one waterproof nightcap; one large camlet cloak, well lined, warm, but light to carry, and soon dried after rain; one leather bottle to carry wine; one leather bucket; one bill-hook, or good small hatchet; one sickle; one claw-hammer; some horse-shoe nails; two large oilcloth covers, one for each load.

Articles made of silver are not advisable; those of tin or other metal are easily replaced if lost. Dishes and drinking-cups should be made to fit into one another.

Part 2
1809

Having at length recovered my health sufficiently to move, I proceeded to the army depot at Belem, and assumed the command of the detachment of the 29th Regiment there, consisting of several officers and about 160 men. Almost all the other regiments of the army had left convalescents there, besides all the baggage and women. There were nearly 800 women there.

This motley assemblage was under the command of General Sontag, a German, a remarkably little man with a remarkably large nose. It was said that he had been employed by government on certain secret services, in which he had acquitted himself with great address. But a spy he never could have been, as no disguise could change his appearance. Be that as it may he had rather a troublesome command, as may easily be imagined, when it is considered that the majority of his force consisted of women. These were quartered in a barrack by themselves, under the charge of a few married sergeants and men, who issued their rations, and were answerable that they were all present, and locked up, every night. Instructions having arrived that most of these women were to be sent to England, where on their arrival each was to receive a guinea and have their expenses paid to their own parishes, the general sent his *aide-de-camp* to announce the intelligence to them. They one and all resisted. None would draw lots to decide who were to go. The *aide-de-camp* said he would report their conduct to the general. They shouted defiance, and all swore that if he ventured to show his nose amongst them again they would tear his wig off and souse him under the pump.

Belem is situated on the banks of the Tagus, about two miles below Lisbon, of which it may be deemed a *faubourg*. It has rather an elegant appearance. It has a fortified castle which commands the river, military barracks, handsome public buildings and private houses, a magnificent convent, and two royal palaces. When the French were here they had seized all the pictures of any value that they could find, and here they still remained in the packing-cases in which they had packed them to send them to France, when we detained them as public property. Even the royal aviary did not escape the rapacity of the French. One of their generals took possession of all its feathered inhabitants, and when we were there it was empty.

I was fortunate in getting a tolerable billet. The proprietor had been private secretary to one of the ministers, and was particularly intelligent. I acquired much information from him regarding the manner in which the French governed Portugal during their occupation.

Reports began to be circulated that the French army in Spain had received large reinforcements, and that Napoleon himself was expected or had arrived to take the command; and a few days afterwards it was whispered that the English army was retiring. We were not left long in suspense. On the 9th January, 1809, Major Richard Egerton and Lieutenant Stanhope returned to Lisbon. They informed us that the 29th Regiment, after having reached the frontiers of Spain, had been obliged to retreat because a column of the French army had advanced so far as to intercept their communication with our army in the north, and that consequently they had received orders to fall back on Abrantes, and that all magazines and stores which could not be brought off from Castello Branco and other depots were ordered to be destroyed. The regiment arrived at Lisbon on the 20th January, and were quartered in the convents. The officers got billets in the country. I marched next day with my detachment to join the battalion. I had the good fortune to get an excellent billet in the Rua d'Ourize d'Ouro, in the house of a priest.

This gentleman was an Italian. He seemed to have some independent means of his own, and appeared to he more a visitor at Lisbon than one of the ordinary clergy of the place. He received me most kindly, gave me a pretty saloon, with a neat bedroom at one end, and insisted on my breakfasting and dining with him every day. He took me with him when he made his evening calls on several noble families, and he procured opera tickets for me.

We heard reports that the Spanish armies had been defeated by the French, that Napoleon was at Madrid, and that, consequently, our army, not having been supported by the Spaniards, as was expected, was left exposed, and liable to be pressed on all sides by an overwhelming foe under Bonaparte himself, and had been obliged to retreat. Soon afterwards the news arrived of the battle of Corunna, fought 16th January, which victory proved what British soldiers can do under the most adverse circumstances, and added to the glory of our arms. But from the untoward events which had occurred, the only alternative left was to embark, which the army successfully accomplished, without leaving even a gun as a trophy in the hands of the enemy.

The certainty that our army had returned to England proved rather a damper to us. It was provoking to think that the laurels we had gained were now likely to prove fruitless. We dreaded being ordered home also. Affairs assumed a most gloomy aspect, and rumours were rife that the French were threatening to invade Portugal with a large force, and that Marshal Victor was at Alcantara with a corps ready to advance against Lisbon. Reports were also spread that we intended to abandon the Portuguese, so that we were looked upon with great suspicion. They had lost much confidence in the British owing to the Convention of Cintra, and the unfortunate results of Sir John Moore's operations in Spain tended to increase their want of confidence.

In consequence of the failure of Sir John Moore in Spain, great gloom and consternation prevailed in Portugal, particularly as it was known that Bonaparte was at Madrid concerting measures for the entire subjugation of both countries. Napoleon, however, dreading the warlike preparations of Austria, suddenly left Madrid on the 22nd January, and took the Imperial Guard with him to France. The citizens of Lisbon were forming themselves into volunteer regiments of various descriptions, some as infantry, others as cavalry or artillery, or light corps. After their business of the day was over and their shops were closed, they used to drill in all the public squares. Besides occupying the citadel we had strong posts in several parts of the city, and inlying piquets every night ready to turn out at a moment's warning, besides patrols.

The 29th Regiment, having received drafts of men from England, and most of the wounded men having returned to their duty, became once more a most effective corps. It was received by the commander-in-chief, Sir John Craddock, in the Rocea Square on the 27th January, and he gave it his most unqualified praise for the high state of discipline it displayed and the soldier-like appearance of the men. Two days afterwards, it was our turn to give the guards for the day. The usual grand guard mounting had taken place, and just as every man was filing off to his respective post, the halt was sounded, and verbal orders were given that everyone should repair to his barrack, instead of going to his post, and that the regiment had received orders to be in readiness to embark at a moment's notice. We all, of course, hastened to our quarters, and as none of us was encumbered with much luggage, we soon had our traps in movable order, ready for anything. Our destination was kept a secret, and we could form no conjecture what it might be.

The force destined for the secret service, consisting of the 29th, 27th, and 9th Regiments, and a brigade of artillery under the orders of General Sir George Smith and General Mackenzie, embarked at eight o'clock on the morning of the 31st January. The departure of this small expedition nearly produced a serious commotion in Lisbon.

The people being aware that our army had retired from Spain, and had returned to England, were led to suppose that all the English troops in Portugal were also going away, and thus abandon them to the mercy of another French army. They rose in a tumultuous manner, and endeavoured to stop all our baggage.

The convoy sailed from the Tagus on the 2nd February, 1809. We then learned that we were intended to secure Cadiz, which, it appeared, was then threatened by the French. We arrived there on the 5th February, and came to anchor in the harbour. The governor declined our assistance, and we were not permitted to land. In this refusal he was supported by a party who were in the French interest. But the inhabitants in general and the merchants were most anxious that we should garrison the place, as it was known that a column of 5000 French, favoured by some Spanish traitors, were secretly approaching with a view to surprise this important city. They likewise discovered that all the cannon on the walls pointing to the land side were loaded with sand. This confirmed the suspicion of the people, and brought matters to a crisis. A commotion arose between the two parties. The captain of the port, accused of being a partisan of the French, was killed. All the people armed themselves, frequent skirmishes took place between the parties, and many lives were lost. These troubles were attended with considerable effect. They put the governor on his mettle. The place was put in a proper state of defence, and the French, finding their object foiled, gave up the attempt and retired. But the governor still entertained the absurd notion that we would take possession of Cadiz and retain it, as we had done Gibraltar. Although the troops were not allowed to land, yet the officers individually were permitted to go on shore, and were on all occasions received with great enthusiasm by the people.

The governor's apprehensions and dread of our gaining an entrance continued unabated; and when General Sir George Smith, who commanded the expedition, died after a short illness, only one company was allowed to land to attend his funeral, and the men were permitted only to have side-arms. While we were detained here waiting for further orders, we managed to make our abode on board the transports as agreeable as circumstances would permit. We lived remarkably well; provisions and poultry were plentiful and cheap, green peas and other vegetables were in high perfection even at this early season, most excellent sherry was to be had at about ninepence a bottle, besides a numerous variety of other wines. Nor did time pass heavily. Boating was a favourite amusement and by this means a friendly intercourse was constantly kept up with the other vessels, visits being paid and returned. In the evening we went on shore to stroll on the Alameida, or to attend the theatre.

As to myself, I found it particularly agreeable. My gallant friend, Captain Sir James Gordon, who was then in command of the fine frigate *Active,* being there, I used to go on board to dine with him. One day I met there my old acquaintance, his brother, John Gordon, the great wine merchant of Xeres, and his father-in-law, Monsieur Bigbeder. Captain Gordon also introduced me to the Honourable

Mrs. Rawdon and her daughter, who were on their travels, and to whom he had offered a passage in his frigate to England.

On the 12th February, I paid a visit to Port St. Mary, and saw the Gordons. I found the place dull and stupid.

About this time we heard that Zaragoza had succumbed to a siege of two months' duration, and that the garrison had made the most gallant resistance on record.

Notwithstanding the discouraging events which had happened in Spain, the British government determined to support by fresh exertions the noble cause of liberty in the Peninsula. In the first place, the defence of Portugal was decided on. Sir Arthur Wellesley was appointed to resume the command of the army, and reinforcements were announced as being on their way from England. General Beresford was appointed commander-in-chief of the Portuguese army. Sir Robert Wilson organised a corps of Portuguese troops from the Lusitanian Legion at Oporto, and with this body acting as partisans he occupied a line of posts along the Spanish frontier near Almeida, and kept open the communications with Cuidad Rodrigo.

Reports were circulated in February that Marshal Soult was preparing to invade the north of Portugal from Galicia with 24,000 infantry, 4000 cavalry, and 60 guns, and that General Lapisse was to cooperate with him by Almeida, and General Victor by Alcantara and the line of the Tagus. In the beginning of March we learned that Soult had entered Portugal, and was directing his march on Oporto. We were aware that that city had been prepared for defence, a line of works having been established to cover the line from the Douro to the sea, and was well supplied with cannon, and that a large garrison and the armed population were determined to make a second Zaragoza of it. So at least said the Portuguese.

Soult continued to advance, but his march was not so rapid as he wished. The peasants and militia were anxious to oppose him, and because General Freire wished to retire on a strong position, they accused him of treason and murdered him. Baron d'Eben, a German, holding an English commission in the Lusitanian Legion, succeeded him in the command of this undisciplined force. Soult attacked him and defeated him with great slaughter. The French then pushed on for Oporto, which they reached 26th March, and carried by assault three days afterwards. The military abandoned the defence and fled, and the inhabitants, seized with terror, took flight also. All hastened pell-mell to the bridge over the Douro, pursued by the enemy, cutting them down in all directions. The fugitives got jammed on this bridge; some were pushed over, none could advance, and the French kept plying them with grape and musketry. They told us that several thousands of the inhabitants were either killed or drowned.

Disastrous news also reached us from Spain. Sebastiani, we were told, had defeated the Spaniards under Cartoajal at Cuidad Real, and Marshal Victor had defeated the army of Estramadura under Cuesta.

After remaining nearly five weeks at Cadiz, pent up on board our transports, we at length received orders to return to Lisbon. The convoy sailed on the 6th March, 1809, and after a stormy passage we once more anchored in the Tagus on the 12th. We disembarked next day, and the men were quartered in a convent, and the officers in billets. We were all delighted to get on *terra firma* again, and no wonder, when it is recollected that from the time we sailed from Portsmouth last year to the present time we had been nearly nine months out of fourteen on board ship.

The person on whom I got a billet having rather a small house and a large family, procured rooms for me at a hotel. Many of the officers of the 87th, or Royal Irish Regiment lived at this hotel, where they all messed. They had a grand gala on the 17th March, St. Patrick's Day, which they kept up till an early hour next morning. There was a constant round of toasts and cheers, alleviated with songs and the band playing national airs, much to the surprise and amusement of the Portuguese, who had congregated in vast numbers under the windows.

The sudden recall of our expedition from Cadiz was now readily accounted for. It appeared that in consequence of the unfortunate termination of Sir John Moore's campaign in Spain, Marshal Soult had been enabled to enter Portugal with 20,000 men, and was already in possession of Oporto. Great alarm prevailed at Lisbon. Exaggerated reports were spread that Soult was pushing on, and would soon sack the capital. It appeared that we were determined to defend Portugal if possible, and the commander-in-chief lost no time in making such necessary dispositions for that purpose as the small force and present circumstances would permit, while waiting for reinforcements which report stated were coming from England.

Our whole force in Portugal did not consist of more than 7000 men. In addition to the regular regiments two provisional battalions were formed from the men at the depot at Belem. These consisted of wounded or sick men belonging to the regiments which had gone to Spain, and of stragglers from the army who had found their way back to Portugal.

Our little army marched on the 18th March, and took up cantonments in the beautiful villages of Loires, Lumear, and others adjacent, about eleven miles north-east of Lisbon.

This is one of the finest parts of Portugal, being in a high state of cultivation, and the country sufficiently undulating to give it a very picturesque appearance. The high road from Lisbon is studded on either side with numerous villas, surrounded with gardens, orange-groves, and vineyards. The Portuguese are excellent gardeners, and in this warm climate, where much artificial moisture is requisite, they manage the system of irrigation with great skill. They always select, when possible, ground which has a declivity or slope, on the highest portion of which they have a marble fountain, with a tank or reservoir of water, generally from 20 to 30 feet square and some feet deep. From this the water is conducted morning and evening by longitudinal furrows, intersected by cross ones leading downwards to the next one, to every plot and border in the garden, and from thence to the orange-grove, which is always open ground, well cleared of weeds. The orange-trees at this season are truly beautiful, being covered with green, yellowish, and deep golden fruit, according to their degree of ripeness, interspersed with pure white blossoms, all variegated with the deep rich verdant shining leaves. Nothing can be more agreeably delightful than to stroll in the fresh of the morning in these groves. The ground, being covered like snow with the fallen blossoms, imparts a balmy fragrance to the surrounding atmosphere. Then it is delicious to enjoy the luxury of a refreshing cold bath in the pure crystalline waters of the spacious tanks, protected from the scorching rays of the morning sun by the pleasing shade of gentle weeping-willows, which are always an appendage to the fountains.

I had the good fortune to get one of those villas assigned as quarters for our company. The men occupied the lower part and out-offices. The proprietor had removed the greater part of the furniture to Lisbon, leaving only a few tables, chairs, bedsteads, and some cooking utensils. But this was of no consequence, because, being so near Lisbon, we got at a cheap rate every necessary or luxury the town or country could afford. We formed a mess at the house of a baker in the village, who made pies and puddings in great perfection.

While living in these pleasant cantonments in seeming quietness, I had reason to know that the heads of departments looked for the expected reinforcements with great anxiety. It was reported freely that the advancing. French were advancing, and had such been the case, we would have been in an awkward predicament, as our small force would not have been sufficient even to make a show of resistance. Indeed, we understood that, in the event of the enemy pushing on, a plan was arranged for our embarkation at Castoes Bay, where some field-works were to have been thrown up to cover our retreat. The French must certainly have had very bad information not to have advanced on us while we were in this helpless state.

The British government, seeing that hostilities were likely to be resumed between France and Austria, decided on renewing operations in the Peninsula, and hence they determined to increase the army at Lisbon. To the great satisfaction of all, large reinforcements at length arrived, the first under General Sherbrooke, and in April another under General Hill. Everyone appeared reassured. We all looked forward with great ardour to the opening of a new campaign.

Nor was our own army alone restored to a fighting condition. It was determined to reorganise and discipline the army of our friends the Portuguese, which, as formerly mentioned, had been broken up by the French. General Sir William Carr Beresford was announced as being appointed commander-in-chief of the Portuguese army, with the rank of field-marshal, and officers from our army were allowed to volunteer into that service with the understanding that they were to get a step of promotion in it. This was understood to be an advantageous offer. Our captain availed himself of it, and in accepting it became a major and a field-officer, and many followed his example. But for me, who was then only a young subaltern, the prospect did not seem so brilliant. I should probably only have been a supernumerary captain. Besides, I deemed that the Portuguese force would not be in an efficient state to take the field for some time. Hence I did not quit my own regiment, which was on the eve of being actively employed against the enemy. Perhaps I was wrong, but such at the moment was the feeling of all the officers of our corps.

Marshal Beresford established his headquarters at Thomar. All our arrangements for taking the field being completed, dispositions were made for our advance on Coimbra. This was done by the army marching by brigades in succession, and by different parallel routes, for the greater convenience of procuring provisions and quarters.

We commenced the campaign on the 8th April, 1809, by marching to Bucellos. The men were billeted on the inhabitants, and I and three other officers were quartered in one house. Bucellos is a neat, small country town, situated in a valley between ranges of heights in front and rear. These ranges are highly cultivated, being covered with vineyards producing the excellent wine called Bucellos. We visited several of the cellars. The wine is kept in casks or tuns of very large dimensions. We saw it in different states of preparation, both for home consumption and for the English market. The new wine previous to being fined appeared something like whey. That for Lisbon was of a clear amber colour, rich and mellow, while that for London, being well dosed with brandy, was strong and fiery.

After remaining three days at Bucellos, we marched on the 11th April to Sobral de Monte Agraco. On the 13th we moved to Marciana, and next day to Cadevale, both but indifferent villages, through a well-cultivated country, and the weather was remarkably fine. We reached the fashionable watering-place of Caldas on the 15th, after having been completely drenched with torrents of rain. However, I got an excellent billet, and availed myself of the warm baths. The bath in which I bathed was like a large saloon with a cupola roof. The bath was an oblong square, about three feet deep, and had small dressing-rooms all round. The water was of a bluish-green colour, and you could see it bubble up through the sandy bottom. It was so warm that on my entering it rather hastily it made my nose bleed. From this the water passes to another bath for poor invalids, and after that it runs into a place in the open air for horses and other animals.

I took advantage of our halting at Caldas to make a pilgrimage to the Heights of Rolica, of such glorious memory to our regiment. The day unfortunately proved dull and misty, and was consequently very unfavourable for a proper inspection of the whole position. However, I went step for step over the ground and up the steep ravine, which had been so daringly forced. It was melancholy to observe the bones, hair, and pieces of uniform of our brave comrades and gallant enemies lying strewed about. Ravenous wolves had scratched up the graves of friend and foe, and had devoured the remains. Although eight months had elapsed since the action, there were quantities of French shakos, pieces of broken muskets and other arms lying about. Our regiment had a memorial monumental stone, with a suitable inscription on it, erected here in memory of our gallant Colonel Lake, to mark the spot where he fell. A handsome monument was also erected in Westminster Abbey. Both of these were defrayed by subscription of so many days' pay from officers and men.

It being certain that Marshal Soult had pushed his advance posts across the Douro, and reports of the enemy's advancing being rife, we began here at Caldas to establish out-piquets. We moved on the 20th April to Alcobaco, rather a long march. After leaving the vicinity of Caldas, the road passes through a dreary pine wood, on a white sandy soil, for some miles, and then over some steep heights, down to the vale of Alcobaco. Part of the troops were quartered in the grand convent. The monks, who were all of noble families, invited all the generals and officers to dinner. This monastery is a superb building, and was one of the richest in Portugal. It had a valuable library and splendid saloons, such as the Sala dos Rees. The kitchen was of great dimensions. The walls were lined with glazed tiles, which gave it a light and elegant appearance. It was fitted up with every attention to cleanliness and utility. Besides the dressers of wood, there were others with white marble slabs. There were one or two fountains of spring-water in it, and at one end a stream of water from the river Alco runs through, and serves to carry off all refuse.

I and three other officers were quartered in an excellent house. The proprietor very hospitably invited us to dine with him, but not wishing to give him trouble, we declined. However, he pressed us very much, and overcame our scruples by saying to us:

"Come, you shall eat your own dinner. Give me your rations, and let me cook them for you."

This he did, and many additions he made to the king's own, and plenty of excellent wine of a choice vintage he gave us.

Next day, the 21st April, we proceeded to Batalha, a village of no great size, but very remarkable for its magnificent monastery and church. In a side chapel of the church, separated by a curious screen of beautiful fretwork, in a splendid tomb raised on four steps, and with a movable lid, lies the body of King John IV., father of Katherine of Braganza, Queen of Charles II of England, dressed in his robes of state. His hands form a St. Andrew's cross upon his breast. Being embalmed, the whole was in a high state of preservation. The features of his face were as perfect as on the day he died (1655). His suit of armour, two-edged sword of an enormous size, and his battle-axe, with his scutcheon, and coat-of-arms, are suspended on one of the side walls. The monks invited the officers to dinner.

We marched on the 22nd April to Leiria, a distance of two leagues, principally through olive-groves. This is rather a pretty country town, and has a picturesque appearance, being nearly surrounded by a range of swelling hills, intersected with charming valleys, all highly cultivated with vineyards, olive-groves, and studded with numerous villas and gardens; while the old Moorish castle perched on a rocky height commanding the town has a fine effect. Lower down is the Episcopal palace, of large dimensions, but of no particular elegance. The cathedral, however, is a structure of some note, and the public hospital is a fine and commodious building. Here the corps of the army, which had marched by different routes, concentrated. We were billeted on the inhabitants, and the artillery were posted in the Roceo, or large public square. We heard reports that Sir Arthur Wellesley had been appointed again as commander-in-chief of our army, and that he had landed at Lisbon on the 22nd April. This was confirmed by general orders on the 25th April. The news was hailed with great satisfaction, not but that Sir John Craddock, our present general, was an excellent man, but Sir Arthur having already proved a successful general, was a greater favourite, in whom all seemed to have the most perfect confidence. Sir John Craddock was displaced so far in an honourable way that he was appointed governor of Gibraltar, then esteemed a post of the utmost importance. But this certainly did not reconcile him to giving up the command of an active force in the field, which appeared evident from his general orders in taking leave of the army.

We understood that our forces amounted to nearly 30,000 men. Sir Arthur Wellesley was likewise appointed a marshal, and commander-in-chief of the Portuguese forces, and was invested with the supreme command. From this time a new impulse was given to our hitherto tardy operations. Decision and energy became apparent. General Mackenzie was detached with a corps of 4000 men towards Abrantes to watch the Tagus, and Marshal Beresford was sent with another corps to act on the upper Douro.

In the afternoon of the 29th April we received sudden orders to march to Pombal. This seemed to corroborate current reports that the enemy had made a move forward. After a tedious march of five leagues through rather a desolate country, we arrived very late at Pombal, the approach to which is by a fine road through low ground, having rows of poplars on each side. The town is rather a neat place. It is commanded by a range of heights, on which stands an ancient Moorish castle. On the west side the land is flat and swampy.

We marched next day, passing through pine-woods, over some heights to Redenhan, and then on to Condeixa, in all about four leagues.

On the 1st May we proceeded through an undulating country, finely cultivated, to Coimbra, about two leagues. The men and most of the officers were quartered in the convents of monks. I and three or four other officers got a billet on a canon of the cathedral. He had an excellent house, fitted up with many English comforts. He was a gentlemanlike person, and very liberal. He insisted on giving us our dinner every day. We made him, however, take our rations, to which he added many capital dishes, confections, dessert, and wine.

Coimbra is the Oxford of Portugal. Here the young men of all ranks, and from all parts of the country, resort to study at the university, which possesses great celebrity in the country. Coimbra is a charming place. The view of the town from the hill in approaching from the Condeixa side is truly magnificent. It is situated on a sloping hill on the right bank of the Mondego. The cathedral and numerous churches with their spires, the convents, the university and other superb public buildings, the clean white private houses, with their verdant gardens and terraces, form a fine and pleasing effect, enhanced by the surrounding scenery. The river Mondego dashing out from between stupendous banks, on each side richly cultivated, passes close under the town, where there is a bridge. At some distance below this the valley opens and spreads out into an extensive plain, called the Campi, and celebrated by Camoens for its salubrity. Through this plain the Mondego glides gently along, now a lazy stream.

The people were much delighted to see us. They had for some time past been in constant dread of a visit from the French; indeed, so much so that the university, the grand library, the archives, the observatory, the laboratory, and the valuable museum were all in a dismantled state, all the valuable articles being packed up ready for removal in case the enemy had pushed on. The colleges were all empty. The students had very gallantly formed themselves into two light corps, under Colonel Trant.

On the 3rd May our favourite commander-in-chief arrived. The grenadiers of the 29th Regiment had the distinguished honour of being selected to form the guard of honour to receive him. His entry was quite a triumphal march, thousands having turned out to meet him.

Things began to look warlike. We knew that the French had begun to push their advance-guard forward, and were two or three days' march in front of Oporto. We were all on the *qui vive*. Our outposts were increased, and were maintained day and night; we had also strong inlying piquets. The army was rearranged. Some of the best disciplined Portuguese regiments, which had English officers attached to them, were now incorporated into our army, one battalion being in general placed in each of our brigades. The 16th Portuguese Regiment, under Colonel John Milley Doyle, was placed in our brigade, which now consisted of the 29th Regiment, the 16th Portuguese, and the 1st Provisional Battalion of detachments, comprised of parties of the 28th, 38th, and 92nd Regiments, the 43rd and 52nd Light Infantry, and the 95th Rifle Corps.

We understood that the plan of operations would be the following: Sir Arthur Wellesley was to advance direct on Oporto, to attack the enemy in front, while a corps under Marshal Beresford, consisting of Major-General Tilson's Brigade, the 87th and 88th Regiments, and some squadrons of cavalry, was to proceed by Vizen to cross the Douro, and, in conjunction with the Portuguese under Silveira, to turn the left flank of the enemy and to operate in his rear. Another corps under Major-General Mackenzie, consisting of the 27th, 31st, and 45th Regiments, a brigade of cavalry, and some thousands of Portuguese, were posted at Abrantes and Santarem, to protect the line of the Tagus against Victor, having the Lusitanian Legion and some Portuguese militia at Alcantara in his front, under Colonel Mayne.

On the 5th May Sir Arthur Wellesley reviewed the united army of the British and Portuguese forces in the Campo de Mondego. We learned from the Portuguese that Soult was still at Oporto, but that his advance-guard was at Oliveira, and his outposts extended to the Vouga.

The first preliminary to the opening of the campaign was the formation of the advance-guard, consisting of our brigade, the 29th Regiment, the 16th Portuguese, and one battalion of detachments, under Brigadier-General Richard Stuart, the 14th and 16th Light Dragoons under Sir Stapleton Cotton, with a brigade of artillery. This corps was pushed on to feel for the enemy, and marched on the 7th May to Mangaforaz. A division under General Hill marched on a parallel road along the coast leading from Aviera and Ovar to Oporto, in order to turn the enemy's right flank.

We moved on next morning, and passed through Aguada to Mureska, a small village near the left bank of the Vouga. Being now within a league of the enemy's advanced corps, the strength of our piquets was increased, and patrols of discovery were sent out to observe the enemy, while the whole force had orders to be ready to stand to their arms at a moment's notice. We, however, passed the night in tranquillity, and to our surprise remained inactive all the following day, the 9th May, as we anticipated that something was about to take place, being aware that the piquets had received orders not to allow any of the inhabitants to pass over towards the enemy.

As evening advanced, we gave up all hopes of moving forwards, and had lain down in our cloaks to get some rest. About midnight, however, we were awakened by the orderly-sergeants, who came to tell us that we were to get under arms, with as little noise as possible—no bugles to sound, or drums to beat—and to march immediately.

We now understood that we were about to endeavour to surprise the enemy's advance-guard, under General Francesche. We accordingly marched in great silence, and crossed the river at the Ponte de Vouga. The night was intensely dark, and we kept groping our way with some difficulty, and at last came to a standstill. During this an order was passed from the head of the column, "Send Lieutenant Leslie to the front."

I accordingly proceeded up as fast as I could, and found that my services were required to act as interpreter. The chiefs, the brigadier and his staff, were puzzled, not being able properly to understand the Portuguese guides, or to explain to them the route it was wished to take. I soon put matters to rights, and we again proceeded. The road was extremely bad, and we had not got very far when we were brought to a halt, as it appeared that the artillery had missed their way. While so detained I crept up a bank on the roadside to rest, and soon went fast asleep. It was near daybreak on the morning of the 10th when we began to move again.

We reached Albergaria Nova about dawn, but the enemy had fled an hour before, leaving a few sick men and lame horses, and occupied a wood at no great distance. We pushed on through the village and entered an extensive plain. Our cavalry, under Sir Stapleton Cotton, were formed in order of battle in two lines to the left of the road, while our light troops and the battalion of Portuguese students pushed on to feel for the enemy.

Some warm skirmishing soon commenced, and a few pieces of artillery got up to support our men. The enemy made no stand, but retired, keeping up their fire. We continued to follow them closely up, drove them rapidly through the town of Oliveira, and took some baggage and provisions. They, however, took up a position just outside the town, where some of their advance-guard had had a bivouac. We were halted in the streets, waiting until the whole of our artillery could come up, previous to attacking them. While lying on our arms in this manner, a person asked me if we would like the church bells to be rung to celebrate our arrival. I said, "By all means, if you choose to do so."

No sooner said than done. In a few minutes all the bells struck up a merry peal, and presently the people came to tell us that the French had fled. Whether this was caused by the loyal display, or by other reasons, I know not, but certain it is that they retired to a more respectful distance. Our outposts were placed close up to theirs, so that the hostile sentries were within half musket-shot of each other.

We occupied the French bivouac, which was laid out in the most tasteful manner. The huts were arranged in regular streets, many of them being adorned with evergreens round them, and devices cut out in the grass, such as *"Vive l'Empereur!" "Vive la France!"* &c., and all were well provided with tables, chairs, and cooking utensils, brought out from the Portuguese houses in the town. This had been a sort of permanent outpost.

The French exercised great cruelties in order to strike terror into the inhabitants, and to prevent them from acting against them. We observed near the entrance of Oliveira three bodies hanging on one tree. On inquiring, the people told us that they were the priest, the chief magistrate, and the town-clerk. This atrocity was committed because the people had gallantly encountered a French reconnoitring party, the commanding officer of which had been killed in the skirmish. The Portuguese peasants merited the greatest praise for their patriotism. They, as *ordinazas*, or resident militia, had erected fire-beacons on all conspicuous points, and along the road from Coimbra up to the nearest French outposts. Each of these beacons was guarded by armed parties ready to set fire to it, and thus give notice to the rear the moment the French advanced in force. This precluded the enemy from getting any accurate accounts of our movements. These brave people had no uniform, and were but badly armed, some having only old muskets and others pistols.

We were under arms long before daybreak next morning, the

11th May. Our piquets reported soon after dawn that the enemy had disappeared from their front. We immediately advanced in pursuit, but they had got the start of us so much that we saw nothing of them until we reached a wood about ten miles farther on. Then we observed the enemy's advanced posts. Two companies of the 29th Regiment, to one of which I was attached, were thrown into the wood on the right of the road, as a patrol of discovery, and also as a flanking party to protect the flank of the advanced column, by clearing the wood of any parties of the enemy. We had a Portuguese guide with us, and I acted as interpreter. We extended a subdivision, and advanced in skirmishing order, but the enemy's party withdrew without any resistance. We, however, held the wood until we were relieved by riflemen of the German Legion under Major-General Murray, when we were withdrawn and rejoined our regiment.

The enemy, about 5000 men, were posted in position on the heights above the village of Grijo, which is situated in a valley. The woods in the low ground and the village were occupied by their light troops, all under General Marmont, who had been pushing on for Oporto on his learning that the British were advancing.

We halted on a height on the side of the vale directly opposite to them, the 29th Regiment being formed in line, the 16th Portuguese on our left, and the cavalry and artillery on the right, on the main road, all ready to move on to the attack. Our light troops, consisting of the light company of the 29th Regiment, with the detachments of the 43rd and 52nd Regiments, and the 95th Rifle Corps, all under the command of Major Way of the 29th Regiment, dashed on, and were soon warmly engaged with the enemy in the woods below. During this we were ordered to lie down. Sir Arthur Wellesley and his staff were immediately in rear of our colours. The enemy's shot was passing through and over us pretty thick. One passed between myself and an officer who was in the act of handing me a cup of wine, nearly dashing it from his hand, and it fell just in front of Sir Arthur's horse.

The skirmishing still continuing with great obstinacy, and the enemy not seeming inclined to give way, Sir Arthur Wellesley said:

"If they don't move soon, I must let the old 29th loose upon them."

He ordered the 16th Portuguese, under Colonel John Milley Doyle, to move down through the wood, so as to gain and turn the enemy's right, while the column of the German Legion threatened their left. This had the desired effect. The enemy, finding both flanks likely to be turned, while we were ready to attack in front, they, after returning a few volleys from the Portuguese and Germans, hastily withdrew, and retired with great celerity. The 14th Light Dragoons were immediately sent in pursuit. They attacked the rear guard, and took many prisoners. We moved on through the village and were halted in the French bivouac, at some distance in its rear. The huts appeared to have been only recently erected, and the straw in them quite clean, so that it would seem they had not expected us. They likewise left cattle slaughtered in the village, which they had not had time either to serve out to their troops or to carry off.

We thus became indebted to our gallant foes for food and shelter. We made a capital dinner of their beef, and slept well and comfortably in the huts they had left standing.

Our light company suffered very severely in this affair, owing in some measure to a ruse practised by the French. While warmly engaged with them in the wood, the enemy's skirmishers hastily retired and got over a stone wall. Our gallant fellows instantly dashed up after them, when, to their surprise, a French battalion was lying concealed behind the wall. Several of our men, who in the hurry and excitement of the moment jumped over without looking before them, were instantly bayoneted. Lieutenant Stanhope had got on the top of the wall, and was seized hold of by a French soldier, who endeavoured to drag him down, but he was fortunately rescued by turn of his own men, who succeeded in pulling him back.

About two o'clock in the morning on the 12th May, we were aroused by the noise of a loud explosion which shook the ground. We immediately got under arms, and soon afterwards learned that the enemy had retired across the Douro, and had blown up the bridge of boats.

It was now clear that our commander was determined to force the passage of the Douro, and to drive the enemy from Oporto. By some mistake no orders arrived for our moving on, and we were kept waiting for some hours in an anxious state of suspense. However, orders at length arrived, and we proceeded with great expedition to Villa Nova, which is a suburb of Oporto, situated on the left bank of the Douro. We were halted in the steep narrow streets, and the column of sections well closed up. The inhabitants told us that from the top of their houses they could see the French under arms in the streets and squares in the town opposite, seemingly without any apprehension that a formidable enemy was so near them. We could not venture to go up to look at them, because in the interim the regiment might have moved on. Word was passed from the rear to open right and left to let the guards pass, but we resolved that no one should go before us, and passed the word back that we were so crowded that it was impossible to open out to let anyone pass, so we remained at the head of the column, and near the edge of the water, concealed from the view of the enemy only by some houses.

In the meantime Sir Arthur Wellesley had ordered the artillery to take post in the garden of the convent of St. Augustine, which is situated on a commanding height at Villa Nova, and commands the city on the other side of the river. We soon afterwards heard a partial cannonade, and then volleys of small arms. This, we learned, proceeded from General Hill's division, which was crossing over immediately above the town, under protection of our artillery, while a division of Germans, under General Murray, crossed the river four miles higher up at Avintas.

Soult now observing that the attack became very serious, and that his retreat might be endangered, began to evacuate the town. This being observed, we were ready to take advantage of it. Signs were made to the inhabitants, some of whom, availing themselves of the confusion in the enemy's army, instantly brought over several boats. The 29th Regiment immediately jumped into them, and pushed across in the frail barks, for many of the boats were in a dangerous state, being much shattered by the explosion the previous night. We succeeded in gaining the opposite shore with no other opposition than a few straggling shots, as the enemy hastily retired to the upper part of the town on our landing and forming on the quay. We immediately entered the town, and advanced up the main street, amidst the acclamations of the people, and the ladies, who from the upper windows and house-tops kept cheering, waving their handkerchiefs, and shouting, *"Viva! Viva!"* The doors and shops were all closed, and the streets as we advanced were strewed with French baggage which had been abandoned in their haste. On gaining the upper part of the town we observed some of the enemy through an opening. We then turned down on our right where the high road enters from Valenza, on which the enemy was retreating to Amarante. Here our leading company, the Grenadiers, began to fire upon them. They made little resistance, and made off in haste and confusion, abandoning a brigade of artillery and some ammunition wagons, and many were killed and wounded by our fire. We left sentries to protect the wounded, as the Portuguese mob was threatening to kill them.

On getting clear of the town we turned to our left into an open space enclosed with walls, in passing which, the enemy, who occupied a rocky height on our right, opened a smart fire upon us. We did not stop to return it, but pushed on, gained an opening, and immediately attacked the enemy, whom, after a smart skirmish, we drove from the heights. This was their last stand. We now had a splendid view of their whole army in full retreat. We reformed and rushed down after them. They made no fight, every man seemed running for his life, throwing away their knapsacks and arms, so that we had only the trouble of making many prisoners every instant, all begging for quarter, and surrendering with great good humour.

The 29th were the first troops that crossed direct into the centre of the town of Oporto, and, led on by Sir John Sherbroke, overtook the retreating enemy ere they quitted the town, and opened a fire on their rear, in consequence of which several pieces of cannon and ammunition wagons were captured. We afterwards drove them from a rocky height, and continued pursuing them very closely, they running away as hard as they could, cutting off their knapsacks, throwing away their arms and ammunition, &c. Many came out of houses and surrendered themselves prisoners. We were now rapidly gaining on the enemy, and those we overtook were begging for quarter. During this melee an order was passed from the rear to halt, and then open to right and left, when two squadrons of the 14th Light Dragoons, under the command of Major Harvey, led by

Major-General Charles Stewart, passed through us and dashed at the enemy, who, on perceiving the cavalry, immediately got over the fences on each side of the road, and opened a destructive fire on the dragoons, by which Major Harvey lost his arm, and many of his men were killed or wounded, with little or no loss on the part of the enemy; whereas, if the infantry had been allowed to proceed, there is little doubt the whole of their rear-guard would have laid down their arms and surrendered.

We continued still moving on, when the Duke of Wellington came up and asked me:

"What regiment is this? Where is Colonel Whyte?—where is Colonel Whyte?"

I went and found the colonel, to whom the duke gave orders to move the regiment up a height to the left of the road, and to form line along a wall on the edge of a wood which was in front, and not to move without his own positive orders. There we remained till about seven o'clock p.m., when we were marched back into the town. A street was given up to the regiment, and the officers were allowed to choose the best houses they could find. In the one which fell to my lot I found that the French had been kind enough to leave dinner prepared for me.

I may avail myself of this opportunity of noticing a statement which Colonel Napier has made in his account of the operations of the army at Oporto. He mentions that General Murray did not attack the flying enemy in flank as he might have done, and that in consequence of this, Major-General Charles Stewart and Major Harvey, impatient of this inactivity, charged with two squadrons of the 14th Light Dragoons, cutting up the French rear-guard, and making many prisoners.

It may be very true that General Murray did not attack the flying enemy as he might have done in the flank, but the attack made by General Stewart and Major Harvey, which was no doubt a dashing affair on their part, did more credit to their gallantry and courage than to their judgment.

The passage of the Douro was certainly a daring and dashing enterprise. There was Marshal Soult established, one of the best of the French marshals, with a large and well-appointed force under his command. The town is a very defensible position, having a broad and rapid river in its front, over which he had destroyed the means of passage; and he had secured all the boats of every description, so that a formidable resistance might easily have been made. Notwithstanding all these chances being against us, we overcame every obstacle, bearded the marshal in his den, and in a few hours drove him from his stronghold, which speedily obliged him to make a hasty retreat, and to evacuate the whole kingdom of Portugal.

There is no doubt but that the French had very bad intelligence regarding our force and movements. It would appear that they never dreamed that we would have had the hardihood to attack them in front, and expected that we would have disembarked to the north of Oporto, so as to threaten their rear, and communication with Spain. One of our officers found a plan, which a French officer had dropped in the road, of a section of the country, in which were detailed all the posts and points of defence from the mouth of the Douro along the coast to some distance northward, with the signals to be made should the English fleet appear, and instructions for defensive measures should they attempt to disembark. Indeed, so little was our hostile visit expected, that even the marshal himself had left his dining-table with his dinner untouched, for the benefit of his more fortunate opponent, our commander-in-chief.

When we first entered the town there was not a soul to be seen in the streets. All the doors and lower windows were closed up. The people appeared to have gone to the upper stories and roofs of the houses, but as we advanced and gained ground on the enemy, and French baggage of all description was lying strewed about, the rabble, urged by hopes of plunder, began to appear and to seize everything they could lay their hands upon; they had also knives in their hands ready to despatch the French wounded, had they not been prevented by us.

One fellow, a shoemaker, I imagine, came out very oddly accoutred for the fight. He had got a skin of thick sole leather tied on in front as a shield, from his chin to his toes, with a sword in one hand and a pistol in the other. He marched alongside of us, shouting, "Death to the French!" but when the French balls came whistling rather fast about our ears, he, with more prudence than valour, quietly dropped to the rear.

Our gallant commander, Sir Arthur Wellesley, with his usual foresight in making his dispositions for the campaign, had detached a force of British and Portuguese troops, under Marshal Beresford, to intercept the retreat of the French.

Owing to our supplies not having been able to keep pace with the rapid advance of the troops, and the difficulty of getting them across the river, it was found impossible to follow up the pursuit of the enemy. As our brigade had been for the last four or five days continually employed in most harassing duty, fighting and marching, and having gone over upwards of eighty miles of country in that short period, constantly in presence of the enemy, we were allowed three days to halt at Oporto. The inhabitants received us very hospitably. They opened the theatres, and invited us to attend. We had also the means of good living, the town being well supplied with provisions, and wine cheap.

On being driven from Oporto, Soult first directed his retreat upon Zamora, so as to unite with Loison; but on reaching Penafiel at night, he found that Marshal Beresford and Silveira had driven Loison from his post on the Tamega, so that his retreat was cut off in that direction. He therefore decided to retreat by Braga, which he did by forced marches. Having learned at Guimaraens that we were endeavouring to reach that place before him, so as to intercept his retreat into Galicia, while Marshal Beresford was marching on Chaves to cut him off in that direction, he was reduced to great extremity, his rear-guard was overtaken at Salamonde, and some made prisoners. However, he determined to save his army at all hazards, so he abandoned his remaining baggage and stores, and availed himself of bye-paths through mountainous districts, and finally made his escape over the frontiers to Montalegre, which he reached on the 17th May.

The tables were thus turned. But four months previously Soult had been engaged in active pursuit of the English army, without defeating them. Now the British, after defeating him, were in their turn pursuing him, and that so closely as to compel him to abandon his artillery, baggage, and stores to the victors.

Our brigade left Oporto on the 15th May, and proceeded to Villa Nova, a small village about four leagues northward, where we had some difficulty in finding cover to protect us from the rain. Next morning, the 16th, we moved upon Braga, hoping to reach that place before Soult, but he had succeeded in attaining his object, and had escaped. We halted there that night. Next morning, the 17th, we stood to our arms before daybreak, and left Braga after dawn. When we had marched three leagues, we learned that the French had escaped across the frontiers, destroying the bridges to retard our pursuit. We were immediately counter-marched, and moved into cantonments at Povo de Lanhoso, a small village in a wooded country. Although our accommodation was but indifferent, we were well pleased, the weather being very stormy, wet and cold for the season. There being now no enemy to dread in this quarter, we were allowed to take a nap in the morning. But our prospects of repose were of short duration. We got reports that Marshal Victor, with a *corps d'armee,* had taken Alcantara, and was threatening to enter Portugal by Castello Branco, and that our army was to move with as little delay as possible in that direction.

We commenced our march southward on the 20th May, and reached Braga that day. This was one of the neatest country towns, and the most thriving-looking place, we had seen in Portugal. It is noted for its manufactures of silk and woollen stuffs, especially a fleecy sort of shawls and night-caps.

This part of the country, *entre Douero y Minho,* is remarkably fine, being well cultivated, and the fields laid out in the English style, some with hedge-rows, others with rows of trees, on which vines are entwined, producing excellent grapes.

We moved to another Villa Nova on the following day, entered Oporto once more on the 22nd May, and reinstated ourselves in our former billets.

The army having been now all reassembled at Oporto, the various brigades received different routes of march to Coimbra, some by the inland road, others by the coast road. Our brigade took the latter. We left the city on the 24th May, repassing the Douro by the bridge of boats to Villa Nova; then leaving the road we had advanced by, we marched off to the right, and after going nearly two leagues through a fine country, we reached the small village of Municoso. My billet was in a peasant's house. An old man and his daughter constituted the family. We could get little or nothing to purchase in the place. We showed money, and asked for bread, fowls, &c. The only answer from one and all was, "*Nao!* the French have robbed us of all!—all!" There was, however, a fine promise of fruit. I observed in the small cottage gardens, almond, peach, orange, citron, plum, quince, cherry and fig trees, &c., all in full bloom. The following day we marched to Ovar, a distance of two leagues, through a flat, sandy country. Here we were detained waiting for boats until the 27th, nor did we embark until late in the afternoon of that day, when we proceeded down the Vouga, and across its mouth, which here assumes the appearance of a lake, or rather an arm of the sea, about seven or eight leagues broad. We did not reach Aveiro until after two o'clock in the morning of the 28th May, after a tedious and unpleasant voyage. The boats had only a small bit of deck at the stern for the steersman to stand upon, and under this we crept as the only shelter from the rain and cold.

On the 29th we proceeded four leagues to Venda Nova, a small wretched village, and on the following day, after a march of four leagues more, through a well-cultivated country, we again entered the fair city of Coimbra, and I lost no time in repairing to our hospitable friend, the worthy canon. We left Coimbra on the 3rd June, and marched two leagues through a beautiful country covered with gardens, vineyards, orange-groves, &c., to Condeixa. On the next day, the 4th June, we reached Pombal; here we left the high road to Lisbon, our march being directed to Abrantes on the Tagus, in a south-easterly direction. After a long march of five leagues through a barren country, we reached Cao de Maqao, *the land of apples*, a small village surrounded with gardens. From this place there is a most picturesque view of the town and old Moorish castle of Orem, situated on a high peaked hill.

We moved on the 6th to Payalvo, and on the 7th reached Punhete. This is a neat small town, prettily situated on a high ridge or tongue of land at the juncture of the Zenzere with the Tagus.

We proceeded next day, the 8th June, up the right bank of the Tagus two leagues, through a flat country covered with olive-groves, to Abrantes, a town situated on a conical hill, commanding the passage of the Tagus. Here there is a bridge of boats, hence it is considered a point of great importance. I got a very good billet on a priest, who was very civil, and made his servant cook for me.

We now learned that the French column, under Marshal Victor, which had threatened to enter Portugal in this direction, on finding that we had defeated Soult and driven him out of Portugal, and were marching to meet them, had withdrawn, and had retired to Talavera de la Reyna, and that a Spanish army, under General Cuesta, was on the Tagus watching the motions of the French.

Our commander-in-chief now determined that we should become the assailants, and march into Spain to attack the enemy. For this purpose the army began to concentrate, and preparations were made for the campaign. The men were supplied with shoes and other necessaries brought from Lisbon.

As our numbers increased by the arrival of reinforcements, the troops were ordered to be encamped. We left Abrantes on the 12th June, crossed the Tagus by the bridge of boats to the left, or southern bank, and occupied a position about a league distant from it. There we bivouacked and erected huts in regular order. For a camp-life it may be said that we lived here remarkably well, being plentifully supplied not only with the necessaries of life, but with many of its comforts, as our suttlers had great facility in bringing goods from Lisbon by water carriage.

The plan of the campaign seemed to be, that we were to advance up the valley of the Tagus on Placentia, and after uniting with Cuesta's Spanish army, to push on to Madrid: while Venegas was to push across the Tagus at the same time, and to advance on the capital simultaneously with us. Beresford, with 12,000 Portuguese in the vicinity of Almeida, and the Duke del Parque, with 10,000 Spaniards in the vicinity of Cuidad Rodrigo, were destined to watch Soult. The passes of Perales and Banos were to be occupied by a Spanish force, to prevent Soult from attempting to advance against us by Placentia and Salamanca. The French armies were so placed that either Soult or Victor would be able to act against the rear of an enemy who should advance against either of them.

Hence, it was evidently Sir Arthur Wellesley's object to concentrate our and the Spanish armies at Placentia, so as to leave the French commanders in doubt which line of operations he would follow, and then by a rapid march to make a dash at one of them. He, it appears, decided on trying his luck against Victor, as having a chance of also gaining the capital, Madrid.

The army broke up from Placentia on the 18th June, and took the line of the Tagus. Sir Robert Wilson about the same time advanced from his position on the Tietar, and moving on our left flank, reached Escalona on the 23rd, and was thus in the rear of the right of the French army under Victor.

When Joseph Bonaparte received at Madrid accounts of this decided move of the English army, he immediately brought all the troops he could spare, and formed a junction with Victor and Sebastiani near Toledo, while orders were sent to Soult to unite with Ney and Mortier, whose whole united forces were to proceed by forced marches through the passes of Perales and Piceto de Banos on Placentia, so as to act in rear of the English army. By these dispositions of the French armies they had concentrated 50,000 men in front of Sir Arthur Wellesley, and a like number threatened his rear.

Before the commencement of our operations in this campaign we understood that the positions of the different French armies were nearly as follows.

Marshal Victor, with about 25,000 men, was on the Tagus, having fallen back from the frontiers of Portugal on learning that Soult had been driven from Oporto. Sebastiani with about 20,000 men, was in La Mancha. General Kellerman, with a division of cavalry, was between Burgos and Madrid. All these corps may be said to have been in our front. Marshals Soult and Ney, with 60,000 men, were in Galicia and Leon. These last would be more or less on our left flank as we advanced into Spain on Madrid. The French had likewise a large force in Catalonia, but these were too far distant and too much occupied to have any immediate effect on our intended proceedings.

The British army of nearly 21,000 men were bivouacked at Abrantes, ready to march into Spain. The Portuguese army, under Marshal Beresford, consisting of 12,000 men, with a force of 10,000 Spaniards, under the Duke del Barque, was in the neighbourhood of Cuidad Rodrigo. The Spanish army of Estramadura, of about 37,000 men, under Cuesta, was on the left bank of the Tagus, and covered the bridge at Almarez, and was thus directly in advance, and between us and the French corps under Victor. Another corps of about 18,000 men, under Venegas, was in the

Carolinas. Sir Robert Wilson, with the Lusitania Legion and some Spanish light corps, was stationed on the Tietar, ready to act according to circumstances. Romana, with about 15,000 men, was in Galicia, opposed to Marshal Ney; Blake was at Valencia with 20,000 men.

By a reference to a map of the Peninsula it will be seen that a broad expanse of mountainous country separates the valley of the Douro from that of the Tagus, and forms an almost impassable barrier, there being practicable roads only at the east end by the Escural to Segovia, and near the west end by the road from Salamanca to Placentia, by the strong pass of Piceto de Banos, through which cavalry or artillery could be brought.

The officers of each company of our army got one bell-tent, which held three or four persons. All the arrangements for the approaching campaign being completed, the army broke up from the encampment and commenced the march towards the frontiers of Spain on the 27th June, 1809.

We proceeded through a barren, undulating country of low hills and hollows, covered with green *cestos*, a plant of three or four feet high, bearing a white flower with dusky green leaves, covered with a sticky, clammy substance, and emitting a sickly smell. We bivouacked at Gavion, a small miserable country town. The next day we passed through the same sort of country and reached Niza, a tolerably-sized town surrounded by old Moorish walls with square towers. On the 29th we continued our march through a desolate district, and reached the Tagus by a steep descent. The river here flows between two rugged mountains forming the celebrated pass of Villa Vilha, being one of the keys of Portugal. We crossed the river by a floating bridge of boats, and bivouacked near the old castle on the opposite bank. The scenery is wild and grand in the extreme. On the following day, the 30th June, we marched to Cemadas, a distance of only two leagues, to give time to get all the baggage and stores over the river, and for the rear-guard to close up.

On the following morning, 1st July, we marched to Castello Branco, a distance of three leagues. It is rather a neat town, situated on a hill, and has an old Moorish castle with walls and towers, from which there is a splendid view. On the west and north are high precipitous mountains, the Sierra d'Estrella, but to the east and south the eye is carried over unbounded plains extending towards Spain. This place is considered as a kind of frontier advanced post.

On the 2nd July we passed over an open, plain, uncultivated country, covered with rough grass, and at intervals with brushwood, for four leagues, and bivouacked near the village of Ladoeeira. Next day we proceeded four leagues farther, through the same sort of country, to Zibriera, also a small village, at both of which places the troops had warning not to enter, as a contagious typhus fever was raging in them.

On the 4th July we passed under Salvaterra, a small frontier town situated in a commanding position on a hill, not far from the right bank of the river Elga, which divides Portugal from Spain. The column waded across the river, which is here of some breadth, but not very deep. After proceeding about two leagues we were encamped at Zarza Maior, a small Spanish town. Here several of the soldiers' wives, having preceded the column, had taken the liberty of helping themselves to various articles in the shape of vegetables and other eatables. On complaint being made by the injured inhabitants, Lord Hill consigned the delinquents to the provost, *who exercised schoolboy discipline* on a few as an example to the rest.

The surprising difference in the appearance of the Spaniards and Portuguese in dress, manners, customs, and habits, is very remarkable, they being such near neighbours.

We halted at Zarza Maior two days, and Sir Robert Wilson joined us with his Lusitanian Legion. On the 6th July we marched on to Moralega, on the 7th to Coria, on the 8th to Galesteo. On the 9th we passed the River Alagon by a temporary bridge formed by cars, and encamped near Placentia, a remarkable ancient town, situated on the south of the high ridge of the mountain which separates Spanish Estramadura from Old Castile. The town stands in the mouth of one of those difficult passes which command the two districts. It is beautifully situated on a rising ground on the verdant bank of the river Alagon. The appearance of Placentia is very imposing. The cathedral, the churches, with their spires, the convents, the bishop's palace, form conspicuous objects, and add to the venerable appearance of the town, which is also ornamented with gardens, vineyards, and olive-grove. It is considered the capital of High Estramadura. Near the town in a pleasant locality Charles V. had his retreat.

The people neither here nor at the different places we had passed through since we entered Spain displayed that enthusiasm which might have been expected. We had a plentiful supply of all sorts of vegetables, fruits, and wines at a remarkably reasonable rate. The army was halted here for some clays, to give time for the military stores, provisions, and ammunition to come up, and also to wait for several regiments which had arrived at Lisbon to reinforce the army.

During our stay at Placentia, a sergeant of our grenadier company being appointed orderly to the adjutant-general, the Honourable Sir Charles William Stewart, used to go into the town every morning, and returned again in the evening. One day on his way back, just on quitting the town, he was met by two persons, one of whom spoke English remarkably well. They addressed him, saying that an English soldier was lying intoxicated at some distance off, and offered to accompany him to show him where the man was. To this the sergeant agreed. They took the direction to some high broken ground, covered with large rocks and brushwood. After searching about for some time, and getting more and more into a remote lonely hollow, they alleged that they were tired, and sat down upon a large stone. The sergeant did so likewise. After some conversation relating to the English army, in which they endeavoured to discover its numbers, and what place they were likely to go to next, finding that the sergeant evaded their questions, they turned fiercely upon him, and presenting pistols, declared they would shoot him if he did not disclose everything he knew. They told him that they were aware that he was employed by the adjutant-general, and that he must know the number of brigades, the names of the generals, and the destination of the army, whether going to move on Madrid or go through the passes to the north. They kept urging him until nearly daybreak next morning, and on his still refusing to answer their questions, they said, "Now we must be off, and we shall shoot you!"

Both started up; one of them presented his pistol, on seeing which the sergeant threw himself back, in doing which his right hand was raised. A ball went through it. Fortunately he put his hand to his face, which being covered with blood, the men imagined that he was mortally wounded, and also, no doubt, dreaded that the report of fire-arms might bring someone to the spot. They ran off in great haste, and were soon out of sight. From the sergeant's description of the two men, one must have been a French officer in disguise and the other a regular spy.

After a few days good wine became scarce, owing to the great demand made for it by our army. I strapped on my canteen one day, and went into town. While strolling about in search of a place likely to afford the desired beverage, I spied an elderly, portly-looking *signora* peeping out at the wicket of a large gateway. So I asked her, "Do you sell wine?"

She at first hesitated, and seemed shy of answering my question, but on looking about and seeing no other military near, she stepped back, and making a sign with her hand, said, "Enter, *signor*," and immediately bolted the wicket. She then led the way across a court, and opened a cellar door. I took off my canteen and gave it to her to fill, and remained at the door, not wishing to intrude into her secret depot. On perceiving this, she came back and begged me to come in, saying, "Pray enter, *signor*; do not fear anything, we are old Christians"—*Viejos Christianos* (not "converted "Jews).

During this campaign there appeared in our bivouac a peculiar race of men, retailers of lemonade, who continued to accompany the army throughout the whole war as regular followers. They were fine large muscular fellows, of swarthy complexion, expressive dark eyes, black-bushy hair, all natives of Valentia, and dressed in a most unique costume. They had sandals made of a sort of wild grass, or of goatskin, on their feet, their legs bare, short, wide petticoat trousers scarcely reaching to the knee, like a kilt, jackets made of some light-coloured cotton stuff with slashed sleeves to admit the air, large red sashes encircling their loins, their bronzed necks perfectly bare; a broad-brimmed *sombrero*, or hat, shaded their open, manly countenances. Each had a ticket stuck in front of his hat, indicating his name and number, so that no spies under such disguise could enter our lines. On their backs by a cross-belt were slung a sort of long slender barrels of churn form, having a tube and turn-cock near the bottom, and a basket with glasses of various sizes. This was their stock-in-trade. They promenaded the camp or accompanied the column on the march, vending at a moderate price their cool and refreshing beverage, bawling out, *"Limonada! Limonada fresca!"* The chief of each party had a donkey loaded with common sugar, &c. They resorted to the coldest springs before daylight, and there prepared their lemonade. When our ration wine was bad, or so hot as not to be palatable, which was but too often the case, we indulged in a glass of punch-royal, which was most easily made. We hailed one of these lemonade sellers, and purchased a quart or two of his lemonade, to which we added a portion of his Majesty's ration rum, with a glass or two of suttler's brandy, and our punch was made.

About midday on the 15th July I was warned for detachment duty, and got orders to proceed immediately into the town of Placentia, and to report a myself to the quartermaster-general, Sir George Murray. On my presenting myself, he told me that I was to proceed with despatches, and directed me to adjutant-general, Sir Charles Stewart, who gave me a sealed packet of confidential despatches addressed to Captain Rhuman, who was employed in the secret service at Avila do Formes, or wherever else I might find him. I got likewise an order to the commanding general to give me a certain sum of money in gold doubloons, which was also to be delivered to the captain. I then had to go to Sir Arthur Wellesley's secretary to get an order on the *junta*, or town council, to provide a guide, and to furnish me with a horse to start with, and others on the road, for which I was to pay eight *reals* a league. All this being arranged, I returned to Sir George Murray, who gave me another packet of despatches, with a written memorandum of the direction in which I was to proceed to Avila de Formes, and the distance, which was stated to be five leagues; also instructions that I was to proceed there without delay, and to follow the captain wherever he might have gone, in order to deliver my despatches, to receive any which he might have to send back, and to return with all possible expedition. I was about to leave the office, when Sir George Murray very good-naturedly said, "Sir, perhaps you have not dined?"

On my replying that I had had no time that day to attend to so essential a point, he politely requested me to take a seat at his table. There was no resisting so tempting an offer to one who had been living on camp-kettle soup, roasted hearts, and little else, and that too squatted on the ground in a tent, for nearly two months. It was no small treat to sit down in a comfortable chair to a decently-dressed dinner.

I then took my leave, and having folded the doubloons in a handkerchief as flat as I could, I tied it round my waist under my coat, At five o'clock p.m. I mounted my mule, that is to say, I found myself on a large flat pack-saddle, my legs a mile apart, and two wooden boxes dangling one at each side, as stirrups to put my feet in; but off we went at a smart pace, my guide leading the way. Shortly after quitting the town, a peasant, who was sitting by the roadside, started up and kept running alongside of me. I took no notice for some time; but finding that he continued to keep up with me, notwithstanding our going at a good pace, I, having in charge so much public money and important despatches, began to be apprehensive of some danger, so I stopped, and began to cross-question the guide about the man. He then informed me that he was the owner of the mule on which I was riding, which had been pressed into the public service, and that the poor fellow, dreading that he would never see his property again, was resolved to accompany it in our expedition. I remonstrated with him, and told him how absurd it was to give himself so much trouble. I assured him that his mule should be well taken care of and safely restored to him on my return. All arguments, however, proved fruitless, so on we went, and the activity which the poor man displayed was really surprising.

Our route was through one of those difficult passes which led through the mountains which separate Estramadura from Old Castile. At some distance from Placentia we entered the gorge or entrance of a large *strath* or glen, as they call it in Scotland, down which rushes a mountain stream, up which our course lay. On the left bank of this stream stands Aspenilla, a neat village at the mouth of the vale. The grandeur of the scenery in this region was strikingly superb. On casting the eye up the great *strath* towards the north, you behold the summit of the mountains, which terminated the view, covered with snow. On looking to either hand, you found yourself amidst sweet gardens and orchards of cherries, almonds, olives, and other fruit trees, attached to the neat villages and detached cottages, which bordered each side of the river. Next succeeded rows of rich vineyards, olive-groves, &c., and above them, up to the foot of the craggy rocks which cover the summit of the low hills, was rich luxuriant verdure, or these hills were covered with woods, consisting principally of cork trees or chestnuts, which offered food for herds of swine and goats.

The mystery of this delightful landscape was easily explained. The people, invited by the constant supply of water in the river, and the rills and fountains on the hillside, established their residences along the stream. The farmers of the plains had also their habitations here. In October they went down to the plains and scratched up the soil with a rude plough, sowed their wheat or other grain, and harrowed it with the branch of a tree. Then leaving their crop to a benevolent providence, they hastened back to their charming retreats. When reaping time came in June, they, with their friends and neighbours to assist them, descended to the plains, erecting rude bivouacs or sleeping in the farm-sheds, cut down the grain, which was immediately threshed out, put into sacks, and transported by mules to the several homes.

My route lay up the course of this river, which in some places is still and deep, and at others it rushes over a rocky bed, gradually becoming narrower as you proceed. Our road dwindled into a mule track which frequently crossed and recrossed the stream in its various windings. I reached Mabaconcejo about eleven o'clock at night. On going to the *alcalde* and demanding two fresh mules, he professed great willingness to forward the public service, but assured me almost all the animals had been embargoed for the army, and that as it was so late he could not possibly procure mules for two or three hours. As I had no means of compelling him to get mules, I was obliged to submit.

He gave me a billet on one of the best houses. The landlord was very civil; I got a hasty supper of some sausages and a bottle of excellent wine. I told him to call me in three hours, and turned into a bed, the first time I had enjoyed such a luxury or slept without my clothes for nearly seven weeks. Mine host was punctual. At the appointed hour, 3 a.m., he awoke me and most kindly brought me a cup of capital chocolate which I gladly accepted. He refused all compensation. I mounted again, and after riding a league, I came to Cabizuelo, and two leagues farther on to Jerte, both small towns. The valley began to narrow very much, and the road became steep. We reached Tornabacos after another ride of two leagues. This is the last place in Estramadura, and is situated on the mountains at the foot of the pass. The road now became very difficult, being very narrow, and winding at some places along the sides of steep acclivities, at others mounting by zigzags up most abrupt ascents. Here an action had been fought, as we saw some shot lying about.

After a tedious ride of three leagues more, we at length arrived at Puerto de Tornabacos, at the top of the pass. This is a small desolate place, situated in the region of eternal snow, and is the first frontier place in Old Castile. I stopped here at a wretched *posada* in order to refresh the mules, and to get some breakfast. They prepared for me a mess of black pudding, eggs and bacon, all fried together in oil, and seasoned with garlic. Hungry as I was, I could not manage to eat this, so after some delay they procured me some milk, with which and a loaf of good bread I was obliged to be contented. The muleteer, not being so fastidious, regaled himself with the horrid compound of bacon, eggs, oil, and garlic. A red coat never having been seen in this part of the world before, I became an object of great curiosity. Crowds of people assembled in front of the hostelry, others, pushed their way inside. Many asked various questions relating to ourselves and the French, but most stood mute, gazing at an *Inglese*.

On resuming my journey, the road rapidly descended into Castile, and the country became more open, and cultivation resumed its sway. Fields were enclosed, bearing crops of hay, &c., so different from the southern parts of Spain. I continued on for about three leagues farther, and at length arrived at the place of my destination, Bario d'Avila, a small neat town situated on the bank of the river Formes.

On approaching the place my guide preceded me, keeping about ten yards in front. He went cantering briskly along, cracking loudly over his head, by a peculiar knack, his short-handled, long-thonged whip, which Spanish couriers use; while the small globular bells which decorated the head and neck of his ambling mule kept continually tinkling. The people, as we flew through the streets, turned out to inquire the news.

I here found Captain Rhuman, a German by birth, who held an English commission in the Lusitanian Legion. He was a most intelligent person, a capital linguist, and was employed in the secret service, being well qualified for such an office. I delivered to him my despatches and the money all safe, which was a great relief to me. He was on the eve of going out to meet by appointment a chief of a band of *guerillas*. He wished me much to accompany him, that I might see what sort of gentry these outpost warriors were; but however anxious to satisfy my curiosity on that head, I felt obliged to decline his invitation, as my orders were peremptory to return without any unnecessary delay.

After resting three hours, and having got the captain's despatches, including secret reports and official returns of the French armies in this quarter, Spanish and Paris newspapers, &c., I took my departure, and reached Tornabacos late at night. I immediately went to the house of a family to whom Captain Rhuman had given me a letter of introduction. They received me in the kindest manner possible, and assured me it was impossible to get fresh mules at that late hour, or even at any time, the proprietors of these animals being afraid that if they conveyed anyone to the low country, and particularly to where the army was, their mules would be embargoed for the public service. I also got a hint that the proprietor of the mules I had was, for the same reason, contemplating to make his escape and forfeit all the hire due to him. I immediately had him brought before me, and directed him to be ready to move at 4 o'clock next morning, threatening him with severe punishment in case of failure, as his name and address were known; but at the same time I pledged myself that if he conducted me safe to Placentia again, I would ensure him that his mules should not be embargoed, and that I would give him something extra beyond the public allowance.

The ladies of the family were most affable, and I passed an agreeable evening. One of them was sadly puzzled to make out what sort of a place England was. She said they told her it was a country all surrounded with water. She could not understand how this was possible, and even if it were, how was it possible to get there? She had no notion whatever of the sea, and as little of large ships. She had never seen any sort of vessel except a small ferry-boat. After a few hours' stay, I started on my return to Placentia. I was much surprised to meet on the road at intervals herds of cattle, mules, &c., coming up to the mountains. On inquiring, I was informed that the proprietors of these animals, afraid of their being impressed for the use of the armies, were driving them to a place of security. I likewise passed immense droves of sheep. I learned that they were the usual flocks of merinos in their progressive annual march towards the cooler mountain regions, it being their habit during the oppressive heats of summer to pass that period there. For this purpose they begin to leave the plains in the beginning of June, and gradually eat their way up, and about the early days of September they commence returning again to the open plains. This system, however, proves very detrimental, and becomes a great hindrance to improvements in agriculture. The merinos are under royal protection, and the farmers in the plains are prohibited from enclosing their grounds, so that the sheep may have free pasturage on the grass and stubble lands in passing. Each flock consisted of many thousands of sheep, preceded by a shepherd at the head, with a splendid wolf-dog or two, and the rear was brought up with the head-shepherd and his numerous attendants and several of these fine dogs, with fine large asses carrying the baggage, cooking utensils, women, and children. The flocks kept a mile or two distant from each other.

I was much pleased that it had fallen to my lot to perform the duty in which I was now engaged. It proved a most interesting excursion, the scenery was altogether so different from what I had hitherto been accustomed to. Since our departure from Castello Branco, we had passed over immense plains, where scarcely a habitation was to be seen for miles, and little cultivation, but at intervals small patches of wheat, or open woods of black oak or cork trees, the ground and and burnt up, the heat oppressive, and water seldom to be found. How different was the contrast in these delightful, romantic regions! There the people, in their charming mountain vales, lived in the most perfect security, enjoying all the freshness of the cooling breeze, and the varied luxuries their charming retreat afforded. There they had the purest springs, the finest fruits of all kinds, the choicest vines, abundance of excellent bread, milk, and honey. The horrors of war were to them unknown.

I reached Placentia in the afternoon of the 17th July, and on delivering my despatches to the quartermaster-general, Sir George Murray, he expressed surprise that I had not returned sooner, he having begun to surmise that I had been taken prisoner. On my explaining to him that the distance had proved to be nearly double what he had told me previous to my departure, and the obstacles and difficulties I had in procuring mules, he was perfectly satisfied, and most politely again invited me to dinner. I detailed to him from my notebook all I had seen, and the resources which our commissariat might draw from those retired vales.

During my absence the army had marched in advance. Sir George Murray gave me a memorandum of their route, and an order for post-mules to enable me to overtake my regiment. I found that a hospital depot had been established here under the command of Captain Pattison of the 29th, and that there were also one or two other officers of the regiment left on the sick list. The brave captain was in great distress at the idea of being left behind his corps, which was expected shortly to come in contact with the enemy. He charged me to request that our commanding-officer would get him relieved. I got a capital billet, and laid in some necessary supplies for future service.

Next morning, the 18th July, I proceeded. The road lay through a most extensive plain, bordered on the north, or left hand, by mountains, and on the south by the Tagus and the hills beyond it. In some parts there were detached woods of cork and oak trees, but at such open distance that it gave the plain a pretty, park-like appearance. I passed through Tulaquila and Malpartida, miserable villages, and late in the evening I overtook the army, and found my regiment encamped on the river near Majadas.

On the following day, the 19th July, we reached Casa de Centinella, after a long march of four leagues, and bivouacked in one of the cork woods. On the 20th we continued on through the same flat country to Oropeza, which is a neat old town situated on a ridge of land rising out of the plain. This was a most distressing march of three leagues. The heat was excessive, and the want of water was severely felt. We learned that a body of French dragoons had left the place only a few hours previous to our arrival. We halted here on the 21st, on which day the Spanish army, under

General Cuesta, formed junction with us. They passed on beyond us, and took ground in advance to our left.

In the afternoon we were ordered to turn out at six o'clock in review order. We paraded accordingly, the whole of our army forming one continued line of great extent. We then understood that this exhibition was for the edification of the Spanish *dons* who were to inspect us. After standing at open ranks for a length of time, we at last perceived a crowd of staff-officers moving up from the left of the line. As the cortege approached, I perceived four or five cavaliers riding in advance, one of whom was habited in a sort of fustian jacket and a black jockey cap. Our officers were all asking who he was, but nobody could tell. Therefore, as one of the Spanish officers riding with him passed near me, I asked him who the gentleman was. He replied, *"Es mi lor Mac Duffee, Gran Signor Inglese."*

My English friends were still in the dark until I explained that I had the honour of claiming to be a countryman of that great personage, the descendant of the Thane of Fife, the conqueror of Macbeth.

We were under arms next morning by the usual hour, three o'clock, and commenced our march to Talavera de la Reyna, "the Queen's Pottery." For the first league or so the ground was broken and uneven, but afterwards plain and open, with occasional cornfields and patches of cork woods. After advancing about two leagues we passed the Spanish army formed in two lines in the plain on the left of the road. We continued to advance, and soon afterwards we learned that our cavalry, in combination with some Spanish horse, were skirmishing with a body of French cavalry, who were retiring before us. As we approached Talavera and the banks of the Tagus, the plain became visibly much narrower. The mountains on the left tended rapidly towards the south, while the range of precipitous hills on our right, on the left bank of the Tagus, enclosed it on that side, so that the open country was not above three miles in breadth.

The Spanish army, taken as a whole, presented the most motley and grotesque appearance. Many corps were regulars, and many more were irregulars. Their uniforms were of every variety of colour, their equipments and appointments of the most inferior description. All were deficient in discipline and regular organisation. One could not but lament these defects, for the men were remarkably fine, possessing the most essential qualities to make good soldiers, being individually brave, patient, and sober, capable of enduring much fatigue, while their officers in general were the very reverse. The infantry regiments of the line were generally in blue uniform with red facings. The provincial corps, styled volunteers, were mostly dressed in the brown Spanish cloth of the country, with green or yellow facings; some had *chakoes*, others broad-brimmed hats with the rim turned up at one side, and all had cap-plates of tin announcing their designation. Some had belts, others had none. They had no pouches, but a broad band of soft brown leather in which was placed a row of tin tubes, each holding a cartridge, and having a fold of leather to cover them, fastened round the waist. There were several Swiss regiments, also dressed in brown. Two or three regiments, which bad formerly been composed of Irish, still retained the name of Regiments d'Irlanda, de Hibernia, &c., in red uniforms with blue facings, and a harp on the collar of the jacket. They had only a few officers, who were Irish or of Irish extraction, The most efficient corps were the Walloon Guards, who were all supposed to be Flemish Walloons, but they were principally German Swiss, with a number of other foreigners. They wore a blue uniform with red facings, bordered with white lace, and they bad silver epaulets and ornaments. The cavalry consisted of heavy and light dragoons, with some regiments of hussars. Some were tolerably well dressed, in blue uniforms with red facings, others in yellow with red facings. Some had boots, but many wore long leather leggings, which came up several inches above the knee. The horses in general were small, active, and hardy, of the Spanish Barbary breed.

Everything indicated the appearance of an antiquated system; nothing of the new school in the art of war seemed to have been adopted in the Spanish army. The proud Castilians seemed still to believe that they were the same energetic race who maintained a high degree of celebrity in Europe, and became the conquerors of the new world. They still clung to the ancient customs and prejudices, and seemed to be altogether unconscious of their inferiority.

As the army kept advancing, so the enemy continued to March

to retire, covered by their skirmishers. Our cavalry, however, drove them from the town of Talavera, and from the olive-groves in its vicinity, while they, to mask their retreat, set fire to the dry stubble, which created a great smoke and concealed them from our view. They succeeded in joining their main body, which occupied a position on the other side of the river Alberche, about two leagues beyond Talavera. Their left rested on the Tagus, and their right on a bend of the Alberche and some broken wooded heights about two miles from where that river unites with the Tagus. Their numbers were said to be about 55,000 men.

We bivouacked in the olive-groves to the left of the town of Talavera, which is situated on the right bank of the Tagus, over which there is a fine bridge. General Mackenzie's division was pushed on as an advance-guard to watch the enemy.

On the 23rd July we understood that we were to attack the enemy. We were accordingly under arms before three o'clock in the morning, but had moved only a short distance when we were halted, and the men kept standing under arms. No one could tell the reason, but there we were kept for several hours in a miserable state of suspense, all being hungry, and no one having anything to eat. No cooking could be done, as from our not having been dismissed we expected every moment to receive orders to proceed. However, late in the afternoon, we were at last informed that the men might cook their dinners.

We heard that the uncomfortable position we had been placed in was owing to the obstinacy of the old Spaniard Cuesta, who under various pretences declined to assist in attacking the enemy that day, and, among other reasons, it was said that he alleged it was Sunday. He, however, agreed to cooperate next day, the 24th.

About eleven o'clock at night, I being the officer of the day, was called up to take charge of a fatigue party of six men of each company, with orders to proceed into the town and to have all the men's canteens filled with water. So off we went in the dead of night, each man carrying eight or ten canteens. But the puzzle was, after getting into the town, where to find the water in the obscurity of darkness. We succeeded in finding one or two public fountains, but as so many from various other corps were on the same errand, the supply was not equal to the demand. So some knocked at one door, and others at another, all bellowing out, *"Aqua! Aqua!"* The frightened inhabitants, delighted to find that the requisition was of so simple a nature, and not for wine, gladly supplied our wants.

On regaining the bivouac about two o'clock in the morning of the 24th July, we found the troops getting under arms, with orders to make as little noise as possible. No drums were allowed to beat or bugles to sound; it was therefore clear to everyone that we were now about to attack the enemy. After the disappointment of yesterday, everybody was in high spirits. While the parade was forming I had the pleasure to find that my school-fellow, friend and country neighbour, Andrew Leith Hay, who had got a lieutenancy in the regiment, had just arrived with our senior, Captain Tucker.

We moved off in the greatest silence about three o'clock a.m., diverging to our left hand as we advanced towards the enemy. When the column had marched about five miles we were halted. The 29th Regiment, the leading one, was deployed into line. The next regiment did the same at about ten paces in our rear, and all the following ones did the same, so that the whole division stood in column of regiments in line. We now understood that we were within gunshot range of the enemy's position, and that we were only waiting to, hear that our right and centre columns had commenced to attack the enemy's left, for us to dash on and carry the key of his position.

But we waited in vain; no firing was heard, no cheer of success greeted our ears—all was silence. Day was fast breaking. The men became impatient; eager murmurings were heard on every hand, "Why don't we advance?" While we were in this state of suspense, the gallant Lord Hill, commander of our column, came back from the front with evident vexation, and announced that the enemy had retreated and there would be no fighting. This intelligence was received in mortified silence.

Colonel De Launcy, of the quartermaster-general's department, soon afterwards appeared, bringing with him a French officer whom he had taken prisoner. It appeared that the colonel, a most daring and enterprising officer, had during the night gained the flank of the French army. Finding that they were moving off, he secreted himself near the road, so that he could observe their numbers as they passed. After the whole had departed, this officer, having forgot his watch in the bivouac, returned in search of it, when Colonel De Launcy, with his orderly dragoon, pounced upon him, and made him their capture. He was a very handsome young man in green uniform.

We were shortly afterwards counter-marched, and moved back to our bivouac in the olive-groves, in the vicinity of Talavera. That of my regiment was close on the left side of the main road to Madrid, and only about a quarter of a mile in front of the town. On arriving there we found our baggage waiting for us. Our paymaster and his coadjutor, the clerk, were likewise on the *qui vive* awaiting our arrival, it being the 24th—muster-day. He said with a gracious smile, "Gentlemen, I shall now have the pleasure of mustering you all, which is more than I expected."

The great disadvantage of not having attacked the enemy on the 23rd July, as our gallant commander, Sir Arthur Wellesley, had wished, became evident to everyone. Marshal Victor, with only about 25,000 men, had waited for us: we, on the other hand, had 19,000 British and nearly 50,000 Spanish troops, which could easily have defeated the French, and would most probably have succeeded in opening Madrid to us. But owing to the procrastination of Cuesta, this golden opportunity was lost; Victor, learning that Joseph Bonaparte was hastening with reinforcements to support him, fell back to meet them.

Now that the enemy had disappeared from our front, Cuesta became full of fight. He determined to pursue as if the enemy had been beaten and was flying in disorder. He pushed his army across the Alberche, took post at Santa Olalla, and established his advanced posts at Torrigors on the 25th July. Sir Arthur Wellesley prudently sent only an advanced guard across the Alberche, under General Mackenzie, who occupied Casaleguas.

During the whole day of the 25th all seemed to remain quiet. There were no movements in our bivouac, and we heard no reports, but on the morning of the 20th reports reached us from the front that the French had reappeared. Late in the afternoon quantities of Spanish baggage began to pass us to the rear, and soon afterwards many wounded and numerous runaways, who informed us that the French had attacked their advanced post, which Cuesta had been obliged to draw in, and that the Spanish army was retiring.

On the morning of the 27th July we, as usual, turned out and stood to our arms an hour before daybreak. Even at that early hour symptoms of the Spaniards being in retreat began to appear. Herds of cattle, pigs, and sheep, moving to the rear passed us, then followed ammunition wagons and baggage, and a few hours afterwards came the infantry, artillery, and cavalry.

As our tent was within a few paces of the road, I got accounts of what was going on from the Spaniards as they passed. While in conversation with some of them, General Hill rode up and asked me if I could tell him what was going on in front. I detailed all the particulars I had learned. He then said, "All I know is this, that if the enemy advance to attack us, we shall occupy the ground from the river here on our right to the pointed hill on the left."

Captain Melish, of the quartermaster-general's department, told the general that he was going forward to see what was going on, and on his return would let him know.

The truth was, that King Joseph, with a force from Madrid, had joined Sebastiani, who was at Toledo, and had then pressed on to unite with Marshal Victor. The united French forces had then attacked Cuesta's advanced guard with great vigour, and caused the Spaniards to retire in great haste across the Alberche.

Early on the 27th July our cavalry were ordered to the front to support our advanced guard, and to cover the retreat of the Spanish army. About midday the enemy appeared in front of our advanced guard, which then retired from Casaleguas, through a wood, across the Alberche, and drew up at a short distance on the right bank in front of an old ruin or windmill. While resting in this position with piled arms, the enemy, under cover of the wood, had pushed on so very close that they unexpectedly opened fire on our troops. Some confusion arose from this circumstance. Our troops were withdrawn from the wood into the plain, where order was restored, and the whole began to retire in regular order, closely followed by the enemy.

We now had certain intelligence that the enemy was pressing on in force. Wounded men from our advanced guard began to come in, and the report of cannon announced to us that a battle was at hand. We ordered our dinner to be cooked in all haste, and lost no time in despatching it. We then had our tent and baggage packed. This foresight was well-timed, for shortly afterwards the drums beat to arms, the bugles sounded the alarm, and we got orders to move to our left. The Spanish army began to take up their position on the ground we were quitting, forming in two lines with reserves in the rear.

To understand the positions on the field of battle, it may be stated that our line of defence ran from the Tagus on our right to a conical hill about two miles on the left. The town of Talavera, situated on the left bank of the river, was about half a mile in the rear, and the Madrid road running east from it was parallel to the Tagus at a short distance from its bank. On this road, and nearly half a mile from the town, stood a church, in front of which field-works were thrown up, and a battery of Spanish heavy guns placed on it so as to command the road and the space between it and the Tagus. This point became properly the right of our position. From this, and for a mile towards the left, the country was level, but covered with gardens, olive-groves, and vineyards, and was much intersected by thick earthen walls, which rendered it very defensible. Here the Spaniards were posted.

From the edge of these wooded enclosures the ground was open, and began to rise gradually, until it reached the summit of a conical point of a range of green hills on the left. Beyond these hills, which were very steep, on the other, or north side, there was a valley, and beyond that commenced a broken rocky mountainous country, impassable for troops, which enclosed the position on that flank. The whole space from the enclosure to the hills was occupied by the British, who formed the left wing of the army, while some light troops and cavalry were placed in the village beyond.

Near the British right flank, and just clear of the olive-groves, was a large knoll, on which some works were begun to be thrown up, and a brigade of British guns was placed there in battery. The bed of a dried-up stream, coming from the mountains, ran along the whole front of the position down to the Tagus.

Between four and five o'clock in the afternoon our brigade moved off, left in front, between the Spanish lines. The Spaniards appeared very valiant, and cried out, *"Rompez los Franceses."*

We could now hear smart musketry firing going on between our advanced guard and the enemy. The sound of cannon and small arms seemed approaching us very rapidly. On getting clear of the enclosures and gaining the lower slope of the hill, our brigade, the 29th Regiment, one battalion of detachments, and one battalion of the 48th Regiment, was drawn up in rear of the front line. We could now see our advanced guard retiring across the plain, closely pursued by the enemy. A portion of the advanced guard moved directly towards us, and passed through our line, and proceeded to the different places in position. During this the French kept up a continued fire against them of shot and shell, which were now falling thick and fast amongst us. While this cannonade continued we were ordered to he down. As the evening was now closing, and darkness began to prevail, we could discern the shells and time their course from the moment they left the mouth of the howitzers by their fuses burning like brilliant stars as they rose in the air, then rapidly descending right down upon us, or breaking over our heads. Many of us made narrow escapes, but on the whole no very serious loss was occasioned. The firing ceased, and all seemed hushed and quiet. We lay on the ground with our arms in hand. The night became very dark and gloomy. We had continued in this way nearly an hour, when in a moment, about nine o'clock, there opened a tremendous fire on the top of the hill on our left, and which seemed to have been taken up and ran down the first line in our front. It was now evident that the enemy had made a dash at this, the key of our position, and were in possession of the top, as we could, by the blaze of firearms and the flashes of light, distinguish the faces of the French and those of our own troops returning the fire.

The 29th Regiment was immediately thrown into open column, left in front, and instantly moved up the hill to attack the enemy, directing our march between the fire of both parties. Without halting, our left made a dashing charge, and after a short but desperate struggle drove the French off the summit of the position. We then wheeled into line, advanced obliquely to our left, and opened our fire on the French reserves which were pushing up in support of their discomfited comrades. This decided the affair; the enemy was completely overthrown and fled in confusion, leaving the ground strewed with their dead, dying, and wounded, among whom was the colonel of their 9th Regiment, and quantities of arms and accoutrements. During this affair, when we formed into line, our right companies were some way down the slope of the hill. We could see the French column moving up across our front, their drums beating the charge, and we could hear their officers giving orders and encouraging their men, calling out, *"En avant, Francais! En avant, mes enfants!"* but our well-directed volleys and cheers of victory stopped their progress, and their shattered columns returned in dismay. The wounded and the prisoners informed us that they were part of General Rufin's division. The 29th Regiment took possession of the top of the hill, our colours being planted on the summit.

It was evident that the troops posted on the hill had been surprised, owing, no doubt, to the neglect of the common precaution of throwing out piquets and a chain of sentries along their front. We understood that the corps consisted of the German Legion. General Donkin's brigade assisted us to repel another attack made during the night on our position.

How we, the 29th Regiment, who were the right regiment of the brigade, got so gloriously into the fight I could not tell; but this I know, that as we were advancing up to the attack we came upon our next left regiment, the battalion of detachments, who appeared to have got into confusion, and we pushed our way through them to rush at the enemy. The gallant soldiers of the battalion seemed much vexed; they were bravely calling out, "There is nobody to command us! Only tell us what to do, and we are ready to dare anything." There was a fault somewhere. We afterwards found, on re-forming, that we had been the centre regiment, the first battalion of the 48th Regiment being on our left, and the battalion of detachments on our right.

We had the good fortune to rescue our General Hill, who, in leading us to the attack, and being anxious to see what was doing in front, gallantly dashed on a little too far and got into the French ranks. They had seized the reins of his horse, and would have had him prisoner had we not immediately charged on and thus rescued him. But Major Fordyce on his staff was killed, and Captain Gardiner mortally wounded.

As soon as the 29th Regiment had established themselves on the hill, and we had reformed our line in a proper position, a corporal and three men of each company, under an officer, were thrown out as a piquet in front, and a portion formed a chain of sentries, while our line lay down, each man with his arms in his hands, and all upon the alert. Nor were these precautions unnecessary. The French piquets frequently during the night ducked up at various places, gave loud huzzahs, fired a volley, and then as hastily retired again. Indeed, we were so close that we could hear the French sentries challenging their visiting rounds, and calling out, *"Qui vive!"* On these salutes taking place we always stood instantly to our arms, and when the advanced piquet announced all quiet we lay down on the ground again. In some instances several advanced sentries of some of our regiments, being young soldiers, fired, so that the word "stand to your arms" was frequently passed along the line.

The Spaniards had also their alarm on the right, about midnight, but whether real or imaginary never could be ascertained. It was not confined to one spot, for it spread right and left, and they opened a running fire along their whole line, which lasted for some time, until many corps, scared by they knew not what, fled to the rear, and it was only with great difficulty, we were told, that they were brought back into their places in line, again.

From our commanding position on the hill we had a grand and sublime view of this midnight scene. The lengthened blaze of the Spanish fire, running up and down the lines, and the flashing of their artillery had a magnificent effect. While looking towards the enemy in our front, we beheld a kind of illumination moving in advance in certain directions. This was caused, no doubt, by a number of *flambeaux* which they carried at the head of their reserves and artillery to enable them to find their various routes to their proper places in their position.

About one or two o'clock in the morning of the 28th July the moon began to give some light. As it became stronger we could see black patches moving in the plain immediately in front of us, and then become stationary directly opposite to us. This was no other than their columns forming in mass for attack. We could also hear the noise of wheels and the cracking of whips as they brought up their guns to plant them against us. All this was extremely splendid and exciting, but nature will under all circumstances have her sway. No sooner was any alert over than we sank down and dropped asleep. Although I had no greatcoat or covering of any kind, and only an old tin pot which chance threw in my way for a pillow, yet I got two or three profound naps during the intervals we were allowed to rest.

It may be naturally supposed that we looked most anxiously for morning, and as the day began to break all eyes were strained to discern the disposition of the enemy. As things became more visible a very imposing sight presented itself to our view. The whole disposition of the enemy's force could be clearly distinguished. In the first place, immediately beneath us was formed a heavy solid column on the brink of the ravine, with reserves in its rear, with field batteries on both flanks, and the guns already pointed towards us, while light troops were thrown out as *tirailleurs* to cover their front and prepare the way for a grand attack, which was evidently to be directed against us on the hill. At some distance to the right were formed other masses in like manner. Others were also for mod in front of our allies the Spaniards. The columns of reserve, cavalry, spare artillery, and baggage extended a long way back in their rear.

Our own lines presented an animated but not so formidable appearance, owing to the nature of our formation. Our front showed an extended line only two deep, with the reserve placed at various distances along its rear. The disposition made by our experienced commander seemed most perfect to meet the meditated attack, and as, after the enemy's first attempt on the previous evening, all our troops had got into the proper place assigned to them in our position, everything appeared in complete readiness for whatever might happen.

As the sky began to redden with the first blush of the morning sun, a gleam of animation was thrown over both armies, which our elevated position enabled us to survey. The piquets in front were withdrawn, and our light company, and others of the brigade were thrown out as skirmishers to cover our front. The still of the morning was broken by no warlike sound. A solemn silence prevailed on both sides. Our view was extensive, and the scene before, us was most imposing and sublime. While we were contemplating this, Sir Arthur Wellesley rode up in rear of our regiment, the 29th, and then going to the front seemed to survey the enemy with great earnestness. Much about the same time we could plainly discern Joseph Bonaparte and a large suite of staff in his train coming up at full gallop in rear of the French masses in our front.

All was yet breathless silence, when we perceived the smoke of a gun curling up in the air, and heard the report of a single cannon. This appeared to be the signal for putting the enemy's columns in motion. We were not detained long in suspense. In a moment a tremendous cannonade opened upon us on the hill, and on the regiment stationed on the lower part of the slope to our right. We could then see the French skirmishers dash up and push rapidly on, while the columns immediately in front of us got in motion, advancing towards us. It was now evident that the enemy intended if possible to turn our left, and to storm and seize the hill, the key of our position, which they had taken and lost the night before. General Hill, seeing the overwhelming force that was coming against us, gave orders that the light troops should be recalled, and the bugles sounded accordingly. The skirmishers were closing in and filing to the rear with all the regularity of field-day and parade exercise, which the general observing, called out, "D—n their filing, let them come in anyhow."

In order to cover the advance of their columns the enemy continued the terrific cannonade, which became so destructive that we were ordered to lie down flat on the ground. The shot flew thick and fast about us, but it went principally over us, the guns being too much elevated; but not so with the 45th Regiment below us on the right: we could see large gaps made at times in their ranks by the round shots.

At length the French column of attack, which had pushed vigorously on notwithstanding the well-served fire of our artillery directed against them, began to approach us. We took no notice of them, but allowed them to come up pretty close to us, when our brigadier-general, Richard Stewart, said, "Now, 29th! now is your time!" We instantly sprang to our feet, gave three tremendous cheers, and immediately opened our fire, giving them several well-directed volleys, which they gallantly returned; but we checked their advance, and they halted to continue the battle with small arms. We then got orders to charge, which was no sooner said than done. In we went, a wall of stout hearts and bristling steel.

The French did not fancy such close quarters. The moment we made the rush they began to waver, then went to the right about. The principal portion broke and fled, but some brave fellows occasionally faced about and gave us an irregular fire. We, however, kept dashing on, and drove them all headlong right before us down the hill into their own lines again. We kept following them up, firing, running, and cheering.

In the midst of the exultation, about seven o'clock a.m., I received a ball in the side of my thigh, about three inches above the right knee. The sudden and violent concussion made me dance round, and I fell on my back. I immediately put my hand on the wound, which was bleeding profusely, to feel if the bone of my leg was broken, and, to my great satisfaction, I found that it was not. As I found myself unable to rise, I called for assistance, but from the noise and hurry of battle no one seemed to take notice of me. At length my friend, Andrew Leith Hay, perceived me. He raised me up, and then, taking the musket out of the hand of Corporal Sharp of my company, he directed him to conduct me out of action, and to find out the surgeons.

With his assistance, and that of another man, who was wounded in the arm, I limped off. In quitting the field, I passed near Sir Arthur Wellesley, the commander-in-chief. He looked at me, seeing the blood streaming down my white trousers, but he said nothing, I then passed through our second line, which, without, of course, being able to take any part in the action, was suffering much from round shot and shells falling amongst them. Indeed, I was nearly knocked over, and I made a narrow escape of being killed even at some distance in the rear. A shell came whizzing close to our heads, and alighted a few feet in front of us, throwing up the earth in our faces, but it fortunately bounded to the left down the slope of the hill, when it exploded. I soon afterwards reached my friend, Dr. Guthrie, who with his assistants were actively employed in amputating legs and arms.

I have collected from the reports of various friends the following account of the continuation of the battle after I was wounded, and obliged to quit the field.

Our regiment, the 29th, and the battalion of detachments pursued the defeated enemy even across the ravine where the reserve was formed. Our troops were recalled, but in retiring up the hill again they were exposed to a destructive fire from the enemy's guns. They reformed line again a little in rear of the crest of the position, so as to be covered as much as possible from the effects of the cannonade, which still continued along the whole line for upwards of an hour. However, on its ceasing, men from both armies were sent out to collect the wounded. They intermixed in the most friendly terms. Lieutenant Langton, of the 29th Regiment, gave to a French officer two crosses of the Legion of Honour which had belonged to officers killed far up the hill. The destruction we had occasioned in the French ranks was evident to everyone. The whole face of the hill was covered with the dead and dying.

All symptoms of strife had now ceased. The enemy lighted fires and evidently commenced to cook, while our brave fellows had only their morsel of biscuit and a mouthful of rum or wine.

About twelve o'clock noon the enemy begun to get in motion again. Their reserve were seen closing up from the rear. It was evident a renewed attack was about to take place. Heavy masses were formed in front of the centre. Two large columns pointed to the valley on the left of the hill, and a body of light troops were seen moving to gain the distant range of hills on the other side of the valley, clearly demonstrating that they would endeavour to turn our left flank while they attempted to force our centre. To cover this disposition, about one o'clock p.m., they opened a general cannonade along our whole line, and a vigorous attack was made on our centre. The guards allowed the French column to come up quite close to them. When the guards advanced with a hurrah to meet them with the bayonet, they would not stand, but giving a rambling fire, they turned and fled. Flushed by this success, the guards followed them up too far, and left their flank exposed. Of this the enemy took advantage, and opened a destructive fire of guns and small arms. The guards, not having recovered their order after the charge, were in rather a perilous position. Sir Arthur Wellesley seeing this, ordered the 29th Regiment down to cover them; but as the regiment had suffered so much during the previous attack, the 48th Regiment was sent instead. Under cover of this corps the guards made good their way to the rear, where they re-formed, and again took their place in the position. Simultaneously with this attack on the guards, the enemy likewise attacked positions held by the 7th and the 53rd Regiments.

While these several attacks were going on in the centre and right, the enemy also renewed their attempt on our left. A Spanish corps under General Basscourt was moved across the valley to keep the column which had outflanked us in the mountain ridge in check. In this they effectually succeeded. After their defeat in the morning, the enemy did not venture to attack the hill again, but they endeavoured to push two large columns into the valley on its left, with a view of turning our position. To prevent this threatened movement, General Anson's brigade of the 23rd Light Dragoons and the German Legion received orders to check the advance of the French. The cavalry advanced gallantly, regardless of the fire of several battalions of French infantry. Unfortunately, the front of the enemy was protected by a deep ravine which was found impassable for horses. A considerable body of the 23rd, however, succeeded in crossing it, and fell on two regiments of mounted *chasseurs*, which at once gave way. The 23rd was then charged by the Polish lancers and the Westphalian Light Horse, and was surrounded, broken, and half of them destroyed. However, this desperate charge and brave conduct of our dragoons so astonished the enemy, that seeing our other corps of light cavalry also formed ready to advance in the same manner, they brought their columns to a stand, and no further attempts were made to gain possession of the hill.

The enemy being thus repulsed and defeated at all points, and having sustained a fearful loss of men, twenty pieces of cannon, and several thousand stands of arms, towards evening made dispositions for retreating, by drawing off their infantry under cover of their numerous cavalry, and before daylight next morning, the 29th July, they had all retired across the Alberche. General Robert Crawford having joined the army with the light brigade during the night, was instantly pushed on in advance, and he established his outposts on the right bank of the Alberche. The enemy continued their rear-guard on the opposite side until the 31st July, when they retired to Santa Ollala.

The 29th Regiment had the honour of securing two banners,

or small silk standards, termed in French *fanions*, belonging to the column which they defeated. On the top of each staff were plates with screw-holes, indicating unquestionably that eagles had been attached to them. The bearers, on finding their corps routed, had unscrewed the eagles and concealed them about their persons. The banners were picked up lying amongst the dead in front of our regiment. On their being carried to the commander-in-chief he most handsomely desired that the regiment should keep them as a memorial of their gallant conduct.

The brunt of this hard-fought battle fell upon the British. Indeed the Spanish army, it may be said, did nothing, with the exception of their artillery, the cavalry regiment del Rey, and the light corps, who were detached to skirmish and keep the French in check on the rocky hills on our left. All the rest merely occupied their places in the covered ground.

After the grand attack on the centre, the wadding of the guns, which kept smouldering on the ground, set fire to the dry grass and standing corn. The blazing element spread with great rapidity up and down the intervals between the contending armies. This proved a sad calamity, because all those wounded, who were so maimed and that they could not get out of the way, perished this wild fire.

When the enemy made their grand attack on the hill in the morning, our artillery posted on the summit fired over our heads as we advanced to meet the foe. One shot passed so near our brigadier-general, Richard Stewart, and Lieutenant Duguid of our regiment that the wind of it carried off both their cocked hats. In the hurry of the engagement the lieutenant picked up the general's hat and put it on, thinking it all right. But when he returned to our position, after driving the enemy down the hill, he, to his surprise, was accosted by an orderly sergeant demanding the general's hat.

Just as the action was about to commence one of our assistant surgeons, Dr. Kelly, was ordered by Staff-Surgeon Guning, attached to headquarters, to proceed down to our centre, and to inform Sir John Sherbrooke that in the event of any accident happening to him or any of his staff, Dr. Guning would be found at a place indicated in the rear. The young Esculapius hinted that he had no horse, and that it would occupy much time to walk there and back again, during which time his services might be urgently wanted in surgical operations. The good-natured staff-surgeon instantly dismounted, saying, "Take mine, and return without delay."

Scarcely had our young medico started when the tremendous cannonade burst upon us. A cannot-shot which had passed over our heads in an instant carried off the head of the horse as he cantered down the rear of the line. He, more frightened than hurt, gathered himself up and ran back as hard as he could to report what had happened. This was a sad piece of intelligence to the good doctor. His holsters had been well crammed with comforts, his ample military cloak neatly rolled up and strapped over them; but worse than all, his round valise-portmanteau fastened behind, besides a change of linen, contained all his fund of ready-money. The young medico, not being aware of this, or from want of reflection, abandoned all, which of course became a prey to the first roaming plunderer in the rear.

During the grand attack on the centre, the 97th Regiment made a gallant charge. The French broke and fled. In the ardour of pursuit and consequent melee, Major MacCarthy got mixed with the enemy. They had hold of his horse's bridle, and in their flight were dragging him along with them. In an agony of despair he roared out, "Shure is there no Connaught man that will save me?" And sure enough some of his brave countrymen instantly made a dash, with a loud hurrah, and brought him out triumphantly from the hands of the foe.

When our advanced guard was on the Alberche on the 26th July, previous to the battle, Mr. Swinburn, one of our commissaries, was at Santa Ollala collecting provisions. He had gone out in the morning to a village some distance off to procure supplies, leaving all quiet and no immediate apprehension of the enemy. On his return in the evening, not doubting but that the Spaniards and our outposts were still there, he rode quietly into the town, now in possession of the enemy, and was of course made prisoner. He was carried before Joseph Bonaparte and Marshal Jourdan, who questioned him very closely regarding our designs and number. He evaded answering in the best manner he could. They seemed quite incredulous when he mentioned that our commander was Sir Arthur Wellesley in person.

The next morning he was brought into the French lines and made to accompany Joseph and Jourdan during the battle, sometimes at the risk of his life being taken by his friends, for our long shots were flying about their ears. They persisted in cross-questioning him regarding the different divisions and corps of our army, our strength, and the names of the different generals. On his declining to satisfy them Jourdan pulled out a memorandum book and read to him a statement of our force, which on the whole was more correct than could have been expected. They treated him, however, very well, and in a day or two they allowed him to return, as being considered a non-combatant.

When I went to the rear after being wounded and found Dr. Guthrie, our surgeon, he examined my wound and pronounced it to be very severe, but he trusted that it would not prove dangerous. He could not extract the ball, which seemed to have taken an oblique direction downwards. He dressed and then bound up my wound, and recommended me to go to the rear where the baggage bad been ordered to rendezvous, and not to go into the town, as everyone seemed to doubt if the Spaniards would stand their ground, and prevent the enemy from forcing their way into it. So leaving him we fell in with a stray horse, which had either broken loose, or whose owner had fallen. So I was lifted upon it, but my blood was now getting cool, my leg very stiff, and the pain occasioned by the motion intolerable. I therefore got off, and hobbled along with my two supporters. On my way I came up to Captain Poole of the 52nd Regiment, who belonged to the first battalion of detachments, and our Brigade commissary, Mr. Brook. The captain told me that he had been seized with a fever during the attack on the hill on the previous evening, and had not been able to ascend it with his battalion.

Our dispenser of bread, a more daring spirit, made many inquiries about what was going on, and asked me if there was any possibility of his getting a view of the battle. I told him he had only to make haste up to the peak of the hill, and that he might then gratify his curiosity. He instantly started off. Poor soul, to follow such witless advice! Scarcely had he reached the top, and got a peep of the enemy when he was hit in the paunch by a spent ball. The ball and the fright finished him. He pined and died a week or two afterwards.

The captain accompanied me in search of our baggage. We at length found it at a single house on the high road from Talavera to Oropeza, about two miles from the field. I made my way into this empty house. The batman of the company and some women of the regiment got me some straw, and a blanket being spread upon it, I was laid down. The pain of the wound became very acute, but there was no remedy but to grin and bear it. The poor women were in great distress. All came in to visit me, and made many anxious inquiries about the fate of their husbands. I had the satisfaction of assuring four or five of them that their husbands were safe when I left them, or only slightly wounded, but many others were forlorn widows. They most kindly made some tea for me. But the absurd part was their sympathy with the captain. They all asked him where he was hit, and trusted that he was not badly wounded. He seemed sadly worried and perplexed what answer to give. He replied in a faint voice that he was extremely ill with fever. In about an hour afterwards, perhaps nine o'clock a.m., Lieutenant Stanus of our regiment was brought in also severely wounded.

Various reports began to spread; some that the enemy had made another attack, and had succeeded in forcing a part of our line; others that the enemy had sent troops into the mountains on our left, and had succeeded in turning that flank. Cowardly runaways from the Spanish army continued to pass to the rear in increased numbers, two or three of these fellows frequently on one horse. From seeing this we began to surmise that the enemy might really have defeated part of the Spanish force; and as the baggage began to move off farther to the rear, we determined to get on to a bullock car, and to make the best of our way back to Oropeza, the nearest town in our rear.

Our friend the captain, on the first rumours of adverse reports, without waiting to inquire whether they were likely to prove true or false, started up very nimbly, mounted his pony, and set off in all haste out of harm's way to the rear.

I should think we left the house about one or two o'clock p.m. When we had got about three leagues we met General Robert Crawford hurrying on with the light brigade, consisting of the 43rd and 52nd Light Infantry and the 95th Rifle Corps. He directed the surgeon of the 43rd to give us any advice we might require, and made the most anxious inquiries regarding Sir Arthur Wellesley, and what was going on in front. I gave him a short detail of the principal events. He seemed much annoyed when I mentioned that Talavera was about twelve miles off, and that I did not think he could reach it before dark. At this moment Captain Pechell, *aide-de-camp* to Major General Tilson, came up. He announced that the enemy had been defeated at all points, and gave orders to the baggage to counter-march and to return in all haste to Talavera. He said to General Crawford:

"These gentlemen," meaning me and my friend Stanus, "belong to a corps which has had the distinguished honour of charging and defeating a large force of the enemy both last night and this glorious day."

We proceeded on our weary way. The bullocks moved but slowly, and it was dark before we reached Oropeza. I got a good billet, and Stanus got one on the opposite side of the street. My servant had me carried in and laid on the bed, and went off to procure some necessary comforts. Wearied out with loss of blood, and exhausted with fatigue, not having had much rest for the three previous nights, I fell into a profound sleep. My man, not wishing to disturb my repose, allowed me to lie too long, and I awoke cold and comfortless, my leg as stiff as a poker, very much swollen up, and the pain most tormenting. But I got some warm tea, and then was undressed and put properly into bed. I consoled myself with thinking how much my situation was better than that of many others.

Although I passed rather a restless night I felt upon the whole better than I expected next day, the 20th. My friend, Lieutenant Stanus, sent over word that there was good accommodation for another in his billet, and begged me to get moved across. In the afternoon, Colonel Jenkinson of the Guards was brought to my door in a cart. As the people did not seem disposed to admit him, I intimated that I would go over to my friend. This was soon accomplished, as they carried me across mattress and all. The poor colonel, who was wounded in the knee, took possession of my billet. He was seized in two or three days afterwards with lockjaw, and died. A staff surgeon, Dr. MacDougal, announced himself to us as being appointed to take charge of the wounded.

I found our new billet as comfortable as circumstances would permit. Our landlord, a kind-hearted person, procured everything for us we desired. But our wounds began to be very troublesome. Suppuration was proceeding, and sloughing took place, so we were obliged to keep applying bread poultices. I however had the good fortune to have a most charming nurse, no other than a daughter of our host. She was a nun of the Order of Saint Clare. The French having destroyed the convent, the establishment was broken up, and she had returned to take refuge in her father's house. She was dressed in a coarse grey habit. She was young, extremely beautiful, mild and noble in countenance, had a charming disposition and most engaging manner. She did everything in her power to assist us, getting bandages for us, preparing poultices, bringing in chocolate, and amusing us with cheerful conversation, relating to us curious stories of these eventful times.

Fortunately, I understood a little the dressing of wounds. Our only medical attendant was a Spanish barber, who, according to the custom of the country, combined also the profession of surgeon. We employed him to operate on our chins, but dispensed with his attendance in his surgical capacity. After shaving me one morning, he produced a case of rusty instruments, and told me he was going to perform an operation *"mui pelegroso,"* no less than to take off the arm of a wounded soldier, out at the socket.

We heard current reports that Marshal Soult had defeated the Spanish forces at the Puerto de Bannos, had forced that important pass and was pushing on to Placentia, threatening our rear. This appeared to us very extraordinary, as we were under the impression that our victorious army at Talavera was about to push on to Madrid.

On the morning of the 3rd August, we were not a little surprised on receiving a visit from Andrew Leith Hay and Captain Fra, and still more so when Hay informed us that the whole army was come hack, and that they believed that they were going to give battle to Soult, who, after forcing the pass of Puerto de Bannos, had entered Placentia, and captured our military stores and hospital there.

We remained quiet under the conviction that the army on the 4th had marched on the road to Placentia. About one o'clock p.m., however, Dr. MacDougal came in haste to inform us that all the sick who were able to move were ordered to proceed without delay to the bridge of Arzobispo. Our paymaster, who had refused to give us any money on account of pay two days before, although it was then some time in arrears, and we were in great want of it, now passed in, and throwing a month's pay into each of our beds, decamped in a hurry.

We then learned to our dismay that our army, instead of going to fight Soult, had gone off to their left, and had crossed the Tagus by the bridge of Arzobispo, that the English commissary was going to leave the town, and the French might be expected to enter it before next morning. It was now high time for us to endeavour to make our escape; not a moment was to be lost. We sent to our commissary to the *alcalde*, requesting to be supplied with mules, but he answered that every animal had been embargoed for the army, and it was impossible to afford us any assistance.

We began to make up our minds to become prisoners of the French, when the Spanish force under Basscourt, which had been sent in advance on the road to Placentia, began to defile through the town. The Spanish drummers were beating to arms, and those inhabitants who did not relish the French were quitting the place in all haste.

I fortunately observed General Cuesta's coach. I got our landlord to write a note stating that two English officers, badly wounded, would feel much obliged to his excellency if he would issue an order for them to get mules to join the English army. This was handed into his old lumbering machine of a coach. He immediately sent an *aide-de-camp* to inform us that orders had been sent to the *alcalde* to provide us with what we required.

The Spanish army continued marching past. It was provoking to observe that the Spanish government had provided plentifully for their own army, while, after having assured Sir Arthur Wellesley of every sort of supplies, they had failed to do so for the English in every particular, although our commissaries were ready to pay for everything. The near approach of the French caused them to produce stores which they had concealed from us, and most of the Spanish soldiers had some loaves of bread stuck on their bayonets, while others had pieces of bacon.

After a tedious delay, an old lame mule, the most worthless animal our good allies could find, was brought to our quarter. There was no time for remonstrance. So I prepared to mount the crippled brute, and Stanus his horse, which had a desperate sore back. Just as we were going to depart, Lieutenant Bagwell of the 87th Regiment arrived from Talavera, very badly wounded. The ball had entered at his right side, passed round the front of his stomach, under the skin, and coming out again at his left side, passed through his arm close above the elbow joint. On the morning of the 27th July, when skirmishing on the Alberche, as the advanced guard was retiring on the position, Lieutenant Bagwell observed his captain, MacCreagh, knocked over by a musket-shot quite close to him. He caught him in his arms, and in the act of doing so, he received this terrible wound. As the enemy were pressing very closely, he laid the captain on his back, and was obliged to retire. The ball had hit the captain's watch, which it broke, and forced into his groin. The French treated him in the kindest manner. His wounds were dressed, and the watch extracted; and they, seeing that his wounds were mortal, sent him in next day, with a flag of truce, that he might breathe his last amongst his countrymen, and not amongst strangers. I got Lieutenant Bagwell established in our billet, and sent off for the surgeon, who sent back word that he was going to dinner, but would attend afterwards. Our amiable nurse, the good nun, provided us with a supply of wine and some excellent bread, with many expressions of kind wishes for our safety.

We found ourselves in a wretched plight, owing to the motion of the animals and the hanging of our legs in riding. Our wounds became much irritated and very painful, while the poor hobbling animals were almost done up. After a few miles we fortunately overtook some covered Spanish provision wagons. We offered the driver of one of them a dollar or two to give us a lift, which was accepted. We got on for some miles farther in this way easily enough, but at length the road became so blocked up with artillery, baggage, stores, &c., that the wagon could not proceed. We therefore remounted our Rosinantes, and passed through the Spanish army drawn up in two lines in front of the bridge of Arzobispo. We continued on and crossed the bridge, then turning down the left bank of the Tagus, we reached our bivouac about two o clock in the morning.

Our people were just then getting under arms to march off; we, however, secured one of the cars appointed for the wounded, and then stretched ourselves on the ground near a large camp fire. We rested our exhausted frames while our servant prepared fresh poultices for our wounds, which being dressed, we continued our route in rear of the army, not in a triumphal car, but in a vehicle of the most modest construction.

We understood that Sir Arthur Wellesley, immediately after our victory at Talavera, had intended to follow up the defeated foe and push his way to Madrid, but that owing to the Spanish government having failed to afford him the requisite supplies which they had promised, he was obliged to delay the intended movement. In the interim he received intelligence of Soult's movements from Salamanca, and when the news was confirmed that Soult had forced the pass of Puerto de Bannos, and was expected at Placentia, thus threatening his rear, he proposed to General Cuesta that he should remain at Talavera to keep the French in check should they attempt to advance again on that post, and also to cover our hospitals and protect the wounded left there, while he would move back to Oropeza, and give battle to Soult. To this arrangement Cuesta agreed, and even ordered General Basscourt's division to march on the 2nd August to Oropeza, preceding the British army, and acting as its advanced guard.

Sir Arthur Wellesley appointed Colonel Mackinnon to take charge of the sick and wounded in the hospital at Talavera, and on the 2nd August marched with the whole of his force to Oropeza, where he made the necessary dispositions for attacking or receiving Soult, according as circumstances might require. During the night he received a despatch from Cuesta announcing various movements of the French armies, and stating his determination to retire from Talavera. And sure enough, before daybreak on the morning of the 4th August, Cuesta came in with his whole army, bag and baggage, thus leaving our rear exposed, and all our brave wounded compromised. In order to extricate himself from this difficulty, Sir Arthur Wellesley had no alternative left but to get across the Tagus, so as to place it between him and the enemy, and thus secure his way back to the frontiers of Portugal.

Not a moment was to be lost. He despatched orders for the recall of Basscourt's Spanish division, which had already moved off in advance on the road to Placentia. He then moved off to his left, and after a march of three leagues he crossed the Tagus at the bridge of Arzobispo. Then he turned to his right, down the left, or southern bank of the river. At a short distance farther the army bivouacked, while the Light Brigade under General Crawford was pushed on to gain by forced marches the bridge of Almarez, and to support the Spanish troops posted there for its defence. All those of our wounded who could be moved were brought from Talavera.

Thus the perverse obstinacy of a weak-minded man thwarted all the skilful plans of our energetic and experienced commander. As a further proof of this there was a song current, accounting for our not proceeding to attack the enemy on the 23rd July, after we had marched off for that purpose, as before stated. The reason given was that Cuesta had refused to fight that day, but on the following day he was full of fight when the enemy was gone; that Sir Arthur Wellesley had said they never had held a council of war but once, and on that occasion there were only three persons present—himself, his adjutant-general Sir Charles Stewart, and old Cuesta, and that one of them was a traitor.

Owing to this untoward turn of affairs, Soult, finding no hindrance, got possession of Placentia without opposition, and captured our hospitals and stores left there. When the commandant, Captain Pattison of the 29th Regiment, received positive intelligence that Soult was about to enter the place, he determined to leave it with all the sick that could be moved. When about to depart, the staff surgeon who was destined to remain, and, of course, to fall into the hands of the French, having a remarkably fine English horse which he did not wish to share his own fate, requested the captain to take charge of it for him. After the captain had got some distance from the town with his convoy, he began to think that it would be very absurd of him to retire without having himself seen the enemy. He therefore, desired the convoy to push on, while he returned towards Placentia, acting with great caution; and keeping a good lookout ahead as he passed through a wood, he at last perceived a cavalry patrol of the enemy advancing. He instantly wheeled round, and started off at speed to get away, but to his great horror, after going a few hundred yards, he found his retreat intercepted by a party of French cavalry which had got ahead of him by passing his flank stealthily in the woods while he was advancing, anxiously intent on reconnoitring the enemy. Escape was impossible, so he submitted to his fate, and was led back captive, and his friend's horse became a prize of the enemy.

Our route led through a broken hilly country along the left or south bank of the Tagus, the army proceeding by forced marches to secure the floating bridge at Almarez, Sir Arthur Wellesley dreading that the French might force the passage, in defiance of the Spanish troops stationed to guard it, and, by throwing a corps across, intercept his retreat towards the frontiers of Portugal.

I accompanied the army on a vehicle of the most primitive construction, being no other than a few planks nailed on a rude frame, with a pole in front to which oxen were yoked. The frame was placed in two low wheels, each consisting of solid pieces of wood, into which the axle-tree was blocked, so that instead of the wheel going round the axle-tree, they all went round together, there being two pieces of wood under the frame on each side scooped out to fit the axle tree. The friction was very great, and occasioned a noise when in motion like the drone of the bagpipes. On this miserable machine we placed some straw covered with our blankets, and we were then laid upon it, with our small modicum of baggage for pillows. Four sticks were stuck into holes in each corner of the frame, and a blanket fastened on them, to form a canopy to protect us from the scorching sun; and two lean kine with slow and measured steps dragged us along. Such was our equipage.

The road was extremely bad, passing alternately over steep, rugged, rocky heights, or across ravines and the stony beds of dried-up mountain torrents, so that at times we were obliged to get off and limp after them, while the wretched cattle were scrambling up such abrupt ascents. Numbers of these frail cars loaded with stores and ammunition broke down. All the horses whether of the cavalry or artillery which got lame were instantly shot.

We passed through several villages, but not a living being was to be seen. The inhabitants had all fled to the mountains. From the slow progress we made with such cattle in such a country, night was fast approaching. We gave up the idea of reaching the bivouac at Pesetada de Gabin, and resolved to take up our quarters in a smith's shop. Fortunately there was a fire remaining in the forge; we roasted morsels of beef on the points of ramrods, and served them up on a hard biscuit for a plate. This was the only meal we had that day. We carefully reserved the little bread we had to make poultices of. We then stretched ourselves on some straw in a corner.

We recommenced our car march next morning, the 6th August, about five o'clock, and proceeded on our weary way. The road proved, if possible, worse than what we had already passed. We were stopped on a dreary hill by an officer of the 31st Regiment, who, according to orders from General Hill, had remained there with a butcher or two, with directions to kill some sheep, which were served out to the sick and wounded ready cooked, as they came up. We had a delicious mutton chop, but the want of any sort of bread was a great drawback. This was a most kind and humane act of the general.

There were many poor fellows who were unable to keep up left destitute on the road. One of them, Private Jackson of my company, was walking alongside with his head tied up. I inquired where he was wounded. He produced a tooth stuffed with lead. The ball had entered his left cheek, and passed out at the back of his neck.

In passing a village we had feasted ourselves with the idea of being able to procure some bread, but not a creature was there, not a morsel of food of any kind to be found. Our only prize was a few crumbs in an old basket, which we greedily seized. On reaching another village we had the good fortune to find one of our companions, Mr. Ogilvie, who very kindly supplied us with a couple of mules. We now got on more briskly.

In passing over a high ridge, we observed two huge columns of the enemy moving in the plain on the opposite side of the Tagus. They seemed to be on the road from Noval Moral to Oropeza. We could trace their route by the glittering of their arms. We passed through Meza de Ibor, and reached our bivouac in the afternoon. Our surgeon examined our wounds; the dead parts had sloughed off, and the inflammatory symptoms had disappeared, which was a great satisfaction.

The following day, the 7th August, by means of our mules we passed the army in the march, and reached Delitosa, thinking, as the name denotes, that we were going into a delightful place; but disappointment was our lot—it was a scene of woe and misery. Both the Spanish and French armies had passed and repassed this road, and all the places had been ransacked by friend and foe. We got into an empty room in a dilapidated house. A little bread and some honey were all that we could procure. There being no remedy, we made up a couch of straw blankets as usual, and endeavoured to console ourselves by courting oblivion of our hardships in sleep. Lieutenant Popham of our regiment, severely wounded in the leg, and who had made his escape from Talavera, joined us at this place.

On the morning of the 8th August we received notice that all the wounded and sick were ordered to be assembled at a convent about three miles from Delitosa, and there place themselves under the orders of Colonel Mackinnon. We consequently proceeded in the afternoon to that place. On our arrival, rather late in the evening, we found the greater part of the buildings in ruins, having been partly destroyed by the French. All the habitable rooms were already occupied, while the large church of the convent was filled to suffocation with wounded soldiers. Nor could we find any official, civil or military, to inform us where we were to go, or what we were to do. We at length got possession of a small side chapel, which was in a miserable state of dilapidation, chill, and damp. There we were, without anything to eat or to drink, not even straw to rest on, and keep our aching limbs from the cold bare bricks. We made the best shifts we could to supply those wants, and to remedy all inconveniences.

The boxwood edgings of the flower-beds in the garden of the nuns, plucked up and put head and head together, served the purpose of a mattress. A morsel of meat from the commissary's butcher, put into a camp-kettle lid and frizzled, with a biscuit the size of a dollar, for each, were all we could procure. But when cooked the difficulty arose how to find it, since it was now almost pitch-dark, and light we had none.

In this dilemma a sergeant of the German Legion, hearing our complaint, most good naturedly, and very ingeniously, invented a new kind of lamp which was made by putting a little oil into a small tin, and then tearing a strip off the tail of his shirt, he made a wick of the rag. This temporary illumination being of course soon extinct, we were left in darkness again, and endeavoured to compose ourselves to sleep. Vain attempt! Our ears, instead of being saluted, and our minds soothed, with the melodious notes of the holy nuns singing their evening hymn in the choir, were stunned with the shrieks, and our hearts made sad with the lamentations, of the brave but unfortunate fellows obliged to undergo amputation. The nuns had fled from their former abode of retirement and peace. How changed the scene now! In this, their own choir, was now the place where all the horrors of war were displayed, as the medical officers had made it the surgery where all operations were performed, and they with many lamps were actively engaged in the stern duties of their calling.

We remained in this abode of misery the whole of the 9th, when it was announced that all were to be moved to Elvas, in Portugal. On the following morning, the 10th, the wounded and sick being placed on cars or mules, set out for their destination, but by some mischance no means of transport was provided for me. This was rather awkward. My servant, however, fortunately discovered a mule in a back yard, having been left there in the confusion. This made me independent. Mr. Stanus, Mr. Popham, and myself determined to keep together, and we followed the convoy; but owing to the delay occasioned in my getting an animal, we took a road which varied a little from the route which they had taken, so we missed them. We therefore resolved to push on and find our way through the country to Elvas, the best way we could. After passing through the defiles at Jaricejo, leading to the bridge of Almarez, on the Tagus, we turned off to the left in a south-westerly direction, and reached Truxillo, rather a neat and tolerable sized country town. It is remarkable for some remains of Roman antiquities, and also for Pizzaro's house and monument.

We found the town in a state of great confusion and apprehension, full of detached parties and runaways from the Spanish armies. Accounts had arrived that Cuesta, after passing the bridge at Arzobispo, on the 6th August, had left a corps there under the Duke of Albuquerque to defend it against the French, and retired with the remainder of his force to Paraleda de Garben; that the enemy had on the 8th August discovered a ford above the bridge, and passed over a body of troops to turn the flank of the Spaniards while the bridge was forced in front; that the Spaniards had been surprised, defeated, and fled, abandoning all their artillery. The inhabitants were therefore in great alarm, thinking that we were retiring and that the enemy would shortly follow. The people were very uncivil. We could not succeed in gaining admittance to any house without a billet, and the magistrates were too busy with their own fugitive soldiers to attend to us who bad fought and bled for them.

We were sitting in the *plaça* or great square in this forlorn situation, consulting what we had best do, when my friend Captain Langton of the quartermaster-general's department happened to come by. He most kindly assured me that he would get us a billet. After a considerable delay, he at length returned with one, and informed me that it was with no small difficulty that he had obtained it, because on his requiring one from the *junta*, they seemed to demur, and on his demanding one in his capacity of quartermaster-general, they had the audacity to order in the guard and wanted to turn him out. He, however, dared them to do that at their peril. They gave way and obsequiously gave him our billet.

We immediately proceeded to take at possession, but this proved a mutter of no small difficulty. Although the house appeared tolerably large and neat, a person showed us into a small filthy kitchen. This we scorned to take, and insisted that we should get a decent room. We made our way to one close at hand, but on attempting to enter we were stoutly opposed by two good-looking *senoras*, who, observing that we could only hobble along, kept us at bay by their vociferations and an animated war of words. We, however, by a vigorous charge with our crutches, at length succeeded in effecting an entrance. Their stormy raving instantly subsided into sullen silence, but they were not to be defeated. Furious with rage, they seized the bed-clothes from off the bed, determined that not one of us should make a comfortable lodgement there, and started with them out of the room. Then returning with various domestics, they rapidly carried off the bedstead, tables, chairs, &c. In short, the chamber was stripped of every article, and we were left to our meditations to repose on the cold bricks. In our disabled situation resistance was impossible. We submitted to the outrage in contemptuous silence, and with the aid of our pack saddles and blankets, we formed an uneasy sort of couch. We, however, here got bread, chocolate, and some meat to purchase, which proved great luxuries after the privations we had endured for the past week. Our poor wounded, many of whom had undergone operations on the preceding day, were obliged to remain in the streets without any comforts or cover.

We were delighted next day, the 11th August, to quit our inhospitable quarters. After a journey of about three leagues over open country, we reached a small village. We found the inhabitants in great consternation. Scarcely had a week elapsed since they had returned from the mountains, where they had fled from dread of the French, when they were now preparing to pack up all their valuables so as to he ready for a move, thinking that as they saw us going towards Portugal, they would soon have another visit from the enemy. It was very affecting to witness the distress occasioned by the invaders in the various places we passed through. We here got into a house, but found few comforts. No beds were to be had. The people spread out some mats for us. Our cloaks and blankets formed all the bed furniture. Our wounds by the continual application of poultices, if not mending, were at all events kept in a healthy state.

As the weather was excessively warm, we determined to follow the custom of the county, by setting out betimes in the morning, to repose at the first halting place during the heat of the day, and to complete the remainder of our day's journey in the cool of the evening. Accordingly, next morning, the 12th August, we were on the alert by peep of day. After proceeding some way, we overtook a friend who had passed us on the road, the day of Talavera. On that day he came cantering after us on horseback, in plain clothes, and told us that he was severely wounded, being shot through the arm, that two of his ribs were broken, and without further explanation went on, leaving us lost in conjecture who he could be. When we overtook him now, to our surprise he was tramping on foot at a swinging pace, warbling an Irish tune, accompanied by a dozen dogs of all descriptions and sizes sporting round him, having been attracted by his whistling *View Hullo*! On our expressing our wonder that a person who had had his ribs stoved in should be walking so gaily, he with great naiveté replied:

"Oh! It was all a mistake, the ball only went through my arm, but it gave me such a confounded rap on the side that I thought; my ribs were surely broken."

He accounted for his being on foot by saying that he had had a horse but no saddle, while his friend had a saddle but no horse, so he allowed him his horse to put the saddle upon. We thought this a most good-natured piece of friendship on his part. He it appeared, had come out with his friend from Ireland, both with appointments as majors in the Spanish army, which they had joined only a few days previous to the battle of Talavera, and consequently had not had time to furnish themselves with uniform, but had put the distinguishing mark of the rank of major in the Spanish service (two strips of silver lace) on the cuffs of their blue coats. When the French made their grand attack on our centre, the Spanish regiment to which they were attached happened to be the one on the left of the Spanish line, and of course the one next the British right flank, which was the 61st Regiment. When the enemy's column pressed rapidly on, this Spanish corps, instead of manfully waiting the attack, went to the right-about, and scampered off, leaving our two friends, who gallantly stood their ground. Fortunately, the Spanish regiment of cavalry del Rey, ashamed of the conduct of their infantry, immediately dashed forward, and not only filled up the gap left vacant by the dastardly corps, but on the French corps being routed by us, they charged them with great effect. The two majors, disgusted with this sample of their troops, tore off their silver lace, and instantly joined the 61st Regiment, each taking a musket, and putting on a cartouche box taken from some of the slain, and they fought most bravely as volunteers until both were severely wounded. We found the major a remarkably good-tempered and very interesting gentleman.

We reached a neat country town about ten o'clock a.m., and got into a clean house. Here we got for the first time since we had left Oropeza an excellent breakfast of chocolate, eggs, bacon, and fruit. While we were enjoying these luxuries a doctor of the German Legion walked into the room. We offered him some refreshment, but he, looking earnestly at the *ci-devavnt* major, said:

"Are you the schentlemans I affronted last night?"

"Sure, and I am the self-same man," replied he; "and if you have aught to say to me, here I am."

But the doctor mildly said that he was sorry he had annoyed him. Our friend said there was no offence at all, at all.

"Come, man," he said, "sit down and take something."

But the doctor declined the offer and retired. The major told us that in the miserable village where he had passed last night, he had been so fortunate as to get a billet with a comfortable bed in it, and in which he anticipated the indulgence of a sound repose, but having gone out to forage some eatables, he found on his return that a stranger had taken possession of his snug berth, and was absolutely ensconced in his bed. But he was not to be done out in this manner, so, without further ado or explanation demanded, he seized the intruder by the heels and dragged him to the door, where he bundled him out and threw his habiliments after him, neither knowing nor caring who the individual was. This gentleman, who rejoiced in the name of Hercules White, and his friend had both been recommended by Sir Arthur Wellesley for commissions on account of their conduct in the action, and the first *Gazette* afterwards announced their appointments as ensigns in the 61st Regiment.

During the heat of the day we closed the windows, and upon mattresses laid on the brick floor we took a quiet *siesta* until about five o'clock p.m. We then proceeded over the same open country for about three leagues to Alvila. The *alcalde*, a jolly-looking honest farmer, gave us excellent billets. We got some capital wine, and passed a most comfortable night. The next day, the 13th August, we reached Merendella, a tolerable village. On the 14th we continued on to Merida, situated on the left bank of the Guadiana, which we crossed by the old Roman bridge. We found it a very neat town. It had formerly been of some importance. There are, besides the bridge, still some remains of Roman antiquities, such as the amphitheatre, aqueduct, and baths.

We started on the following morning at an early hour, breakfasted, and took our siesta at Lobon, a small country town. We proceeded in the evening to Talavera del Rey, a tolerable town situated on the left bank of the Guadiana, which runs close under the steep acclivity on which the town stands. After a pleasant ride of about three leagues in the cool of the morning of the 16th, we came to a view of the fortress of Badajos, the capital of Spanish Estramadura. In approaching Badajos we passed through a succession of cultivated land, fields of melons, olive-groves, vineyards, gardens,

&c. The town is situated on the left bank of the Guadiana, which here runs through a narrow pass, betwixt a height on one side and a range of hills on the other.

Badajos is a place of considerable strength. Its fortifications are very complete, and they seemed to be in good repair. The town stands on a slope from the plain to the height on the north, on which stands the castle or citadel, which commands the whole. On the other side of the river, immediately opposite the citadel, on the peak of a hill, is Fort St. Christoval, which serves as an outwork on that side.

Next day, the 17th August, we passed the bridge over the Guadiana, which runs close under the west side of Badajos, and proceeded over the plain on our way to Elvas. After a ride of six miles we reached the Cayo, a small river which here forms the boundary between Spain and Portugal. Eight miles farther brought us to the fortress, which was our destination, a general hospital being there established for the sick and wounded of the whole army, several convents and other public buildings being appropriated for their reception.

I was fortunate enough to get a billet in a tolerably good house. The people were very civil, and gave me the upper storey entirely to myself. Having more room than I required, I accommodated one of the assistant surgeons of our regiment, so that I had excellent medical attendance at all times. Provisions of all kinds were plentiful and cheap, wines and fruit excellent.

After all the hardships and privations we had endured, the quiet repose of a fixed residence afforded us great relief, although it could only be of a temporary nature. After a time my wound began to show symptoms of healing up, but there was still a considerable discharge, so that for nearly a month I was confined to my quarters. After that I began to hobble about a little on crutches, and to take a drive in a one-horse sort of *calash*, hung on leather instead of springs, to visit or dine with my wounded comrades.

Elvas is a frontier fortress of great importance, but the nature of the ground on which it is placed prevents it from being a place of such strength as might be wished. It stands on the ridge of a hill rising from south to north. The lower portion of the works are regular and of sufficient strength, having Fort St. Lucia situated on a lower height at a short distance in front, on the road to Badajos, but on the north the city is commanded by a steep, high hill, separated from it by a deep valley. On this hill stands Fort de Leppe, which commands the city, and, consequently, whoever possesses the fort must ultimately get possession of the city.

The environs of Elvas are very charming, being well cultivated. Many of the orange-groves and gardens are adorned with neat small country houses, which give them a lively appearance. The interior of the place is not so brilliant as might be expected. The streets in general are very steep and narrow, and by no means kept particularly clean. The houses for the most part are of a second-rate description. All this was particularly striking to one coming from Spain, where the houses are of a superior description and of a different style, and the streets always remarkably clean. In the upper part of the town there is a *plaça*, a sort of square, in front of the cathedral.

We had little or no intercourse with the Portuguese families; indeed, all the people of any fortune or distinction had withdrawn to Lisbon, many of them dreading that in the course of events the place might stand a chance of being besieged.

We heard that General Venegas, who had failed to make a demonstration on Toledo in rear of the French army during the battle of Talavera, as had been intended, had been defeated by Sebastiani on the 21st August, at Almonacid. Towards the end of August reports began to spread that the French indicated symptoms of threatening Portugal.

In the beginning of September, we learned that our army, after remaining two weeks in the passes of Jaricejo, where it had taken up a position, on the 11th August, to guard the passage of the Tagus, at Almarez, had, in consequence of certain movements made by the French armies, fallen back on the frontiers of Portugal. During their sojourn in the wild mountainous district of Jaricejo, our men suffered much from want of good water and regular supplies of provisions, because the Spanish government had not only failed to procure us all necessary supplies for payment, as had been agreed upon, but, in more instances than one, actually seized what our commissaries had secured for our own army.

Sir Arthur Wellesley, now created Lord Wellington, established his headquarters at Badajos, on the 3rd September, which was also garrisoned by a strong English force. An advanced guard was left at Merida, and troops at Lobon and Talavera del Rey, the intermediate towns between it and Badajos.

General Hill's division was cantoned on the right bank of the Guadiana, in various villages, such as Montijo, Puebula, &c., and on the extensive plain; while another division was stationed on the left bank, dispersed in various cantonments, such as Olivenzes, Albuera, Santa Martha, &c., on the south-eastern road to Seville. The remaining divisions were moved over the frontier into Portugal and posted at Canipo Mayor, Portalegre, Castello de Vide, &c., on the northern road leading to Castello Branco, Almeida, and Cuidad Rodrigo. By this admirable arrangement every approach to Badajos from the south, east, or north was protected, while at the same time the heads of our columns pointed equally in all directions, ready to press forward on any, as occasion or circumstances might require, or all the forces could be easily concentrated if requisite.

The troops cantoned on the low plain bordering either bank of the Guadiana began early in October to get very sickly, some being attacked with typhus fever, others with bilious fever, and many with fever and ague, which occasioned a great mortality. The hospitals at Elvas became crowded to a serious extent from the numbers sent in from the out-quarters. These diseases appear to have originated from a combination of causes. In the first place, the men had been constantly in the field for upwards of five mouths, during the various operations of the campaign of Oporto and Talavera, during the whole of which period they had almost never a night or two in quarters. The excitement which kept them up during these daring enterprises was now gone. They were crowded into small rooms in small houses, with only their blankets and bare bricks or day floors to lie upon. In the second place, the wet season had commenced, which prevented outdoor exercise or field movements; and lastly, the damp and chilling mists which prevail at that period along the borders of the river. What was most to be deplored was that the finest and most robust men were in general the first who fell victims to these scourges. Our brave fellows died in such numbers that the contingent allowances made to captains of companies for all purposes could not cover the expense of coffins, so it was ordered that the men should be interred in their blankets only. But their comrades who were still in health, with a commendable fine sense of feeling, begged to be allowed to subscribe the amount necessary to procure coffins for their unfortunate brothers-in-arms.

During the whole month of October, the vast number of fever patients sent in from the army to Elvas, and the want of sufficient accommodation, prevented them from being kept separate from the other sick and wounded. The contagion unfortunately spread to these also, and many who had narrowly escaped the effects of honourable wounds fell under the ravages of disease.

While at Badajos, the commander-in-chief, Lord Wellington, paid a high compliment to the 29th Regiment. It had suffered great loss at the battle of Talavera, and Lord Wellington, in a letter to Lord Castlereagh, 12th September, 1809, says:

> I wish very much that some measures could be adopted to get some recruits for the 29th Regiment. It is the best regiment in this army, and has an admirable internal system and excellent non-commissioned officers.

My wound was now quite healed up, but a general stiffness of the limb remained, accompanied at times with considerable pain, owing no doubt to some of the tendons having been injured, or the ball, which still remained in, pressing on some tender part. I however determined to rejoin my regiment, and accordingly on the 5th November I proceeded to Badajos. I got a billet in a handsome house, and found the lady of the mansion equally so, being a very interesting pretty young woman. She received me most graciously, showed me to a commodious apartment, and assured me that her husband would be happy to have me in his house. On my inquiring what her husband was, she replied that he was a *colonello reformada*—a colonel on the retired list. On my expressing surprise that one so young as she was should be the wife of an old veteran, as I supposed her husband to be, she with great naiveté replied, "He is a retired colonel, to be sure, but he is very robust, and very loving, still." He proved rather a gruff person, nearer sixty than fifty. They very kindly cooked my dinner for me, making several savoury additions to my ration beef, and they sent me fruit and wine. Next morning they provided me with an excellent breakfast, and urged me to pass another day in their house, but duty called me to go on.

I proceeded next day, the 6th November, through Talavera del Rey, crossed the Guadiana by a ford, and reached the headquarters of my regiment at Puebula de la Calçada in the afternoon. This was a large agricultural village. The houses, like most others in these places, were constructed of mud, beat hard in frames, afterwards whitewashed, and roofed with tiles. They in general consisted of only one storey, with attics above. The inhabitants were chiefly farmers and their servants, shepherds, &c. Large tracts of wheat land and other grain, with fields of melons, surrounded the village for miles. Beyond that, on the wide plains, were flocks of merinos, with their numerous shepherds and large dogs.

Here was the first place where I observed the method they have in the south of Spain of preserving their grain in pits. In the vicinity of each village a place is allotted for this purpose. The pits are constructed in the following manner: a wide pit is sunk in the earth, about fifteen feet deep. The bottom is then laid with flags; on this they build a circular wall of bricks about twelve feet in diameter and eight feet high, over which they throw an arched dome, leaving an aperture in the top, about three feet wide, which is continued up two or three feet more, like a chimney, so that the pit is shaped like a bottle with a neck. This neck does not rise to within two feet of the surface or level of the surrounding ground. Perhaps a hundred of these are made in rows in a square portion of land, forming, as it were, a honeycomb. Each farmer has one or two, or more, according to the size of his farm. When the grain is threshed out in the plain, it is carried in and poured into these subterranean granaries. Large slabs are placed on the mouths of each, and the earth is thrown over them, so that potatoes and other vegetables can be planted in the ground, and the hidden grain secured from the rapacious hand of the invader. This is one of the many Moorish customs still prevailing.

About the end of November the people appeared much cast down. They informed me that bad news had arrived, that the Marquis of Areizaga, who had been appointed to the command after Venegas, of the army of La Mancha, had been defeated on the

19th November, at Ocaña. This defeat they felt the more because the marquis by previous boasting had led them to expect that he would drive the French from Madrid. We afterwards learned that he was a young officer without any experience, or capacity for a commander. He was vain enough to suppose that because he had a numerical force of 60,000 men, he could defeat the well-disciplined veteran troops of France, and expel them from the capital. With this view he left his strong position in the Sierra Morena, and advanced in the direction of Madrid. The Spanish army was attacked at Ocaña on the 19th November by King Joseph. The Spanish infantry fought gallantly, but the whole of the cavalry gave way, creating great disorder in the infantry reserve in the rear, while those who stood their ground in front, being overpowered, the whole lied in the utmost confusion, pursued by the French cavalry, who in the disorder found little or no resistance, and sabred the fugitives without mercy. It is said that upwards of 5,000 were slain, 13,000 taken prisoners, and all the artillery and baggage captured. This sanguinary battle proved a deadly blow to the Spanish armies, and a sad disaster to the Spanish cause, as it laid open the whole of the south of Spain to the invader.

Misfortunes never come alone. The news likewise reached us that the Duke del Parque had also been defeated by Kellerman, at Alba de Formes, on the 17th and 18th November.

In our camp the officers of each company formed a mess, and we lived very comfortably, provisions of all kinds, and wine, being plentiful. We frequently interchanged dinner parties, with a card club in the evening. Sometimes we had horse-races, and frequently coursing matches, this place being celebrated for its breed of greyhounds. The queen of Spain, who was very fond of the sport, used to get all her greyhounds from Puebula.

The fever continued to rage, notwithstanding that the weather was becoming more settled and cold. Captain Newbold, of our corps, was carried off after a few days' illness, and shortly afterwards, in the beginning of December, I was seized with it myself—a most malignant attack of bilious fever; but however ill I might be, I had great confidence in my medical adviser, the clever and experienced Dr. Guthrie.

Early in December it was reported that the French, having

defeated the Spanish armies in various parts, and particularly the Duke del Parque at Alba de Formes, were now collecting a large force at Salamanca, seeming to threaten the northern frontier of Portugal, by Cuidad Rodrigo. This news appeared corroborated, because on the 10th December an order arrived for all the sick to be removed with as little delay as possible to Elvas, in Portugal, and for all the troops to march in that direction on the 14th. We further heard that our whole army was destined to proceed to the north of Portugal, and that the troops at Portalegre, Campo Mayor, &c., in that country had already marched.

On the 14th December, my friend the doctor told me candidly that he did not consider that I was in a fit state to be moved, being still subject to attacks of fever, and labouring under great debility. He left it to my own choice, either to endeavour to proceed, or to remain amongst strangers without a chance of medical assistance. I determined if possible to get out of the place, which held out no other prospect than a grave. I had continual hiccup, and nothing would remain on my stomach.

Next morning, the 13th December, I was carried from my bed wrapped up in blankets, and placed on a car with two privates ill of the same maladies, while my servant mounted my horse, and rode by the side. In this uncouth conveyance we jogged on at a slow rate, and suffered much from the jolting, owing to the many ruts in the track across the plain. In fording the Guadiana I heard the men calling for water. I desired my servant to give me some also. He at first hesitated, but on my insisting he gave me a tin full. I took a draught, and to my joyful surprise it remained without any symptoms of vomiting, as had hitherto been the case.

On arriving at Talaverilla I was put into bed, but I was unable to take any nourishment. I observed a row of *jarros* placed along one side of the room. These are pitchers made of porous clay. When filled with water it oozes through the pores, and damps the outside of the vessel; evaporation then takes place, which cools the contents, and the warmer the weather, and the greater the draft of air, the cooler the water becomes. During the night, finding myself feverish and parched with thirst, I called my servant, and got a glass of this water, I shortly afterwards fell asleep, and did not waken for some hours. I repeated the dose of water and felt much refreshed, and was able to take a little sago for breakfast. Being again placed on the car, we reached Badajos in the afternoon of the 14th; but this was no triumphal entry, no cavalcade with the glitter of arms and nodding plumes. I was left stretched in my humble vehicle, exposed in the public square to the gaze of the idle crowd until a billet was procured. My difficulties did not end here, for on being dragged to the door of the destined abode, the proud Spanish Don of a landlord scorned to admit a stranger coming in such a guise into his mansion. He flatly refused to give me admission. I was in no state to stand up for my right, so I despatched my servant to get another billet, which, although of a humbler description than the former one, the owner was of a more charitable disposition, and showed me every attention my situation required.

The change of air and scene worked a wonderful change in my complaint. I got a good night's rest, and felt so much better next day, the 15th, that I was able to mount my horse and to proceed to Elvas.

In consequence of the English army leaving this part of the frontier, it became necessary to increase the Portuguese garrison of Elvas. To make room for these, all our convalescents, who were able to move, were ordered to proceed to Estremos, six leagues back on the road to Lisbon. After remaining a week at Elvas, I found myself so much recovered that I obtained leave to go thither, where I was aware that some of my brother officers were. I set out on the 21st, and reached Estremos the same day. This is a tolerably large town, once of some importance, but having now the appearance of decay. It is encompassed with a wall and ditch, both in a state of great dilapidation. The environs however are very pretty, and the surrounding country well cultivated. We formed a small mess, and I passed a merrier Christmas than I had done for the two preceding years.

The inhabitants told us that the strong fortress of Gerona, after a most gallant defence from July, had surrendered on the 10th December, 1809.

My health being now re-established, I determined on rejoining my regiment, and Lieutenant Duguid, also of the 29th Regiment, proposed to accompany me. But where to find it was the difficulty. All we knew was that our army had marched to the north. We resolved to follow the same route in the hope of overtaking it.

We set out on the 29th December, and reached Ervidal, a small village, the first night, and Fonte de Sor the following one. The weather was splendid—a clear cloudless sky, with genial warm sun. The country was rather flat, with low undulating heights, in general rather barren, and covered with green *cestos*, and only partially cultivated on the borders of the streamlets. On the 31st December, we arrived at Abrantes, where, to our great satisfaction, we found our regiment. We learned that while the army under Lord Wellington had proceeded to the north, General Hill had been left to watch the Tagus. and the province of Alentejo, with a *corps d'armée* consisting of the second division, composed of three brigades of infantry, two brigades of artillery, and a due proportion of cavalry, also a division of Portuguese, under Sir John Hamilton. The following is a detail of the second division, under General Sir Rowland Hill:

The first brigade consisted of the 3rd Buffs, the second battalion of the 48th, the 66th, and the 31st Regiments under the Honourable Sir William Stewart.

The second brigade consisted of the 28th, 39th, and 34th Regiments, under Sir William Lumley.

The third brigade consisted of the 29th, 57th, first battalion of the 48th Regiment, under Major-General Houghton.

Also three companies of the fifth battalion of the 60th Rifles, two brigades of artillery, and some cavalry.

The Portuguese division, under Sir John Hamilton, consisted of two brigades of infantry, a brigade of artillery, and a force of cavalry.

PART 3
1810-11

Lord Wellington, having received reinforcements from England, made a fresh distribution of the army, which was now divided into seven divisions, and also a division of light troops.

The Portuguese army having been reorganised, under Marshal Beresford, some of the best disciplined regiments were incorporated in various English brigades, and the others were formed into divisions and brigades under English officers.

The English army occupied a position in rear of Almeida, and the light division was pushed on to the Spanish frontier towards Cuidad Rodrigo.

After remaining a few days at Abrantes, our brigade, under Major-General Houghton, marched on the 5th January, 1810, to Punhete, two leagues on the road to Lisbon. Punhete is a remarkably neat country town, situated on a high tongue of land at the junction of the Zezere with the Tagus. This was a very pleasant quarter. We had little or nothing to do. The weather was splendidly fine, bright sunshine. Our great lounge was on the bridge of boats over the Zezere, where we used to watch the fishermen hauling their nets to catch savey, an excellent fish of the salmon kind and flavour, except that the flesh was nearly white. Supplies of all kinds, and even luxuries, were to be had here, as boats were daily arriving from Lisbon. But the difficulty was to get money to purchase them; of that commodity we had little or none. Our pay, instead of being paid a month in advance, as is usually the case, was now nearly three months in arrears, and it was only by borrowing from richer friends that we could get any. Very few could afford the serious loss attending getting cash for a bill on England, because the paymasters and commissaries, instead of paying the dollars at four shillings and twopence, their current value, charged them from five shillings to seven shillings and sixpence, and we, although fighting, bleeding, and starving for our country, were subjected to a deduction of ten *per cent*, income-tax, stopped out of our pay. This seemed too bad. Indeed, at this period of the war, English credit suffered much all over the Peninsula, owing to the want of proper arrangement in the departments of the commissary-general and paymaster-general. For instance, I have been told, a contractor went out to a village and bargained with the farmers for cattle. When they were brought in, the commissary, instead of paying cash down for them, as was expected, gave each owner an order on the paymaster-general, who in his turn gave them a bill payable in Lisbon! A good bill, it is true, but of no value to the holders. They could not go two or three hundred miles to Lisbon, and there were no banks in any of the villages or towns to transact business. The poor men took the pieces of paper, first looked at one side of it, and then at the other, but could not fathom how this was to give them hard dollars for their cattle. They would then proceed to the plaza and get some wise head in the market to read the document for them, but this made them no better off. No one would give them one *maravedi* for their bills, so in despair they returned to the commissary and asked what he would give them for the bills. It was said instances were not wanting where certain commissaries of the lower grades got such bills at a large deduction. They got the dollars for them at Lisbon, with which they accommodated those who wished to draw bills on England at the high rates above specified. This glaring oppression on the inhabitants, so injurious to British honour, was soon afterwards remedied by pay offices being established in the various different provincial towns, where the owners of the bills had only to apply to get their money.

While here, my friend, Andrew Leith Hay, and I live together. Our last dollar was expended; our only resource seemed to me to apply to a saving compatriot, who, I knew, had always a reserve fund. To him I went. On stating my distress, and requesting a loan, his reply was, "Guid faith, I've no a penny, I was just coming mysel' to borrow frae you." This source failed me. I told Hay that we must go on short commons, that ration beef and biscuit must be our future fare. He said, "Let me try my luck." Out he went, and on his return, rattling money in his pocket, he threw a handful of dollars on the table, saying, "Now let us have a blow-out." On my inquiring from what friend he could have extracted so much treasure, he replied, "Never mind now, I will tell you after dinner." On my repeating my inquiry while discussing a good bottle of wine, he said, "Why, from Sandy Young, to be sure." I felt thoroughly convinced that my friend's power of persuasion and skill in raising the wind was far superior to my own.

Having some friends in the 10th Portuguese regiment quartered at Thomar, only three leagues off, we went over to pay them a visit on the 16th January. They, with some of the wealthiest native officers of the corps, had formed a tolerably good mess. After an agreeable dinner, it was proposed that we should attend the soiree of the Marquis and Marchioness of A——. To our surprise, we observed there a great, stout fresh-coloured Englishwoman, dressed in a riding habit, and sitting between two young and handsome daughters of the hostess. Colonel Oliver immediately said to us, "This is too bad; do not speak to her." We cut our visit as short as decency would permit. It then appeared that this madam was a trooper's wife, and that an English commissary then attached to the Portuguese army, and stationed at Thomar, a natural son of the notorious Lord George Gordon, had not only taken this soldier's trull under his protection, but had the impudence to introduce her to this and other noble families, and thus bring disgrace on the British character. The colonel went next morning, and communicated to the marquis the whole circumstances, and begged to express how much the English officers felt the disgrace that a countryman should have been guilty of such conduct. The marquis was struck with horror, and clasping his hands, exclaimed, *"Jesus! una puta in mia casa!"* She was immediately bundled out.

Thomar is a thriving handsome town, situated in a valley, near a river, on which are some manufactories of cotton and cloth. On a steep bank, immediately in rear of the town, stands the noble Convento de Christo. The church is very magnificent. The canons' seats, the pulpit and the choir, are splendid specimens of carved work, both in oak and Brazilian wood. The walls are adorned with many pictures by the ancient masters. The organ is remarkably fine. They showed us a barrel or pipe standing detached, but which, when attached to the instrument, had such a powerful effect, that it shook the whole of the massive building. It appeared some twenty or thirty feet high, and about a foot and a half in diameter.

The French, in consequence of their various victories over Spanish armies, were now masters of all the south of Spain. Soult, with 50,000 men, forced the passes of the Sierra Morena in the end of January, and pushing on with the utmost celerity, by Baylen, Cordova &c., he appeared before Seville, which surrendered on the 4th February, and King Joseph entered it on the same day. This was a sad disaster for the Spanish cause, and it proved of immense advantage to the enemy, as it gave them possession of the very place where the seat of the chief government was established, and of the great national foundry of cannon. The supreme *junta* of government fled to Cadiz, but several of its members submitted to Joseph, and suspicions were entertained that others were more inclined to favour the French from interested motives, than to support the cause of their country.

Cadiz now became of the greatest importance, not only as being the seat of government, but as being the great naval station, the emporium of the Spanish trade, and the port where all supplies of bullion from South America could most safely arrive. The French, fully sensible of the great acquisition this important place would be to them, pressed on a force to seize the prize, which seemed almost within their grasp; but the Duke del Albuquerque, a true patriot, although he had received orders from the *junta* to proceed in another direction, foreseeing the danger which threatened Cadiz, most prudently determined to save this last stronghold. He hastened towards it by forced marches, with a body of 12,000 men, and so closely pursued by the enemy that as he passed over the drawbridges on the 3rd February, to enter the advanced posts at the Isla de Leon, the French troops appeared on the heights overlooking the city, and in three days the place was closely blockaded by a strong French force. The garrison was reinforced by an English and Portuguese force under General Sir Thomas Graham.

While Soult had moved on Cadiz, General Regnier, with a

corps d'armée, advanced into Spanish Estramadura, thus threatening Badajos and our line of operations on the Tagus. To counteract this movement, General Hill was ordered to move to Portalegre, so as to protect the province of Alentejo, and also to support Elvas and Badajos should they be attacked.

We left Punhete on the 15th February for Abrantes. Next day we reached Gavion, and on the day following Gaffete, both miserable country towns situated in a dreary district, generally covered with green *cestos*. On the 18th February we entered Portalegre. Here General Hill established his headquarters, and the whole of the infantry and artillery were quartered in the town. The cavalry were posted in advance, in the direction of Badajos and Elvas. The Portuguese division was cantoned in Crato, Castello de Vide, and other adjacent villages.

In taking possession of my billet, a ludicrous circumstance occurred. When troops were placed in cantonments, the usual mode of taking up quarters was for the quartermasters of the several corps to proceed in advance to the town, where an officer of the quartermaster-general's department, having divided the place into districts according to the different brigades, gave over to each quartermaster certain streets for his corps. The quartermaster then selected the best houses for the commanding and other field officers, marking the same with chalk; then the next best for the captains, and so on. Those for the men had the number they were destined to contain also written in chalk on the door. When my billet was pointed out to me, I observed marked on the doorway, which was closed, 'One officer and two soldiers.' The soldiers were as servants. I knocked repeatedly, but no notice was taken or answer given to my demand for admission. After waiting some time, I imagined that the proprietor had gone off. As military men are not very ceremonious after a fatiguing march, I gave orders for the soldiers to force the door. Just as they were about to do this, I heard a female voice in the inside say: "*Spera, spera, senhor*—Wait, wait, sir! What do you want?" I of course replied that I had got a billet on the house, and was entitled to immediate admittance. She began to use all sorts of persuasive arguments to induce me to believe that the house was not fit for the reception of an English officer; but these making no impression, and

I, getting impatient, again directed, the men to force the door; when, to my great surprise, a gruff voice called out, "Hell to your sowl! What is it ye want here? Don't spake to me in aney of your gibberish of Portuguese." It required no wizard to find out that the obstreperous host was a native of the Emerald Isle. So I said: "Good Mr. Pat, no more blarney! If you are not content to take me and my two servants in, I shall take possession of a neighbouring house where there are twenty-five men, and will transfer the whole of them to yours." This threat had the desired effect. The gateway was unbarred. I entered in triumph, brushing past a little, sharp-countenanced man, looking timid and scared, as if the blue devils had got possession of him. A capital quarter I found it, the rooms being fitted up with many English comforts. There was also a tolerable collection of English books, which formed a source of amusement.

My conjecture proved correct. The *patron de casa* was a native of Ireland, who gloried in the patronymic of Pat Maloney. He was a manufacturer of cloth and a dyer by profession, which accounted for the diabolical colour of his visage at my first interview with him. This place is remarkable for its woollen fabrics, conducted principally by Germans and Irish. A great portion of the blue cloth used as uniform for the Portuguese army is made here. Our host had also a countryman as an assistant, who, he told me, had been condemned and was about to be hanged on the bridge at Wexford, when he was pardoned on account of his youth, on condition of his expatriating himself to a foreign land. His crime was having printed or engraved some manifesto of the rebels in 1798, he being then an apprentice to an engraver.

The situation of Portalegre, as the name denotes, is very charming, and the surrounding scenery very romantic. It stands on a spur of a high ridge of hills, which divides Portugal from Spain. The principal part of the town is on the hill, which overlooks an extensive plain stretching to the west and south, richly cultivated with olive-groves, vineyards, &c., bounded by a range of steep hills which give it a grand amphitheatre appearance. The view of the town from the plain is particularly striking. The large churches, their numerous spires, the other public buildings, and in the background the several convents in picturesque situations on the wooded hills above the city, have a magnificent effect. As a military position, at this particular period, it was of some importance, to render effectual the defence of the Alentejo. It gave us the command of the road from Badajos to Lisbon, while, by an easy communication with the Tagus, we could draw all our supplies from the latter without any risk; and, being a central point, our corps was at all times ready either to move south to protect Badajos, or to proceed to the north, as circumstances and events might require. Indeed, the mere fact of our having occupied Portalegre had the desired effect. The enemy, on learning our arrival there, immediately withdrew some leagues back from Badajos.

The garrison consisted of ten regiments of English infantry, two brigades of artillery, and a few squadrons of cavalry. Our sources of amusement were very limited, and we had but little intercourse with the inhabitants, as the principal inhabitants had retired with their families to Lisbon, and many of the young ladies took refuge as boarders in convents, as places of security in these wretched times.

The rainy season had now set in, the weather being chill and damp, and as there were no fireplaces in any of the rooms in Portugal, they were very unpleasant abodes at this season, however well adapted they might be for the usual genial climate. The only comfortable places were the kitchens. We accordingly, as soon as dinner was over, used to adjourn there, and in front of a blazing fire, sip our wine, roast our chestnuts, and crack nuts and jokes together. The landlord of the billet, where our small mess held their merry meetings, was a blind poet, who had many nourishing names. He styled himself Don Francesco Picauzo Cabrae de Souza Tavaorez. This genius used to squat himself on a low chair in a corner inside his large kitchen chimney, which, as usual, extended almost from one side of the place to the other, and there spout verses for our edification. During this wet season the light wines of this part of the country afforded little comfort to the inward man. To remedy this we used to put a certain quantity into a *pancello* or earthen jar, and heat it on the fire, with all sorts of spices, and then, beating up the yolks of eggs, make a capital flip. On presenting our friend with a glass of this, he gave us a specimen of his composition, proposing a toast:

Esto vinho es excellente,
Esto Copo es e primero,
Viva e principal Regente,
Et tainben George Feriero.

We occasionally visited a convent of nuns, which was prettily situated at a short distance from the town. Here many young ladies were being educated, and others had taken refuge to be out of harm's way, dreading lest the enemy should pay Portalegre another visit. As the nuns looked upon us as protectors, they received us cordially, and relaxed a little the stringent rules regarding the admission of strangers. Their chanting of vespers was particularly fine.

The people told us that in 1808 General Loison, with a movable column of French troops, was on a roving expedition, raising forced contributions. He came to Portalegre in August, and demanded a heavy sum from the inhabitants, threatening the town in a savage manner with fire and sword if the sum was not paid within a certain time. He made several of the principal inhabitants attend to receive and count the money over to his agents at the house where he was quartered. One day while the money came pouring in, and before the French had time to count it, the startling news suddenly arrived that the English had landed. This created a great hubbub. The drums beat to arms. Loison had received orders to march *instanter*. The heaps of money in gold and silver on the different tables were hurriedly swept into sacks and packed off, and six of the most respectable citizens carried away as hostages, that the remaining part of the contribution, which was not collected should be paid. He even ordered the rich damask silk hangings, which adorned the public rooms to be taken.

Where there was so large a garrison, there were of course many sporting characters amongst the officers. A committee, or miniature Jockey Club, was established, and horse-racing became the order of the day. A tolerably good course was laid out in the plain, and everything was conducted in due form, under the patronage of our amiable commander, General Hill, who himself was a great amateur in horse-flesh, and had always a capital stud.

The 17th March being St. Patrick's day, the Irish members of our regiment determined to celebrate the anniversary of their patron saint, as wont is in their native isle. We all volunteered to make it a general feast. The usual noisy hilarity on such occasions prevailed. Wine flowed freely. Electric flashes of Irish wit delighted the hearers. The band played appropriate tunes, and national melodies were sweetly sung by many a manly voice in this foreign land with feeling and effect. The joyous evening passed as if war existed not, nor an enemy in the Peninsula. And yet this proved the last commemoration of this festive day to several of the brave fellows who were now so happy.

St. Patrick's day having passed off so pleasantly, the English resolved to make a like demonstration on the 23rd April, St. George's day. Every preparation for a magnificent display was in progress. The saloon was adorned with flags and different devices. The cooks were busy in the kitchen. The wines were cooling, and all was in active progress. To further honour the day, and as a compliment to our gallant general, several of the great *dons* and landholders had arranged that there should be a grand wolf hunt. All the daring spirits and sporting characters were astir at an early hour in the morning full of excitement in anticipation of this, to them, new species of sport. Some were already mounted, and were eagerly pushing on to the appointed rendezvous, when, lo!, an express with despatches arrived with intelligence that the French had suddenly attacked the Spaniards, and had driven them out of Albuquerque, a frontier town a few leagues off.

Disappointment was depicted in every countenance, but this fit of chagrin was only momentary. The idea of meeting the enemy soon banished all selfish considerations. The scene was quickly changed from peaceful pursuits to warlike preparations. The delicacies provided for the banquet were hastily distributed amongst the subscribers.

Everyone hurried off to pack up, and all was soon in readiness to take the field. The whole division was in motion by 2 o'clock p.m. After marching about two leagues, we were halted near Alegrete. It was now perfectly dark, and we here bivouacked in the literal sense of the word—that is to say, we were moved a short distance off the road into a wooded plain. Each man laid himself on the ground, on the softest spot he could find, and slumbered with his arms in his hands, ready to start up, or move, at a moment's notice. As our baggage had been ordered to remain in the rear, our only meal consisted of a mouthful of cold meat and biscuit which our haversacks afforded; and as no fires were allowed to be lighted, we kept ourselves as warm as we could by smoking cigars.

Next morning, the 24th April, we stood to our arms long before daylight. Some hours afterwards it was reported that the enemy had retired. We were then permitted to light fires, and our baggage having come up, we got some excellent tea to warm us. We, however, remained on the alert all day, until it was positively ascertained that the French had retreated. We returned to Portalegre, and occupied our former quarters on the 25th April.

During our sojourn in these pleasant quarters, we were rather puzzled, by our pay being kept so much in arrears, how to obtain the comforts of life beyond our actual rations of wine, beef, and biscuits. Fortunately for us, after the paymaster and others had declined to aid us, an extraordinary character appeared amongst us like an angel, to alleviate our distress. This noble-hearted and generous man was not a Christian, but a Moor or Mohammedan, and, except a few words of Spanish, spoke no language but his own. This stranger brought with him a large stock of all the requisite necessaries, and many of the luxuries, of refined life, and opened a store for their disposal. The few who had the means paid him ready money. To the many who had no money he handed a slip of paper with pen and ink. Each one wrote down the articles he wanted, with a promise to pay for them when the money should arrive. No further security was required, so great was his faith in British honour. Now, considering that we were all and each of us liable shortly to go into action and be killed, or to die of fever, he really ran no small risk in giving such unlimited credit, and his charges, even under these circumstances, were by no means exorbitant.

One fine evening, the 3rd May, a party of us—military youths—while strolling about at Portalegre on the frontiers of Portugal, met some Spanish officers who were busily engaged in making purchases of some articles of ornament, and such appliances of luxury as the place afforded. The Spaniards, to our great surprise, notwithstanding their being such close neighbours to our friends the Portuguese, could only make themselves very imperfectly understood; while we, although foreigners, being more *au fait* at the Portuguese terms for the more necessary articles of life, were not a little amused at the circumstance of having to act as interpreters. The Spaniards, who felt sensible of our attention, informed us that they had been deputed on the part of the governor of Valencia d'Alcantara, as a committee of taste, to procure all that was requisite for a splendid ball which was in course of preparation. They most politely requested that we would do them the pleasure of honouring it with our presence. Glad of an opportunity which would afford us some respite from our usual military routine, we readily accepted their friendly invitation; and on the day appointed we started over the borders, not to surprise the enemy, as our gallant and amiable commander-in-chief soon afterwards did near the same place, but to surprise our friends who invited us, they appearing to think that we looked upon their invitation as nothing more than complimentary words of course.

The road, which was of the worst description, passed over a hilly country, covered at intervals with forests of chestnuts and oaks, or intersected at times with deep and verdant valleys, affording scenery of a varied, romantic, and wild character, such as might well have seemed a most fitting locality for *banditti*, had not the reality truly existed, for the district was the rendezvous of fierce *ladrones* and bands of smugglers. We, however, escaped with impunity, and late in the afternoon reached the appointed fortress.

We now began to take into consideration—what we had not thought of before—where we were to put up: hotels there were none; we decided, as in duty bound, that we should in the first place report our arrival to the governor, and trust to his generosity for procuring us accommodation. We accordingly proceeded to the grand plaza, where his house was situated. It was crowded with a most heterogeneous mixture of motley military, the garrison being composed of parties of different corps, who had escaped when the Spanish armies had been worsted and dispersed. My companions deputed me, as being reckoned the most proficient in the noble Castilian tongue, to announce our arrival, and to request the indulgence of billets for us, as friends and allies of his most catholic majesty. I found it a matter of some difficulty, owing to the Spanish formalities, to effect an entrance. After a parley with the sentry, and bullying an old porter, I at last succeeded. Being met by an official person of a nondescript appearance, I was by him ushered into the presence of his excellency *el gobernador*. This potentate, a tall, gaunt personage, advanced in years, was standing at a table, most eagerly occupied in making punch, towards which consummation he was in the act of squeezing a lemon, which, if one might judge from his grimaces, must have been a very hard one. He kept grumbling to himself, seemingly unconscious that a stranger had been announced, while I, in the meantime, was, in my best Spanish, respectfully addressing him with many flowery compliments, and requesting from him, as a comrade in arms, billets and hospitality. He at length directed a vacant stare towards me, exclaiming at the same time, *"Oh, señor official! que quiere usted?"* Between surprise at being thus abruptly addressed, and the endeavour to suppress a titter, I confess I got rather bewildered in my oratory. I, however, began to repeat my requests, when my ears were astonished by the voice of a female addressing me in English, and in the most refined and polished accent, "My dear sir, pray do not give yourself any uneasiness; we were aware of your coming; everything is arranged for your reception." On my turning round, with some surprise, I beheld a large, fine, lady-like person, who had just entered the room. I could not resist giving a look of inquiry, as if soliciting a solution of this enigma. She seemed perfectly to comprehend the meaning of the look, for, laughing very good-humouredly, she said, "Pray go and bring up your companions: there are orderlies ready to take your horses, billets are prepared for you, and you shall know presently by what chance you meet a countrywoman here."

I lost no time in returning to my friends, who were rejoiced at the success of my mission. I introduced them all in due form, even to the old governor, who, after a few unnecessary bows and scrapes, resumed his former occupation. Some of his staff having arrived, they took my friends to show them the lions, while I remained with our fair friend, to learn her history, which was told in a few brief words.

"I am," said she, "the daughter of the late General Mercer. My father was stationed at Minorca. I was then very young, and I there met Pepe" (pointing significantly to his Excellency), "and married him, without even once reflecting that he was a foreigner, and I a stranger to his country." This account of herself interested me very much, because I happened to know several members of the general's family, and a near relation of his was married to a connection of my own family. On my mentioning these circumstances, she seemed much affected. She kindly offered me a seat in her carriage to the ball, and begged I would attend her while she did the honours of the evening.

The *gobernadora* was received in great state, and accepted the homage of the *dons* and *donnas* with considerable dignity and grace. The ball was brilliant, and the *senoritas*, in their singular but most becoming Spanish dresses, were now all animation.

The assembly was particularly full, because this town, being at that period out of range of our warlike operations, was considered as a place of security, and many families from the neighbouring towns and country had taken refuge here; hence, as may be supposed, the appearance of a few English officers created some little sensation amongst the ladies, who seemed determined to be agreeable; and few women possess greater powers of pleasing, accompanied with sprightly, ready wit, than the Spanish ladies.

Nothing would satisfy some of them but that one of us must dance a hornpipe. This, they supposed, was a *sine quâ non* of an Englishman's accomplishments; while we, with equal absurdity, insisted that some of them should dance a *fandango* or *bolero*, both parties being ignorant respecting the national feelings and customs severally pertaining to them. We were thus unconsciously victimising each other. While this friendly altercation was carried on in the utmost good-humour between us and the ladies, it was nearly leading to unpleasant results amongst the military *dons* themselves. Some one of them, out of compliment to us, having very good-naturedly said that they would dance a *bolero*, others, it seems, insisted that such dances were not proper for public exhibition in a ballroom—that they were only performed by the low and vulgar, and never in good society, except occasionally in family parties as a little piece of drollery. This was denied by others; warm words ensued; *desafios* (Anglicé, challenges) were given and accepted; but, on our understanding how affairs were going on, we begged to interfere, and had no great difficulty in bringing these blustering heroes to reason; and happily, or rather unhappily, for us, a Spanish officer got us out of the dilemma of dancing a hornpipe by volunteering to do it himself. This, to our admiration and dismay, he did to perfection. He set to work with heart and soul—footed, hopped, shuffled, and gigged in the true man-of-war style. It appeared he had learned this boisterous dance while a prisoner, having been taken in a naval engagement. This exhibition afforded great amusement to the *senoritas*, who most wickedly seemed to enjoy our confusion. In vain we solemnly protested that it was not a gentlemanly dance, although a favourite one with our brave Jack Tars. Our sole remedy was to join in the laugh at our own expense, which was only interrupted by the announcement of supper. Here refreshments of every kind were in abundance, including the most choice fruits of Spain and her generous wines. Good-humour was the order of the night. The ball recommenced, and continued with great spirit until an early hour in the morning.

During intervals of this festive scene, I had a *tete-á-tete* with her excellency *la gobernadora*. She seemed bitterly to repent, in her years of maturity, the rash step she had taken when, in her youth, she had given her heart to such a companion; for Pepe had absorbed so much punch that he either could not or would not appear. Yet Pepe had been a gay man in his day—had touched the guitar with exquisite feeling, had sung *seguidillas*, or lays of love, and had danced to admiration. But Pepe had neglected the cultivation of his mind, and, having no idea of the quiet comforts of domestic retirement which his declining years required, nor any mental resource, he became peevish and unhappy. His unfortunate lady, who by birth and education was deserving of a worthier destiny, was doomed to live estranged from her friends and the society she had been accustomed to, surrounded by those who had no one sympathy in her feelings, and having no communion of sentiment even with her own husband. Few foreign gentlemen have any idea of that domestic happiness which constitutes an Englishman's satisfaction. They seldom dine with their families: the coffee-room and gambling-table are but too frequently their evening resorts; while the ladies, under these circumstances, are driven to seek amusement from without. Hence the nightly *conversaziones* of Italy, the *tertulias* of Spain, and the loose state of society in France. While I was escorting about our fair countrywoman, little did those who were enjoying the gay scene know or imagine the sorrow which was assailing the heart of her excellency, who, with all the outward show of one perfectly at ease, was condescendingly receiving or returning the numerous friendly salutations or demonstrations of respect.

I have subsequently met others of my countrywomen in a similar position, in various parts of Europe; and the painful recollections of such encounters have given occasion to these reflections. They are not written in a spirit of prejudice against foreigners. I have passed much of my life abroad, and many happy days have I spent on alien shores; but such passing enjoyments do not constitute the happiness of a life—they ought rather to make us reflect that more permanent ones are necessary, and, above all things, necessary for English people. It must never be forgotten that every country has its own peculiar manners and customs. Our countrywomen, whose brightest possession consists in those pure moral feelings and that just self-respect for which they are so extensively renowned, cannot safely associate permanently with those more than doubtful characters so frequently met with in society abroad. Even let an Englishman bring a foreign wife to his country—she never can accommodate herself to our habits and manners: they are too tame for her, and there are too many domestic arrangements to be attended to—she is continually sighing to return. Yet how often does it now occur that, allured by some empty title—or even, perhaps, by some frivolous accomplishment of foreign growth—our beautiful countrywomen sacrifice themselves in forming foreign connections—to reap disappointment and perhaps ultimate neglect. Vanity in a woman is, in many instances, pardonable; but when she abandons all that ought to be most dear—friends, home, and country—to satisfy a false taste, then, indeed, it becomes difficult to hold her blameless.

We returned next day, the 4th of May, all much pleased with our trip over the borders.

Intelligence having arrived on the evening of the 14th May that the enemy were moving on Badajos, we received orders to march at daylight next morning for Aronches, which we reached after a miserable march of four leagues. The rain came down in torrents. The smaller rivulets were rendered in a short time almost impassable. We had to wade, several up to our breasts, the men drawing their pouches up to their shoulders to preserve their ammunition;

the ranks of each section locked arm, and by keeping shoulder to shoulder stemmed the current; but notwithstanding this precaution, one or two men of another corps were swept away and drowned. The baggage could not pass until the water had subsided, and even then those who were unfortunate enough to have their baggage on small mules or asses lost a great portion of it. Nor were our prospects on arriving very cheering. Our regiment was put into a large old convent. Each of us got an empty cell for our billet. There, drenched to the skin, cold, and hungry, we were left to our own reflections. We at length managed to get timber from ruined houses, and made a fire in the courtyard and surrounding cloisters. Some ration beef and sour wine formed our only repast in this wretched place.

Aronches is an ancient town situated on a hill, and encircled with old Moorish walls and towers. The whole wore a melancholy appearance of decay; but the surrounding country seemed tolerably well cultivated. We remained here the following day, the 16th, and in the evening it was announced that we were to return to Portalegre, because the enemy after reconnoitring Badajos, finding that we were on the alert, had again retreated, carrying off with them all the cattle they could collect in its neighbourhood. We returned to Portalegre next day, the 17th May.

Nothing particular happened to us during the month of June. In July the plot of war began to thicken. It was evident that a deep game was to be played.

On the 11th July reports were spread that the enemy were again threatening Badajos. We were, as on the former occasion, marched off in a hurry early next morning to Aronches. This proved a feint on the part of the enemy. General Hill, from the excellent information he always obtained, found out that, although the French had detached a column towards Badajos, their main body was actually moving north towards the Tagus, with the design of crossing that river, and by a *coup de main* to seize Castello Branco, and thus interpose at a most vulnerable point between our corps and the main army under Lord Wellington. Our able general instantly decided on counteracting the French plans, and by rapid marches to reach Castello Branco before them. We were therefore ordered back to Portalegre, which we reached next morning, the 13th July, and on the following day, the 14th, we commenced our march to the north, and reached Apalao, near which we bivouacked. As it was absolutely necessary that we should proceed by forced marches, and the weather being extremely warm, it was determined that we should always make such marches during the night and allow the men to repose during the day.

We started again in the cool of the evening of the 17th July, and bivouacked near Niza by daybreak next morning. During this night's march we first observed the splendid comet, which was seen remarkably clear with the naked eye. Having no tents, nor time to erect huts, and there being no woods in this district, we suffered much from want of shelter to shade us from the sun during the day, so that we got little sleep or rest. We moved again on the night of the 18th, and reached the difficult pass of Villa Vilha, after a long march over bad roads. We here crossed the Tagus by the bridge of boats, and did not get into our bivouac on the right bank until rather late in the day.

It being ascertained that we had anticipated the enemy, and that they could not now reach Castello Branco before us, we were allowed to rest here until the following morning, the 20th, when we proceeded to Cernados. This proved a most oppressively hot day. Men of all regiments fell out and lay gasping on the roadside, unable to move; several of them died, and others dropped down dead. I suffered intensely myself, owing to my horse losing a shoe. I desired my servant to lead him back to a blacksmith's shop which we had passed. I got leave to remain in the rear, thinking that my servant would soon overtake me again, while I slowly trudged on; but my patience became exhausted, and my strength began to fail, and no signs of my *cavallo* appearing, I summoned resolution and continued to push on, seeing that the poor fellows who had thrown themselves on the ground were in a sad condition under a cloudless sun.

On the following day, the 21st July, we reached Castello Branco. We here learned that the enemy, on finding that we had succeeded in occupying this place, had taken possession of Penamacor, a strong post about eight leagues from Castello Branco, commanding the road from it to the north of Spain, and had thus cut off our communication by that frontier route with the main army under

Lord Wellington. There was, however, another but less practicable road across the mountains, farther back in Portugal.

After halting a day we were pushed on, on the 22nd July, to Ladricero, and Atalaha, and bivouacked in a wood within two leagues of the enemy's advanced posts. We remained here about a week, constantly on the alert. The country was rather open, and the enemy were much superior to us in cavalry.

We retired on the 30th July to Finalhas, and in the afternoon of the following day we were suddenly ordered under arms. Reports reached us that the enemy were advancing. After waiting some time we moved off to the rear, and all the baggage was ordered to precede us. We had marched about two leagues when we were halted, in order, I believe, to give countenance to our small force of cavalry which was covering our rear. As they, however, did not appear, and night was fast coming on, we bivouacked on the roadside, every man lying down with his arms by his side, After daylight our piquets were called in, and we continued our retreat to Sarzades, a small deserted village situated on a hill partially covered with wood.

This was a position which had been previously fixed upon to make a stand, in case the enemy should attempt to attack us; and a well-chosen point it was, as it commanded not only the road leading to the pass of Villa Vilha, but also the road to Thomar and the centre of Portugal. Our right was flanked by the Tagus, from whence the bridge of boats could speedily be removed; our left by a chain of mountains running back from the Grand Estrella; and our cavalry were at Castello Branco, three leagues in front, to watch the enemy.

We erected huts in rear of the position, as bivouacs for the men, and opened communications along the whole line, so that the column or the artillery could easily be moved to support any particular point. A strong advanced guard was also posted at a pass about three miles in our immediate front.

We remained perched on the top of this barren hill nearly three weeks, during the whole of which period we were miserably ill off. Our friend the Moor had not followed us into these desolate and dreary regions. The stocks of the inferior suttlers were quickly exhausted. The inhabitants of the miserable villages had fled to the mountains, carrying with them any goods they possessed. We frequently had literally nothing but scanty rations of beef and musty bread; no rice or vegetables to make soup could be procured; we could not even get brown sugar for our tea.

During this period I was seized with a serious attack of fever and ague. The surgeon wished to send me to the general hospital at Thomar, but I declined quitting my regiment while the enemy were in our front. He, however, had me removed into the field hospital, which was only a dilapidated country church, without doors or windows. There laid in a corner, a little straw, with my blankets and cloak, was my sick-bed, which was only separated from those of the privates by a few boards, which were put up to screen me from their gaze. I, however, thanks be to God and a good constitution, got over it, while others sank.

During this time the French had obtained several successes. In June, they had invested Cuidad Rodrigo, which was garrisoned by nearly five thousand men under General Herasti. The enemy met with a brave resistance, but the works were old and ruinous, and after enduring a siege of a month, the garrison capitulated on the 10th July, 1810.

Almeida was also besieged and taken. The French invested the place on the 23rd August. On the 27th a magazine containing nearly all the ammunition of the defenders exploded, and destroyed a great part of the town, killing many of the inhabitants. On the following day, the 28th August, General Cox, who commanded the garrison, surrendered, and the French obtained possession of the town.

It being our turn of duty for advanced guard, which was taken regimentally, we marched out on the 10th September to relieve the former one, and occupied a position on a height commanding a bridge over a small stream which ran along the foot of a range of hills. The point of defence was well chosen, being opposite an elbow of the river which bent towards us, so that field-works thrown up on each side of the road, on which were posted a few pieces of cannon, effectually commanded the passage by their cross fire. We remained here quiet all the next day, the 11th.

On the morning of the 12th September we received sudden orders to withdraw, and to proceed after our division, which had already marched to the rear. We repassed through Sarzedas and crossed a small river which ran in front of very high hills in rear of it. We mounted these by zigzag roads; and at all the most important points which commanded the ascent we found batteries erected and several furnished with cannon. This proved the great foresight of our gallant commander-in-chief, as by providing these defences the militia and peasantry of the country would be enabled to defend these passes in this strong region, through which the road leads on the right bank of the Tagus to Thomar and Lisbon. We found our division already bivouacked on the mountain above the works.

We moved the next day to Zibriera Formosa and halted the following one, I believe to see whether the enemy was making any attempt to follow us or not; but there being no signs of them, we marched to Cortiçada. Both these places are pretty villages beautifully situated in this mountainous range.

We remained a day at Cortiçada. On the 17th September we marched to Cardigas, and on the 18th to Villa de Rey, both mountain villages, and then bivouacked on the bank of the Tagus. In the afternoon there was a most tremendous thunderstorm, accompanied with the heaviest rain I almost ever witnessed. This drove the scorpions and centipedes into our small tents. I found a horrible long brute of a centipede under my pillow and several scorpions in the grass.

We crossed the Zezere next morning and bivouacked in a wood near Villa dos Reys. We here understood that matters were now coming to a crisis, that the enemy under Massena had crossed the frontiers in great force, that Lord Wellington had fallen back to a strong position, and that we were to proceed to join him with as little delay as possible. In order that there might be no hindrance on the road, all the sick, and even the weakly men, with the women and children, were ordered to remain behind, and an officer of our regiment was appointed to take charge of them and conduct them to Thomar, where a depot was to be established. After the officer was named and all the arrangements made, our surgeon, aware that I was again subject to attacks of fever and ague, had gone, it seems, to our commanding officer, Major Way, and represented to him that I ought not to proceed. On the adjutant bringing me an order to that effect I remonstrated, but the major himself peremptorily ordered me to receive the official papers from the officer already appointed and take the command. I had no alternative but to obey. Taking a hasty farewell of my comrades, from whom I had never hitherto been separated when any actual field services were going on, I was left alone in my glory in a desolate bivouac, having only one subaltern left with me under my orders.

On assembling my detachment, which consisted of me belonging to all the different regiments of the division, I found it amounted to 150 of all sorts—the sick, the lame, and the lazy, besides 50 women and 40 children. After some delay the commissary sent me a squadron of mules, on some of which I mounted the most sickly men, and loaded the others with the knapsacks, accoutrements, &c., of all that were able to walk. My instructions were to proceed to Thomar and to form a depot for our division. I hastened on to provide the necessary quarters, and my sub marched at the head of this motley procession and arrived at Thomar late in the afternoon. On application to the *juiz de fora*, he gave me two large empty houses for the men and quartered all the women and children in the wing of a convent of nuns. I went to report myself to an old Portuguese general, then acting as commander of the place. His staff said he was asleep, and further that I had no intercourse with him. I became the English commander, and my garrison increased faster than I could have wished, as for several days numbers of men kept coming in. They reported that in consequence of the division proceeding by hasty and forced marches to the north, they were unable either to keep up with their regiments or to overtake them.

I was now in for another attack of fever and ague. The fit came on not every third day, but every day, so that I was reduced to a state of extreme weakness. The medical officers urged me to take a sick certificate and to proceed to Lisbon; but having a certain responsible command, I declined their advice. I received a report on the 30th September that a battle had been fought at Busaco on the 27th and 28th. As many wounded would consequently arrive it became necessary to remove to Lisbon a portion of the sick now in hospital here; and the surgeon again representing to me that I had no chance of getting well without a change of air, I gave over the command to the next senior officer and proceeded on the 2nd October with a convoy of 150 sick to Barquinha on the Tagus, where boats were prepared for us.

The whole detachment embarked on the morning of the 3rd October, and immediately proceeded down the Tagus, having wind and current in our favour. The vessels were large open boats, sharp at both ends, having only a deck at the stern of a few feet long for the steersman to stand on, beneath which was a sort of small cabin or store-room. Each boat held about thirty men besides the crew. On approaching Santarem the water was unfortunately very low. Some of the boats grounded, and it became extremely dark. We were obliged to pass a cold night on the water, with only a sail thrown over us to protect us from the heavy dew. We, however, reached Santarem to breakfast.

We found the place in the greatest state of alarm. To my surprise the people informed us that reports had arrived that our army was retreating. Terror and dismay were depicted on every countenance. All seemed to imagine that the British were about to abandon them to the fury of a merciless enemy. I got on board again without delay, and in the evening reached Villa Franca, where everything appeared as quiet and still as in the time of the profoundest peace; but on going to the *juiz de fora* for billets, he received me in a state of great agitation, in a very abrupt manner, muttering to himself. As the Portuguese are usually very polite and have a bland sort of manner, I inquired what was the matter. He then told me that he had just received a despatch announcing that our army was actually retiring, and also an order for all the inhabitants to abandon the town, so as to leave nothing but empty houses should the enemy advance. This was rather startling intelligence. The poor man felt great perturbation at having such an unpleasant duty imposed upon him as to communicate such disasters to his fellow citizens.

How changed the scene at daybreak on the morning of the 5th October! Thousands who had gone to bed in peace and plenty now rose beggars and outcasts from their happy homes. It was truly a melancholy sight to behold the poor inhabitants running bewildered about the streets, or crowding in thousands to the quays; handsome ladies with helpless infants in their arms; others with baskets of plate in their hands; some with useless articles of furniture; each one in bewilderment seizing the first thing that came to hand, and all endeavouring to make their escape. The cries of the children and the wailings of despair of the women were heartrending. In the midst of this distressing scene numbers of women, men, and officers were arriving, which added to the calamity, because additional boats were now required to convey them and the military stores to Lisbon, so that numbers were deprived of the means of getting away. Many delicate and interesting *senoras* kept imploring us to give them a passage, but all the boats were so overcrowded that I found it impossible to comply with their request; and, glad to escape from the sight of so much real human misery, I ordered the flotilla to get under weigh.

Villa Franca is a handsome town, the streets very regular and clean, most of the houses of a superior description, it being a favourite summer residence of many of the wealthy citizens of Lisbon. The whole had an appearance of comfort which gave it an English look; and, in a commercial point of view, it was one of the most thriving places in Portugal, because vessels of large size could come up close to the quays. The environs were beautiful, being ornamented with orange-groves and gardens of every description.

I took several wounded officers on board my boat, amongst whom was an *aide-de-camp* of General Sir Brent Spencer.

About a league below Villa Franca we observed a considerable range of heights on the right bank of the Tagus, rising from the town of Alhandra, and stretching towards the west, on which appeared batteries and embankments. I inquired of the boatman what these were. He answered, "Oh, sir, those are the lines." This was an enigma to us, but my friend the *aide-de-camp* solved the mystery. He said, "That is the position Lord Wellington is now falling back upon, and where he means to meet the enemy." This threw a new light upon us. Everyone wondered, and became animated. Each one seemed to take an intense interest in examining the little we could see of such works as we swept along. It was unanimously agreed that our valiant commander had in this displayed the utmost sagacity. His secret had been well kept. None of us had ever heard of these preparations. We reached Lisbon in the afternoon, and disembarked at the Black Horse Square. I delivered over my sick squad to the inspector of hospitals, and had the good fortune to get a billet on a tolerably good house. I felt gratified to find a quiet place after all the marchings, and countermarchings, and toils we had endured for the last four months.

Nothing surprised me more than the state of Lisbon at this critical period. There appeared no agitation, and no tumults of any kind. A stranger coming from a foreign land could never have imagined that the country was at that moment invaded by a foreign foe, that the whole population of a great part of the land were driven from their homes, all their property abandoned to destruction, and left a prey to a numerous enemy led by the most renowned marshals of France, and that their allies and their own army were then retiring to take up a position and fight for the lives and liberties of the Portuguese close to the walls of the capital.

It is true, fugitives were flocking in from the country in vast numbers, but the good citizens opened their doors, everyone offering the unfortunates the best shelter and comforts they could afford. The only real symptoms of alarm were, I believe, shown in the money market. I understood that handfuls of the government notes were offered for a mere trifle for hard money, silver or gold coin. But confidence seemed perfectly restored when it became publicly known that Lord Wellington had determined to defend the lines.

The general hospital and grand depot for the British army was established at Belem, and Captain John Tucker of the 29th Regiment had been commandant since after the battle of Talavera in 1809. He had a billet on the mansion of the Marquis of Marcalva, a splendid palace. This nobleman was represented by everyone, and, I believe, most truly, as the flower of the Portuguese nobility. He had been sent to France on a mission, and had been kidnapped. He was possessor of the principal vineyards which produced the *calares*, a most excellent wine of rich flavour, and reckoned the claret of Portugal. In the absence of the master, his major-domo sold this wine.

On the 7th October, orders were issued that all the men and officers fit for duty were to proceed to join their respective corps without delay. Feeling rather better from the change of air, and excited by the idea of the stormy scenes which I was aware were about to take place, I determined to join my regiment, although I had still three weeks' leave of absence. I accordingly reported myself fit for duty, and immediately received orders to march next day with a detachment to join the army.

On the 8th October, I went to Belem. While the party was forming on parade to march off, I was seized with a desperate fit of the ague, but this was no time to stand on trifles. I hastened to the nearest *casa de pasta*, gulped down a glass of brandy, and, while still labouring under the shivering fit, I with tottering steps moved off the troops in the midst of a heavy shower, which drenched us to the skin. We arrived in the evening at Lumiar, two leagues' distance. Some warm tea and a comfortable bed did wonders for me. We marched next day two leagues to Cabeça de Montecheque, a small village situated on the heights of the second lines. Here the detachments for the different divisions of the army were separated, each taking the nearest route to the part of the lines which his division occupied. I being the senior officer belonging to the second division, got command of those for that division. My orders were to proceed to Alhandra. I started next morning, the 10th October, and a very arduous march I had of it, as our route lay generally by bye-roads, which were in a very bad state of repair, and it rained incessantly On arriving at Bucellos, I was obliged to halt, being seized with my usual attack of ague. I however rallied after a few hours, and reached Alhandra in the afternoon. Colonel White was pleased to see me because he told me that leave of absence for me had recently appeared in general orders.

Every road to Lisbon was covered with unfortunate fugitives of all ranks. Many elderly ladies in cars drawn by oxen or on mules, and their family walking alongside, were everywhere to be met with. Many had taken refuge in the various village churches, or in the chapels and oratories near the roadsides. I entered one and found it crowded with people all on their knees in silent prayer.

Alhandra is a neat country town situated on the right bank of the Tagus, and a place of considerable commerce. Here, as in the other towns which lay in the track of the armies, the miseries of war were displayed in their full force. All the inhabitants had abandoned the place, leaving their shops full of merchandise, their cellars full of wines, and their houses open to the mercy of friend or foe.

The strictest orders were issued that all property should be respected, and that any soldiers found committing depredations or getting intoxicated should be instantly punished; but with so much temptation, and the numerous individuals of worthless character which are found in every army, it is not surprising that a few should have committed themselves. These were seized, all the troops paraded, drumhead courts-martial were held, the offenders immediately tied up and punished. Sir William Stewart addressed the men in a very energetic speech, pointing out how base an action it was to take advantage of the misfortunes of the inhabitants, to plunder their property, and how cowardly it was for any soldier when the enemy were close at hand to render himself incapable of meeting them by getting intoxicated.

Lord Hill, in command of the second division, had only arrived in the morning with his corps, nor had there been time to ascertain the proper positions in the lines so as to assign to each brigade its proper post in case of an alarm or an attack. Nor was it deemed at the moment so very essential, as it was known that the Light Division were still in front in order to cover the rear of our column entering the entrenchments at this portion of our positions. The usual orders were given, as was always the case when near the enemy, that the troops should stand to their arms before daylight, and we only thought of getting early to rest in order to be early up.

I had got a billet on a house, the inmates of which, in common with their neighbours, had fled. Not a living creature, dog or cat, was remaining in it, only myself and my servant. Wearied with my long march that morning and weakened with fever, I had just got some tea and was taking off my coat to lie down on a mattress, about eight o'clock, when the alarm was given. An orderly announced that the troops were instantly to get under arms. In an amazing short time, each brigade was formed in its respective position. We were then marched out of the town, up to the heights, and formed in contiguous close column of battle in rear of the lines which ran from the plain to the west, while the light troops were posted at the entrance in front of the town, and the wet ditches running from the town across a narrow piece of flat ground to the Tagus. Whilst waiting in this order it became pitch-dark, piercingly cold, with incessant showers of heavy rain. There we were obliged to stand, up to the ankles in mud, wet to the skin, sleepy as death, no chance of getting under cover, no possibility of sitting down, not allowed even to move about to keep up a little warmth during the pelting storm of this wretched night. I must confess my resolution was never more severely tried than on this occasion.

The long-looked-for daylight at length appeared, and the enemy not having dashed on as was expected, patrols were sent out from the town, who on their return reported that the enemy's advanced posts were established about a mile in front. The first brigade, under Colonel Colburn was ordered to occupy Alhandra, where General Hill's headquarters were established. Our brigade under Major-General Houghton was to move to Sobral Piqueño, a small village about two miles to the westward of Alhandra, and nearly half a mile in rear of the lines. While waiting for orders, I and a few others had the good fortune to get into a baker's shop, which had been deserted. We lighted a blazing fire with some of his faggots, and standing round it half-roasted ourselves, turning round first one side and then the other, until our soaked clothing became dry as a board. We were then ordered to get into quarters. It fell to my lot to get a small house, where there was only a kitchen and two small chambers on the ground floor. These were occupied by twenty soldiers, and my apartment was little better than a loft, to which I mounted by a rude kind of ship ladder. The poor owners had abandoned their home, leaving all their little winter stores hoarded up here. There were strings of onions and garlic, pots of black olives in salt and water, heaps of chestnuts, bunches of grapes hung across strings, sacks of Indian corn, jars of olive oil, black puddings, and morsels of salted pork, loaves of bread of Indian cornflour, which made a damp, yellowish sort of bread.

An officer of the navy, Lieutenant Eliot, employed in the gunboats which were stationed in the Tagus to flank the right of the lines, at Alhandra, having an engagement to dine with some officers in the lines, a few miles from the town of Alhandra, was proceeding on foot. He observed in a field a fine fig-tree full of tempting fruit at no great distance, in front of one of our sentries. Nothing would satisfy him but he must needs gather some of the fruit. The sentry cautioned him not to make the attempt, at the same time pointing out to him the sentry of the enemy, who was posted on the other side of the field near the tree. The prudent advice was disregarded;

on he went, and when snugly perched on the tree, stuffing himself and his pockets with the figs, the French sentry approached, called him down, made him prisoner, and quietly walked him into the French lines. He was immediately sent out to Massena's headquarters, who, wishing to have a near view of our gun-boats, under pretence of obliging our gallant friend by getting his baggage for him, sent him, accompanied by a staff-officer, to the bank of the Tagus near Villa Franca, on board one of the gun-boats. On learning the lieutenant's fate, his baggage was sent on shore to him. Massena treated him with great politeness, and made him dine with him every day, at his own table, and after detaining him a week or two he sent him back.

There was a height about six or seven hundred yards' distance beyond our lines of defence, where our sentries were posted from daybreak till dark, when they were withdrawn, and the enemy then pushed on their videttes and occupied it until next morning. I used often to walk out to this height to look down on the enemy's camp, which was at a short distance on the other side, having gardens and vineyards intervening. One day I observed a French soldier in full uniform, coming through a vineyard towards us, leading an ass. As he kept dodging and creeping along, I kept my eye upon him, thinking that he was looking out to get a shot at four or five young officers, who, having just joined the army, were standing all together. I recommended them to separate a little, so as to divert his attention, and not present so large an object for him to aim at. While watching him, I observed that he suddenly left his ass, and threw down his arms. He then made a dash right up to us. I instantly knew that he was a deserter. When at a short distance he halted, took off his shako, and waved his hand. One of our visiting patrols happening to pass at the time, I desired the sergeant to send a man down to him, who accordingly descended, and brought him up, arm in arm, in a most brotherly manner. He proved to be a German. He told me that he had deserted with the intention of entering our service, as he had a brother in the Hussars of the German Legion, which, he understood, were then lying at no great distance, which proved to be the case. He took an anxious look down the hill, and exclaimed, *"Ach! mein Esel! mein Esel!"* I asked him if he would like to have his ass, because we would manage to get it for him. He was overjoyed at the proposal. I mentioned to the patrol his wishes. They all volunteered to go down to the vineyard for it. This I would not allow, but ordered one man to try if he could bring it off, which he did in a very short time, absolutely bringing it off from the precincts of the French camp in triumph. Our new friend in an ecstasy of joy kissed and caressed his brute companion. Perhaps fearing that he would not be allowed to keep his ass, he seemed very anxious to dispose of him immediately, and began praising him and describing his excellent qualities. I pointed to a large lump on one of his legs. *"Ach! dass ist, nichts, dass ist nichts,"* he said, "He is a fine animal." I however told him that he and his animal must proceed without delay to the headquarters of the division, as no person was allowed to purchase anything from a deserter until after he had been reported, but that afterwards he would no doubt be permitted to sell his ass. He seemed quite satisfied with this assurance, and mounting his dapple friend, rode off under escort of the patrol.

Massena first became aware of the lines of Torres Vedras on the 10th October. When he found how strongly we were posted, he retreated after it was dark, and did not make an onward movement for some days. Several skirmishes and affairs of outposts took place, but the French marshal seemed to think us too strongly posted to be attacked with any prospect of success. On the 22nd October, a camp was formed at St. Jago dos Velhos, and we used to go to the lines every morning. Massena remained for more than a month in front of our position. His army suffered very much from sickness and want of provisions, as the country people had either destroyed or carried off in their flight all the necessaries of life. On the 14th November, the French army broke up, and entered into cantonments between Santarem and Thomar. Our army also went into cantonments at Alcoentre, Rio Mayor, Azembuja, Alenquer, and Villa Franca, and our headquarters were established at Cartaxo. The second division under General Hill crossed the Tagus on the 18th November, and occupied the villages of Barcos, Chamusca, and Caregiro. During the remainder of the year both armies remained quiet in their cantonments, and few occurrences of any moment took place. We were pretty well supplied with provisions, having the command of the sea, but the French were reduced to great straits, which gave rise to a saying common in their camp: *"Pour être soldat Français il faut avoir le ventre d'un pou et le coeur d'un lion"*—a French soldier should have the belly of a louse and the heart of a lion. Another of their sayings was: *"La guerre en Espagne est la fortune des generaux, la ruin des officiers, et le tombeau des soldats"*—the war in Spain is the fortune of the generals, the ruin of the officers, and the grave of the soldiers.

One evening, the 13th May, 1811, during the first siege of Badajos, it being our turn for duty in the trenches, we marched about sunset from our encampment towards the town, where we could observe numbers of people and many ladies on the tops of the houses looking at us. The gallant Sir John Hamilton happened to be the general of the day, and Don Carlos d'Espagna, commanding the Spanish troops, was also to give a contingent that night for the works. While we were halted under cover of some heights waiting for their conjunction, it came on to rain, and blew very hard. On the arrival of the *don*, who understood English very well, and after the necessary dispositions had been arranged, our distinguished general proceeded to give his orders to the commanding officers assembled round him, in his wonted cool, decided, and offhand way. They were nearly as follows: "We are going to open the trenches tonight within three hundred yards of the walls of Badajos; the ground is perfectly plain, there will be no cover; the utmost silence must be preserved, and no firing must on any account be permitted. The wind and rain are in the enemy's favour—they will come out—they will mix with you—they will fire upon you, but let them fire and be d——d."

The foresight of our experienced general proved correct; all his anticipations were realised, and his orders were strictly obeyed. To have returned the enemy's fire would have discovered us, and have pointed out to them where to make a sortie. After giving these orders, the general, turning round to Don Carlos, and addressing him in his usual good-humoured manner, said: "Now, Don Carlos, whether would you rather be flirting with the pretty *signoritas* inside, or be opening the trenches outside, in this dark and stormy night?"

Don Carlos, whose gallantry was well known, whether in devotion to the sex or to his country, modestly replied that he certainly was very desirous to enjoy the gay society of the ladies, but, as the only chance of being able to lay siege to the fair ones within was to carry on the siege vigorously from without, he would at present prefer the latter, and he felt confident that, by our united efforts, we should not only win the town, but also the hearts of his fair countrywomen, who were sincere admirers of those who, by noble achievements, rendered themselves worthy of their esteem.

The two brave commanders shook hands. We pushed on close under the castle, and, under protection of some companies, who crept on as covering parties, our men began to dig—yes! many, perhaps, their own graves!

We marched in silence to within five hundred yards of the walls of Badajos; covering parties were sent on in front. The men piled arms, took off their knapsacks, &c., and were extended at arm's length from one another. One man got a spade, another a pickaxe, and we stole on to within three hundred yards of the walls. The engineers directed the men to dig a trench, and to throw up the earth towards the town. In an hour or two the men got the trench so far forward as to afford some cover. The enemy began to discover our whereabouts and what we were doing. They commenced throwing fire-balls and blue lights. Our men were ordered to throw themselves flat on the ground, so that no shadow of them could be seen. The engineers were urging the men to work hard, as they expected a terrible fire to be shortly opened upon us, but to our surprise we were ordered to leave off and to return in great silence. We learned that Marshal Soult was rapidly advancing to attack our army, and we received orders to join our army under Marshal Beresford at Albuera.

On the afternoon of the 15th May, 1811, after a long march, the English army took up their ground on the heights in rear of Albuera; but, as the Spanish army had not arrived, General Houghton's brigade, consisting of the 29th, 57th, and 1st battalion of the 48th Regiment, was moved to the right and formed *en potence*. The Spaniards having come up during the night, our brigade, after standing some hours under arms, was ordered, about six or seven o'clock on the morning of the 16th, to resume its place in the line. We had scarcely time to get a little tea and a morsel of biscuit, when the alarm was given—"Stand to your arms! The French are advancing."

We accordingly instantly got under arms, leaving tents and baggage to be disposed of as the quartermaster and batmen best could. We moved forward in line to crown the heights in front, which were intended for our position, and which may be shortly described as follows. The rivulet of Albuera ran nearly parallel to the front of the heights, at about six hundred yards' distance, which sloped down to it, these being perfectly open for all arms; but beyond our right they swelled into steeper and more detached ones. The village of Albuera was nearly opposite the centre of our line, and on the same side of the water; at which point was the only bridge. The banks of the rivulet were at some places steep and abrupt. On the opposite, or French side, they were rather low, and the ground flat and open for some little distance; then gradually rose to a gentle height, covered with wood, particularly at some distance from the bridge up the river, where the French army lay concealed from our view, they having only some detached parties of cavalry in the open ground.

In occupying the position the army was formed as follows: the Portuguese, in blue, on the left; the English, in red in the centre—viz., General Houghton's brigade, the 20th, 57th, and 1st battalion of the 48th Regiment; General Lumley's, 28th, 39th and 34th Regiments; Colonel Colbourn's, the 3rd, the 2nd battalion of the 48th, the 66th, and 31st Regiments; and the Spaniards, in yellow or other bright colours, formed the right. The whole were drawn up as for a grand parade, in full view of the enemy, so that Soult could see almost every man, and he was also enabled to choose his point of attack; which would not have been the case if we had been kept under cover a few yards farther back, behind the crest of the heights, or had been made to lie down, as we used to do under the Duke of Wellington. That part of the 4th Division under Sir Lowry Cole, which had just arrived from Badajos, were posted in second line in our rear.

Before we had time to halt in our position, we observed two large columns of the enemy, supported by cavalry and artillery, moving towards the bridge and village of Albuera, which was occupied by the light corps of the German Legion under Colonel Hacket. The first attack here commenced, under cover of a heavy cannonade, upon the village and our line in its rear. The Germans made a gallant defence, and maintained their post; but as the enemy apparently seemed to make a push at this point, Colbourn's brigade was ordered to move down in support of the troops in the village.

Soult must have been much delighted on observing this movement: it, no doubt, was precisely what he most wished; because the columns which appeared to threaten the village and our line was only a ruse to distract our attention and neutralise the English force which he most dreaded. Our skilful adversary was, in the meantime, throwing his masses directly across our right flank, or Spanish army, which extended to a great distance from us; and it was with no small surprise that we most unexpectedly heard a sharp fire commence in that quarter. The error our chief had been led into now became evident. We were suddenly thrown into open column, and moved rapidly along the heights to our right flank for nearly a mile under a tremendous cannonade, for the French had already established themselves on some commanding heights, which raked us as we advanced, Captain Humphrey and several men being killed. They were, at the same time, attacking the Spaniards with great vigour, having put them into some confusion when in the act of throwing back their right to meet this flank attack. Colbourn's brigade also, which had moved to cover the village, as stated above, had been recalled and brought up in a hasty manner in column, obliquing to their right towards the heights now occupied by the enemy, and formed line at a right angle perpendicular to the first position. It has been understood that Colonel Colbourn wished to move to the attack with the two flank regiments in quarter distance columns, and the two centre ones in one line; but Sir William Stewart, anxious to show a large front, was deploying the whole. The 3rd, 48th, and 66th Regiments were in line, and the 31st Regiment still in column; when a body of French lancers, taking advantage of the thick weather and heavy showers of rain, got round the right of this brigade, made a dash from the rear through those regiments which were in line, broke them, and swept off the greater part as prisoners into the French lines. The 31st Regiment stood firm, and fortunately escaped the disaster; and the Spaniards continued with some difficulty to hold their ground. Just as this misfortune had occurred our brigade came up, the 29th leading. We closed up into quarter distance columns under cover of the heights and deployed;

but before the 57th and 48th Regiments had completed the formation, a body of Spaniards in advance of our left flank gave way, and in making off ran in our front, and then came rushing back upon us. We called out to them, urging them to rally and maintain their ground, and that we would shortly relieve them.

On these assurances, with the exertions of some of the officers and of our adjutant, who rode amongst them, they did rally, and moved up the hill again, but very shortly afterwards down they came again in the utmost confusion—mixed pell-mell with a body of the enemy's Lancers, who were thrusting and cutting without mercy. Many of the Spaniards threw themselves on the ground, others attempted to get through our line, but this could not be permitted, because we being in line on the slope of a bare green hill, and such a rush of friends and foes coming down upon us, any opening made to let the former pass would have admitted the enemy also. We had no alternative left but to stand firm, and in self-defence to fire on both. This shortly decided the business; the lancers bought up and made the best of their way back to their own lines, and the Spaniards were permitted to pass to the rear.

The formation of our brigade being now completed, and Lumley's brigade having taken post on the left, and all being now ready for the attack, Sir William Stewart rode up to our brigade, and after a few energetic words, said, "Now is the time—let us give three cheers!" This was instantly done with heart and soul, every cap waving in the air. We immediately advanced up the hill under a sharp fire from the enemy's light troops, which we did not condescend to return, and they retreated as we moved on. On arriving at the crest of the height we discovered the enemy a little in rear of it, apparently formed in masses, or columns of grand divisions, with light troops and artillery in the intervals between them. From the waving and rising of the ground on which some of these stood, the three or four front ranks in some cases could fire over the heads of one another, and some guns were posted on a bank and fired over one of these columns. Notwithstanding this formidable array, our line went close up to the enemy, without even a piece of artillery to support us; at least near us there were none. We understood that the nine-pounder brigade had been withdrawn in consequence of the disaster above related. On the other hand, Soult has since stated that he had forty pieces of cannon vomiting death at this point. The 29th Regiment being on the right of this line, its flank was *en l'air* and completely exposed without any strong point to rest upon, while the fusilier and Portuguese brigades of the fourth division, which had also been brought up to the new front, were a considerable way to our right on the plain below.

This was the moment at which the murderous and desperate battle really began. A most overwhelming fire of artillery and small arms was opened upon us, which was vigorously returned. There we unflinchingly stood, and there we fell: our ranks were at some places swept away by sections. This dreadful contest had continued for some time, when an officer of artillery—I believe a German—came up and said he had brought two or three guns, but that he could find no one to give him orders, our superior officers being all wounded or killed. It was suggested that he could not do wrong in opening directly on the enemy, which was accordingly done. Our line at length became so reduced that it resembled a chain of skirmishers in extended order; while, from the necessity of closing in towards the colours, and our numbers fast diminishing, our right flank became still further exposed. The enemy, however, did not avail himself of the advantage which this circumstance might have afforded him.

We continued to maintain this unprecedented conflict with unabated energy. The enemy, notwithstanding his superiority of numbers, had not obtained one inch of ground, but, on the contrary, we were gaining on him, when the gallant Fusilier brigade was moved up from the plain, bringing their right shoulders forward. They thus took the enemy obliquely in flank, who, although already much shattered, still continued to make a brave resistance; but nothing could withstand the invincible and undaunted bravery of the British soldiers. The enemy's masses, after a desperate struggle for victory, gave way at all points, and were driven in disorder beyond the rivulet, leaving us triumphant masters of the field.

To the credit of the troops engaged it ought to be recollected that, in all other battles fought either before or afterwards in the Peninsula, our gallant army, under a skilful commander, had only either to march up to the enemy or to await his attack, and that after a conflict of more or less duration the victory was won; but in this terrible contest, error, confusion, and misfortune attended our first disposition. Victory had to be retrieved from a brave and experienced foe, under many untoward and disheartening circumstances, and it seems universally agreed that the annals of war scarcely afford an instance of so bloody a battle having ever been fought in proportion to the numbers engaged.

Mustering the living and recording the dead became afterwards our melancholy duty. On reckoning our numbers, the 29th Regiment had only ninety-six men, two captains, and a few subalterns remaining out of the whole regiment; the 57th Regiment had but a few more, and were commanded out of action by the adjutant; the first battalion of the 48th Regiment suffered in like manner: not a man of the brigade was prisoner; not a colour was lost, although an eloquent historian most unwarrantably stated that the 57th had lost theirs. The 57th lose their colours!—never! Major-General Houghton, commanding the brigade, and Lieutenant-Colonel Duckworth of the 48th Regiment were killed; Lieutenant-Colonel White of the 29th Regiment mortally wounded; Colonel Inglis of the 57th and Major Way of the 29th Regiments were very severely wounded. In fact, every field-officer of the whole brigade was either killed or wounded, so that at the close of the action the brigade remained in command of a captain of the 48th Regiment, and, singular enough, that captain was a Frenchman, named Cemetiere (cemetery).

The field afterwards presented a sad spectacle, our men lying generally in rows and the French in large heaps, from their having fought principally in masses, they not having dared to deploy, as they afterwards told us, from a dread of our cavalry, as they supposed that we would not have ventured to act in such an open country without a great superiority in that description of force.

The French were driven in such confusion from the field that their brigades and regiments lost all order and were completely mixed, so that numbers of our men and several of the officers who had been taken prisoners made their escape out of the enemy's bivouac during the night, and many deserters came over; but notwithstanding their great disorder, which must have been known to our chief, we remained all the next day looking at one another, while the enemy was actively employed in reorganising his shattered forces. It struck many people that if only a demonstration of advancing had been made even on the following morning, their total rout would have been complete, because General Hamilton's division of Portuguese were still almost entire, nor had Hacket's fine corps, or even Lumley's brigade, or our cavalry been rendered unserviceable, and the remaining part of the 4th division, which had been detained at Badajos, were momentarily expected to arrive, exclusive of the Spanish army. On the third day, even after the enemy had recovered his order, as soon as he observed that we were about to advance, he immediately commenced his retreat without offering the smallest resistance.

Some affecting incidents which occurred on this memorable occasion may not prove uninteresting.

When in our first position Major-General Houghton was on horseback in front of the line, in a green frock-coat, which he had put on in the hurry of turning out. Some time afterwards his servant rode up to him with his red uniform coat, and without dismounting he immediately stripped off the green and put on the red one. It may be said that this public display of our national colour and of British coolness actually was done under a salute of French artillery, as they were cannonading us at the time.

There had been a general court-martial held some time previous to the action. The prisoner, Lieutenant Ansaldo, was found guilty and sentenced to be suspended for six months. He, however, instead of quitting his corps during that period, remained with the army, and gallantly went into action by the side of his prosecutor. They both fell; and what is still more extraordinary, the president, General Houghton, the Judge-Advocate, Captain Binning, 66th Regiment, and many of the members and witnesses were also killed and were almost all of them entombed near the same spot.

A few days after the battle five regiments who suffered most were embodied into one, forming a provisional battalion—*viz.*, the 3rd Regiment, one company; the 66th, one company; the 29th, two companies; the 57th, three; and the 31st three companies, placed under the command of Lieutenant-Colonel L'Estrange of the 31st Regiment.

The Duke of Wellington, on hearing of Soult's advance, used the utmost possible exertions to come up, and to have commanded in person. He arrived the second day after the action, unfortunately too late. Some days afterwards, I have been told, his grace, while inspecting the hospitals at Elvas, said to some of our men— "Oh! old 29th, I am sorry to see so many of you here!" They instantly replied— "Oh! my Lord, if you had only been with us, there would not have been so many of us here!"—so implicit was the confidence of even the humblest individuals in this great man.

On referring to the *United Service Journal* of June, 1832, I find a communication from the gallant Sir William Inglis on the subject of Albuera, in which he has perfectly established the cool and steady conduct of our brave old comrades, the 57th Regiment; but as it might be inferred from the complaint then made by a Spanish officer to him, that the Spaniards had been wantonly fired upon, I believe that the above account of the operations of General Houghton's brigade, which suffered such immense loss on that day, will sufficiently prove that the 29th Regiment did not fire on the Spaniards without necessity, and that under the circumstances in which they were then placed they were perfectly justified in so doing. Sir William Inglis has since informed me that he was not aware of the facts at the time above mentioned.

The 29th, 85th, and 97th having suffered very severely in the recent campaign, were ordered to England to recruit in October, 1811. In the general orders issued by the Duke of Wellington, dated adjutant-general's office, 3rd October, 1811, is the following:

> The commander of the forces has received orders from the commander-in-chief to send to England the 29th, 85th, and 97th Regiments. These regiments have all been distinguished, particularly the 29th Regiment, who have been with the army so long.
>
> The 29th Regiment landed with the army three years ago, and they have been distinguished in every action that has been fought in that period.
>
> The commander of the forces is happy to add that the conduct of these troops has been equally regular in cantonment and camp, as it has been gallant in the field.
>
> Under these circumstances, the commander of the forces

parts with these regiments with regret, but the events of the war and the different actions in which they have been engaged, having greatly reduced their numbers, the only chance of recruiting them is to send them to England.

C. Stewart

Major-General, Adjutant-General

Division orders, by Lieutenant-General Sir Rowland Hill, commanding the second division, dated—

Portalegre

7th October, 1811

Considering the length of time which the 29th Regiment has been under his orders, and the distinguished manner in which it has uniformly conducted itself, as testified in the general orders of the commander of the forces of the 3rd October, Lieutenant-General Hill cannot allow it to quit the second division of infantry without expressing to it his warmest approbation and thanks for their good conduct, and his regret at being deprived of their services.

J. C. Rook

Lt. Colonel, A.-Adjutant-General

Battalion order by Lieutenant-Colonel L'Estrange, commanding provisional battalion, dated—

Castello Branco

4th October, 1811

The 29th regiment being ordered for England, Lieutenant-Colonel L'Estrange cannot take leave of them without testifying his entire satisfaction in the manner which they have conducted themselves whilst under his command.

If his approbation can be considered as a great satisfaction by a corps which has distinguished itself on every occasion, he is happy in taking this opportunity of expressing it, as well as his regret at its removal from the provisional battalion.

On the 2nd November, 1811, the 29th Regiment embarked on board the *Agincourt,* 64, commanded by Captain Kent, R. N. We had also on board five companies of the 85th Regiment, and about a hundred Germans, who had deserted from the French army, and were now returning to their own country at the expense of the English government. These men were formed into a company and placed under my command, as being senior subaltern on board, and this saved me from the unpleasant duty of keeping watch. The vessel was old, and the weather rather boisterous, but our captain told us to be under no apprehension, as he had been sixty years at sea, and never had been in a storm. He had a pet, an old gander, which walked the quarter-deck with him, and had been his companion in several vessels, and nearly as long at sea as himself.

We left the Tagus on the 6th November, reached Portsmouth on the 1st December, and disembarked next day. We immediately marched to Havant, having received orders to proceed to Steyning barracks in Sussex. Major Tod Nestor, who had been badly wounded, and myself, got leave to travel at our leisure. We agreed to post it. While changing horses at Havant I went in to warm myself. A person sitting in the room said, "Pray, sir, excuse me, but I am anxious to know if there is a soldier of the name of Saunders still in your regiment. A deed for £500 was sent to him for his signature, and not hearing from him we supposed that he was killed and the bond lost." I replied that the man was not only alive, but was actually coming into the place, as we passed him on the road, he being in the rear-guard. The person started up as if he had been shot, exclaiming, "He is my brother!" and ran off in the direction to meet the troops entering.

During the march some fine pigs happened to pass, and a soldier remarked to his comrade, "My eyes, Jack, them's fine pigs!" This remark being overheard by a patriotic bystander, he exclaimed, "Pigs!—would you like pigs?" and there and then bought them for the men, and the regiment continued its march, driving, not prisoners, but—pigs before (or after) it.

In consequence of their gallant conduct in the Peninsula, the 29th Regiment soon afterwards had the honour of being ordered to Windsor to do duty over His Majesty George the Third. Their entry was quite a triumphal march. All the people came out to receive them, barrels of ale were presented to the soldiers, and the officers were feted by all ranks, and the regimental horse, Black Jack, was a great object of curiosity.

I got leave of absence, and returned to my home after an absence of nearly five years, the whole of which had been spent in active service by sea and land. I left London for Scotland by the mail on the 25th December. On the following day, somewhere in Yorkshire, a primitive, good-looking Quakeress came into the coach. In the course of conversation she happened to find out that I was a military man, and very earnestly asked me, "Friend, hast thou resigned thy profession?" I replied, "Certainly not." She assured me that the time was about to arrive when the swords of men would be turned into ploughshares, in fact, that all the world was to become of her religion, and live as friends and brothers. I agreed with her that war was a terrible scourge, but on my adding that as the world now existed wars were necessary evils, and at all events a defensive war against a foreign invader, like the Spanish war, was justifiable on every principle of common reason, she denied even this. But on my saying to her, "Suppose you were sitting at your own fireside, and that some vagrants were to come in and snatch up your plate from your sideboard, would you not make some resistance?" "Friend," said she, "I would rebuke them." I answered, "Such loose characters would laugh at you, and take your all if you did not take some measures to prevent them." This puzzled her; she was at a loss for an answer, so that I nearly convinced her that the Quaker principle of non-resistance, however amiable for individuals, could not be adopted by ordinary mankind such as compose he majority in the world.

On the 1st January, 1812, I arrived in Edinburgh during a horrid riot in which several people were killed.

On my appearance in Edinburgh in a braided *peliss* frock-coat, fancy vest with silver Spanish buttons, and a forage cap, which had been our usual morning-dress with the army, I astonished the natives of modern Athens. So great was the curiosity to see the first specimen of a Peninsula costume, that my friends, the Countess of Buchan and Lady Helen Hall, insisted on my appearing at their parties in what appeared to all an extraordinary dress, nay, in attending a public assembly in my proper uniform of the 29th Regiment, so much had the people taken it into their heads that I was a foreign count, I was absolutely mobbed by all the ladies in the ballroom. An old and worthy general addressed me after introducing himself, and hoped I was pleased with the appearance of his countrywomen. He added that I was lucky in being a prisoner in England, for that when he in his youth had been taken by the Spaniards, he had been kept a close prisoner. I was ill-natured enough to enter into his humour, and maintained the deception for some time, but he was really mortified when he afterwards found out that I was a Scotchman.

I got charge of a recruiting party at Aberdeen, and succeeded in getting numbers of excellent men; indeed, in credit to the Scotch, it is worthy of being noted that although the 29th was an English regiment, the majority of its best non-commissioned officers were Scotch, and of five sergeants who got commissions for good conduct in the field, two were from Aberdeen.

Part 4

1812–1813

Major-General David Leslie, brother of the Earl of Leven and Melville, then commanded at Aberdeen; and many county families living in the town, we had a gay winter, many balls, dinners and supper parties being given.

The regiment continued at Windsor, and was fast filling up with recruits and volunteers from the militia, and received the greatest marks of honour from the queen and all the members of the royal family. So high was the character of the regiment, that from one militia regiment alone sufficient men came to have laid the foundation of a second battalion, but owing to the drummers of the 29th being all black, some mischievous person posted a placard asking,

"Who would be flogged by a black———?" The men retracted and I lost for the moment my chance of a company.

Having completed its numbers, the corps, in February, February, 1813, received orders to hold themselves in readines to rejoin their old comrades in the Peninsula: but government, considering that the men were nearly all recruits, or very young hands, many still in their militia uniform, and not thinking it just to send a corps who had earned a gallant reputation into the field until more completely organised, changed our destination, and ordered us to do duty at Cadiz, much to the mortification of all ranks, particularly the officers.

I left Aberdeen on the 7th February, 1813. At Montrose a person opened the coach door, it being dark, saying, "Weel, are ye a' fu?" meaning to inquire if the coach was full. It might have been taken to mean, "Are you all drunk?" In he came, and immediately announced that although he had been studying divinity, the glorious despatches frae the Peninsula describing battles, sieges, storms, wounds, death and glory, had inspired him with a thirst for military fame, and he was going to volunteer his services for his country's cause. I asked him some home questions, and let him into some of the mysteries of a military life in the field, which he had never even dreamed of or taken into consideration before. This seemed to stagger his warlike propensities. Poor fellow! When we were seizing a mouthful of supper, he said he could not partake, but if we would allow him he would take a potato. He was in the act of putting it to his mouth, when a wag called out, "There is the waiter, if he sees you he will charge you for the whole supper."

On the 10th February I set out for London, and arrived there on the 13th. I found that the regiment had already embarked at Portsmouth. I consequently, although I had been awake the whole of the two previous nights, set out in the evening to join it. It proved a drenching night of rain, and, as is usual on occasions of troops embarking, so many were going that I could not get an inside place in the coach.

Cold and stiff, I reached Portsmouth on the 14th February, 1813. The weather was most tempestuous and the wind dead against us, so that many of us remained at the George Hotel on shore. On the 10th March we sailed with a large convoy of vessels of every sort. The vessel in charge was a beautiful ship of immense length, with flush deck. She was destined for the American station. When most of the fleet were carrying a press of sail she had no canvas at all, except her maintop sails. The Americans in England had got a plan of her, which they sent to their country before her arrival, and an attempt was then made to blow her up by a torpedo.

The 17th March being St. Patrick's Day, and several of the officers being Irish, daybreak was ushered in by *St. Patrick's Day in the Morning*, and we had a jollification.

On the 21st March, 1813, we arrived at Cadiz. The regiment was disembarked and marched to the Isle of Leon, and quartered in the Galfineras Barracks, erected by us during the siege, on some heights the town.

Cadiz is a remarkably pretty, neat town. The great Spanish

dockyards, naval academy, and all the main departments are here established. It is an island in a sort of island, being separated from the mainland by an extensive swampy marsh, through which runs a narrow branch of the sea called the Rio of San Pietro. The French held the opposite side of the marsh during the siege, and had batteries all along it. A town which has since been named San Fernando is joined to Cadiz by a narrow, low strip of sand about eight miles long, where there is a capital road raised about six feet above high-water mark.

There was at Cadiz a battalion composed of Germans, who had been forced into the French service as conscripts, and had come over to us. They were formed into a provisional battalion, and officered from different regiments in the garrison, each getting a temporary step of rank. It had served during the whole of the siege, having been quartered at the Aquada. The 29th Regiment was ordered to furnish five officers for this battalion. Our commanding officer, Sir G. Way, on making this known to us, said he did not wish to order any officer to leave his own corps, and, therefore, he begged that those who had an inclination to go would give in their names. I saw that there was a probable opportunity of making a lucky hit. I immediately gave in my name. At the same time I received a kind promise from the colonel, that he would strongly recommend me for a company. Four others also gave in their names.

I then left my old corps, the 29th Regiment. On joining the provisional battalion at Cadiz, I instantly got command of a company of about 120 strong. The men were supposed to be all Germans, but many entered as such were French, Italian, or Poles. They were a remarkably well-conducted set of men, no drunkards or idlers. The generality of them were always employed, when off duty, in making fancy-work of all descriptions, carving in bone, plaiting hair-chains, &c., repairing watches, making busts. They had great power in acquiring languages. My servant, although a German, talked French, Spanish, and Italian, and English at last, remarkably well. He had been servant to a French general who was killed at Barossa. He and many others had been in several engagements, fighting against us, when the 29th Regiment had been engaged. Sir George Cook commanded at Cadiz, and from him and his excellent staff I experienced many kind attentions.

Cadiz was at this period one of the gayest places in Europe. Soult had been obliged to abandon the siege. It was the seat of government. The Regent, the Cardinal of Bourbon, the Cortes, all the foreign ambassadors, and many noble English families, the whole Continent being shut against English travellers, were here. All the notables of Spain, with their families, had taken refuge here, and all the votaries of fashion resorted to this city, so that the place was very animated. Our ambassador, Sir H. Wellesley, from the nature of our alliance with the Spaniards, had great sway, and was the leading authority. He used to give frequent dinners, and most splendid balls and suppers, but withal, he was plain in his manners and dress. To the astonishment of the Spanish ladies, he wore nankeen trousers and cotton stockings. I used frequently to attend the sittings of the Cortes. The house of assembly was elegantly fitted up with three rows of mahogany seats and desks, in an oval form, and the debates, in the sonorous Spanish language, had a fine effect from the warmth and energy of the speakers.

I found Cadiz particularly agreeable, as some friends of our family had been long settled here, and at Xeres, a few leagues off. Don Arturo Gordon was a fine hale old gentleman, although nearly ninety years of age, and his wife was equally active. They were most hospitable. I found their house a home indeed. Many other gentlemen kept almost open house. I have dined at the table of a Scotch friend, who was in partnership with an Italian gentleman, where the most of the plate was of solid gold, and at many places I was expected to dine once or twice a week.

We had here free access to Spanish society. There were five or six houses open every night, where grand *tertulias* were held. A friend had only to present you to the lady, who immediately cordially said, *"Esta casa sta a la disposition de usted"* and you had ever afterwards a free *entree*. At these soirees there is a long saloon where dancing is kept up with great spirit, and another, where a long gambling table is crowded with fashionable males and females, all eagerly engaged in the demoralising amusement; nay, you might have seen here young misses as busy as the others, and their mammas engaged in the ballroom; but the society was often rather frugal, which prevented a person playing high, and many persons were admitted who had no recommendation or qualification.

The Alameida generally consists of two or three long walks parallel to each other, all shaded with fine trees, and having marble seats on each side, where the elderly people sit smoking cigars, and exchanging the news of the day, while the young and gay promenade, and bands of music play for the amusement of the people. The Alameida at Cadiz, being on a fortified point which runs into the sea, and commands a beautiful view of the bay, is particularly fine. One enjoys the luxury of a cooling sea breeze. On the *Ave Maria* tolling all stand up; a solemn silence prevails; a few minutes finish the prayer, and all ranks salute one another with, "Goodnight." The hum of busy human voices is again heard, and the promenade is resumed. As evening closes the gentlemen invite the parties of ladies to join them in a glass of some cooling drink, in the shops which are fitted up with tables, and look like coffee rooms, where ices, iced water, iced punch, and confections of all kinds were to be had. In compliment, I suppose, to the English, the punch was getting rather too fashionable. After this they usually adjourn to the theatre, which is a very neat one, and at this time all the royal company from Madrid were there. Some of the light comedies showed a good deal of wit and ready humour. For this they have always a jester, called the Gracioso, or witty fellow, and from the theatre all crowd to conclude the evening at the *tertulias* of their particular friends.

The bull fights at Cadiz are the most magnificent in Spain. The Plaça de Toros, or amphitheatre, presents a splendid appearance when filled with all the beauty that the country can boast of, in full dress. Its proportions are fine, and it is like in form to the Coliseum in Rome. It has two ornamental strong gateways on each side, the arena is enclosed with a wall about six feet high. Next to this are several rows of benches for those that are particular amateurs of the sport. Then come the boxes, elegantly fitted up for the ladies, and covered in. The back seats and roof are occupied by the common people. The prices are determined not only by the benches, or boxes, but also by *sol* or *sombra*, sun or shade. If the bullfight takes place in the afternoon, then the north-west to north-east seats are the dearest, and if it is in the morning, it is the contrary.

The proceedings are carried on with great solemnity and regularity. Previous to the commencement, the arena, or interior circle, is filled with the rabble, all engaged in betting. Handbills indicating the breed of bulls, their respective colours, and the names of the *picadors*, the *chulos*, and the *matadors*, whose duty it is to kill the animal, are announced, The performers are all dressed in neat shoes, silk stockings, fancy-coloured silk small clothes and jackets, bedizened with pieces of coin, shoulder knots, and red sashes; their hair is clubbed in net bags, and they have caps of black velvet. A detachment of troops with a band of music files in, and gets close to the inner wall. At a signal they advance at short stump step, the music playing, and drive everybody before them, so as to clear the arena. It is very amusing to see the imps and urchins giving them the slip and scampering off.

When the arena is cleared, all the performers enter in grand procession, headed by a *novello*, or young bull. They proceed to the government box, where they respectfully salute, and the young bull is taught to bend on his fore knees. After they have retired, the young bull is put at one of the gateways, which is then opened, and the wild animals follow him to the other gate, when each is put into a separate stall, over which there is an opening. Some of the greater beauties are then appointed to place the bows of different coloured ribbon on the shoulders of the several animals to distinguish them. This is done by fastening the bows to a small barbed needle, which is stuck by them on the animal's shoulder.

On a signal the *picadors* enter. These men are mounted, and have long strong lances. Their legs and bodies are protected by stuffed leggings and jackets of buff yellowish leather. Their saddles have a high peak before, and a back which rises six or eight inches behind. They post themselves at different distances near the centre of the arena, while several *chulos*, with coloured silk flags in their hands, stand ready to act as occasion may require to distract the bull's attention. This is a moment of intense interest. Everyone is wound up to the highest state of expectation. A blast of the trumpet, and the door opens. Out rushes the wild animal, roaring furiously and wildly. On he clashes, perhaps towards a *chulo*. He looks confounded for an instant, shakes his head, gets a glance of a *picador*, tosses his hinder heels and tail in the air, and away he dashes. The skilful *picador,* whose keen eye is on the watch, coolly waits for him. Just as the bull stoops to make a rush at him, he manages to get his lance plunged into his neck, which irritates the bull, and will even make him rear on his hind legs. He escapes from this. A *chulo* runs in his way, shakes his flag, or *banderilla*, a barbed dart ornamented with coloured paper flags. The enraged animal makes at him. You think he is annihilated, but the nimble *chulo* leaps right in the air, dropping his *banderilla* on the ground. The astonished animal runs on, and missing his mark, vents his rage on the *banderilla*. He may then try another *picador*. With more caution he stands staring for an opportunity of attack. The *picador* keeps his eye on the bull's eye. The *picador* nods, and the bull does the same. After some time spent in daring one another, on the bull rushes, and is received as before, but if the *picador* misses his aim, down they come, man and horse, while the bull vents his rage on the poor animal, goring him in a horrid manner. The *chulo* during this scene entices the bull to desist. He will then, perhaps, get in rear of the third *picador,* who has not been active enough to get out of his way, or to turn round. He then gores the horse. On the unfortunate animal rushes. I have seen the bull thus raise the horse's hind legs from the ground and push him on before him. Sometimes you might see the *picador* riding about, and the horse's entrails trailing on the ground. At trumpet sound the horses are withdrawn, and the *chulos* run to face the bull. When he rushes at them, they adroitly fix the darts into each side of his neck, and by leaping either on one side or over his head, escape. The *banderilla* have sometimes squibs and crackers attached to them. The moment the darts are fixed in the bull's neck, off go these squibs and crackers, which so bewilders the poor animal that he roars with pain. He has been tormented in the flank at the same time. The last trumpet is sounded, and in walk the *matadors*, who are always received with great acclamations, to which they make most profound and respectful obeisances all round. The *matador* is armed with a stout, sharp-pointed, double-edged sword, and a red flag about the size of a large pocket-handkerchief, fastened on one side to a piece of wood. He advances to the bull, holds this before him with his left hand, while with his right he holds the sword pointed over it. The bull stands looking at him for some moments, then dashes right at him. The experienced bravo stands firm, and by a well-directed thrust the sword runs up to the hilt near the shoulder of the noble animal, which instantly drops dead at his feet. The spectators shout, *"Viva! Bravo!"* &c. Should the *matador* fail, which is seldom, the *chulos* attract the attention of the bull till another opportunity offers of despatching him. Three horses, gaily caparisoned, are then introduced, a noose is slipped on to the bull's horns, and he is dragged triumphantly from the arena. Sand is then strewed over the marks of blood, and everything is shortly ready for another combat. The same exhibition is repeated until generally six bulls are killed. On particular feast days and grand occasions, figures as large as life, filled with fireworks, perhaps representing *Bolera* dancers, or guitar players, are placed in the centre of the arena, which attract the bull's attention. He attacks them, and tosses them in the air, when a noise and brilliant explosion take place.

Should a bull be too tame, and not given to fight, he is proclaimed a coward, and bulldogs are let loose on him. He tosses some of these, and when others of them pinion him down, a butcher with a round steel comes behind, and by one stab behind the horns deprives him of life. Bullfighting is certainly a most barbarous and cruel amusement, tending to brutalise the minds of the people. Yet it is a magnificent sight to behold upwards of ten thousand people of all ages, ranks, and of both sexes, assembled in rows of concentrating circles rising head over head, and when evening begins to close, the twinkling light caused by thousands of persons striking flints to kindle their lamps has a most singular effect.

Although there are no finer peasantry in the world than the Spanish, much cannot be said for the higher orders, or for the inhabitants of towns, who are a lazy indolent race. Their greatest luxury is to stand idly, wrapped up in their large *capas*, smoking cigars, or gambling in the evening. Assassination is horridly common, many being stabbed at noonday. Some of our countrymen were victims, and Lord Fife saved Lieutenant Gibbon, who was stabbed. I have, however, passed through very suspicious places at all hours of the night, and never was interrupted.

The Spaniards had a rooted jealousy of the English. They imagined that we had determined to keep possession of Cadiz, and make it another Gibraltar. When the foreign battalion was quartered outside the town at the Aquada, the officers had permission to go out after the gates were shut. One evening Lieutenant Farquharson wished to enter to his quarters, he desired the Spanish sergeant to open the wicket, which the sergeant refused to do, desiring the Lieutenant to scramble over the railing on the covered way. This he declined to do, saying that if they did not open the wicket he would report them. They in a sulk moved open the wicket, and the lieutenant had no sooner entered than he was shot through the body, of which he died in a few hours. He was so much beloved by the men of his company, although they were all foreigners, that on hearing of the catastrophe, they ran to their arms, and would have stormed and massacred the whole of the Spanish guard had not their officers prevented them.

It was truly melancholy to see how the Spanish regiments were treated. Being in the same barracks with them, we had every opportunity of observing their internal economy. The men were remarkably fine, but their officers were not worthy of them. The drum was always beating. The poor fellows would be under arms at daylight, and kept for three or four hours doing nothing as if waiting for orders, but few or no officers ever appeared. What sort of breakfast, if any, they got I could not find out, but at ten o'clock they had a parade for guard-mounting. The drums again beat the alarm, *row-do-dow*. Then came dinner time, a pretty mess! Camp-kettles containing beans, cooked with red pepper, strewed with morsels of fat bacon, were placed in rows in the barrack-yard. Each company by tuck of drum fell in with a spoon in one hand, and a hunk of bread in the other, and formed a circle in single file round the cauldron. At a signal one advanced and took a spoonful and retired, and then another, and so on till the whole mess was finished. Evening parade followed, and then some eatables of a very doubtful description. The Walloon Guards, who were all Germans, appeared to have a better system. Their officers were men belonging to many of the first families of Europe.

There being no enemy in Andalusia, and Cadiz being in perfect security, there was only our provisional battalion in garrison, so that the duty merely consisted of a few sub-guards which we had to visit; we therefore had leisure to amuse ourselves, and took advantage of this to visit the field of Barossa. We were entertained at Chicalana, a beautiful country town, the favourite retreat of the Cadiz nobility. Here they have cheery-looking country houses. Next morning we proceeded to reconnoitre the field of Barossa. There were still the skeletons of many brave men to be seen bleaching on the brown heath. One officer, on seeing an old shoe lying, gave it a kick over with his foot, and a bright gold Napoleon tumbled out.

My friends, the Gordon family at Xeres, were most particularly attentive. I used to pay them frequent visits, crossing the bay to Port St. Mary's. Xeres was only two leagues off. It is a remarkably neat country town, surrounded by a finely cultivated country, having extensive fields of grain and vineyards. My friends and others here had suffered much loss during the French occupation. Mr. James Gordon, or Don Jacob, as he was called, was married to an uncommonly clever lady of French extraction. When the French invaded that part of the country, most of the Spanish inhabitants fled; but Mr. Gordon, having no house or friends in any other part of the country, resolved to remain and take his chance. Marshal Soult, finding him a person in possession of such a large establishment in farms and stores of wine, insisted that he should assume the office of prefect of the district, under penalty of forfeiting his all. Under these circumstances, he had little or no alternative but to comply. He made use of the authority invested in him to make the burdens imposed by the invader bear as lightly as possible on the people: but he was plundered by both parties—his new masters, the French, and his old friends, the Spaniards. The French took his stock of wines, which had accumulated, he not being able to export them, and distributed them as rations for the soldiers; while the Spanish *guerrillas* came down from the mountains and seized his large flock of cattle as prizes, treating him as an enemy.

The butts of sherry are kept in long sheds, with aisles, like a cathedral. The butts are on rows on either hand, with the bungs always open. A certain quantity of very old wine is always kept on hand to mix with the new, which makes it sooner ripe and fit for the market.

When Lord Wellington came to Cadiz to consult with the government about the future operations of the army, he stayed at Mr. Gordon's house, going and returning. They were astonished at the simplicity of his habits. He had mentioned over night that he wished to be called at seven o'clock next morning. Accordingly, Mr. Gordon had the servants all ready with shaving water, &c., and the instant the hour struck, he knocked at the door, when his

Lordship desired him to come in. He was already dressed, and was rolling up his shaving apparatus, himself having performed that operation with cold water, and was ready to mount and depart. They, with some difficulty, prevailed on him to take a slight breakfast.

It being my turn for detachment, I was sent with 150 men to relieve the garrison of Tarifa. We marched on the 2nd July, 1813, the first day through the Isla de Leon, to Chicalana, where I got an excellent billet on a Spanish family of great respectability.

The gentleman of the house had joined the French interest, and of course had been obliged to flee with them when they retreated. The ladies told me that they had got letters from him in which he mentioned that the French government was much confounded by the brilliant movement Lord Wellington had made in turning the right flank of their line of operation on the Douro, which stultified and defeated the whole of their plans without the English losing a man.

On the next day, the 3rd, we passed through Conel, a small place on the sea-coast, famous for its tunny fishery. These are large fish, something like a porpoise, part of which may be eaten; but it is caught chiefly for the abundance of oil it affords. Here the most interesting object to an Englishman is Trafalgar. The country has a wild, open appearance, with herds of swine and sheep. We reached Vejar late in the day. It is an old Moorish town romantically situated on the rocky point of a steep hill, so that no wheeled carriage of any description was ever seen within the place.

On the 4th we had to bivouac in the open air. We heard the boom of the cannon of Gibraltar. On the 5th we reached Tarifa, also an old Moorish town. The troops were quartered on an island about six hundred yards from the mainland. But during the siege of the place, the British managed to get an embankment made, and formed a road on it so as to connect it with the town. This was an important point gained, for more reasons than one. It facilitated free egress to the works established there; but it was of much greater natural consequences, being the identical spot where all the Spanish gunboats lay concealed during the war with us and molested our convoys. These gunboats started out, took a position beyond the range of musketry, and blazed away at us. Being mere specks themselves on the water, it was difficult for the ships of war to hit them. They did incalculable damage to our trade, hence it was a good stroke of policy to get this dam made, which, by the sea beating on both sides, soon became a dense bank of accumulated sand, so that no person could ever open a passage again.

Tarifa had not recovered from the effect of the siege. Its former beautiful suburb on the western side was still in ruins. It was a depot for the galley-slaves, who were chained in bands, or in twos and threes. The system of punishment did not seem proportionate to the crimes of the slaves. I asked one of them for what crime he was there. The villain coolly answered: *"Un muerto"*—a murder. On asking the next one (a fine young man) he, in tears, replied: *"Un libra de tabacco."* They were employed in erecting a lighthouse on the island, which, by-the-bye, was at the expense of England.

Tarifa, renowned for the gallant and successful defence which a handful of English troops made, when besieged by Marshal Soult in person, is a small old Moorish town, encircled by a single thin wall, with a few towers, but without any exterior works of defence. It is situated on a promontory at the entrance of the Mediterranean. The streets are steep and extremely narrow, nor have the houses, in general, any pretensions to an appearance of grandeur. On a cursory view, it might be supposed that there was nothing of a very interesting description to be found within the place. After a short residence, however, the stranger will be agreeably surprised with attractions sufficient to induce him to prolong his stay; that is to say, should he have the good taste to cultivate the acquaintance of the charming Tarifa ladies. The fair Tarifenias are celebrated no less for the beauty of their features and the symmetry of their forms, than for the peculiarity of their dress, when they appear out of doors. They still maintain the Moorish custom of going, on such occasions, with their heads and faces covered, instead of assuming the open *mantilla* worn in other parts of Spain. This is done in a very singular manner. A piece of silk or other black stuff, about a yard and a half long and one broad, is lined with some coloured silk, and a runner, or drawing tucker, is made along the lower edge. When this is to be used, after the *saya,* or black upper slip is put on, the *tapa,* with the lining outwards, is placed behind, and brought round the waist, the strings are drawn tight, and tied in front, while the upper edge hangs down to the feet. After it has been neatly puckered all round, the upper edge is raised and brought over the head, and so managed with the hands that only one brilliant dark eye can be seen sparkling through the small opening. The ample folds of this unique costume give a fullness to the outward appearance of the bust, which, contrasted with the slender waist, the small foot and ankle, in silken hose and neat slippers, gives a fine effect to the entire contour of figure. But, however becoming it may be, it is certainly not the less tantalising, as one frequently cannot recognise who the fair *incognita* may be. Should you have passed one of these, supposing you knew her, without noticing her, or have omitted the usual salutations, such as, *"A los pies de usted!"* or, *"Beso las manos de usted!"* you would get a smart rap at the evening *tertulia* for having been guilty of such a *bêtise*. Every woman flatters herself that there is a certain indescribable individuality about her which no man ought ever to mistake when in this dress. The dames of Tarifa trip along at a smarter pace than Spanish ladies usually do. The *donnas*, on all other occasions, walk with a graceful measured step and erect carriage, which impart a certain dignity such as the generality of women in other countries never possess. Indeed, they are so justly proud of this elegant acquirement, that to take notice of a lady's air and manner is the highest compliment that can be paid. The ejaculation of *"Que Gracia!"*—Oh, what grace—is esteemed a greater mark of admiration than anything that could be said on the score of beauty or other personal advantage.

The few English officers of the small garrison were admitted to all evening parties on the most friendly footing. Music, singing, and dancing, with sometimes a little loto, were the general amusements, varied at times by games at forfeits. There was one lady, as elegant and accomplished as she was beautiful, who possessed musical talents of the first order—an absolute queen of song. Never, in any country, did I hear anyone who surpassed her as a private vocalist. Her accompaniments on the piano or guitar were perfection. So pleasing were her manners, and so modest her demeanour, that she was the admiration of the men, and yet a favourite with her own sex. Such was Alphonsita, the fair daughter of a colonel of engineers. Another fascinating Tarifenia, rivalling Alphonsita in charms, but not possessing all her acquirements, so captivated a noble lord, then on an amateur military expedition in these southern climes, but who, of course, had more opportunities of displaying his gallantry in devotion to the fair than in active operations in the field, that he proposed to place his heart and fortune at her disposal; and, on his proceeding to England on urgent affairs, he, with the consent of her parents, placed her in a convent on a handsome allowance, in order to finish her education, or perhaps to place her out of the way of other rivals. His lordship, however, proved no true knight. This Dulcinea, had Don Quixote been in existence, might fairly have called upon him to redress her wrongs. She, however, most sensibly, took the matter very quietly; came forth from the convent, and consoled herself by marrying a man of her choice, who being her own countryman, was a more suitable match.

The stranger ought not to omit visiting Guzman's Tower, famed in historic recollections, and the splendid scenery from this point of view. The blue, deep water, rippling on the beach beneath, appears like an expanded lake, reposing in the bosom of the surrounding hills and magnificent mountains. The traveller, on reflecting that he is standing in Europe, and beholds Africa opposite, with the passing crowd of vessels and majestic ships of war intervening, discovers that appearances are very deceitful—that he gazes on a branch of the ocean—nay, that he is, perhaps, actually perched on one of the supposed pillars of Hercules, commanding the Straits of Gibraltar. The above tower, as history tells us, derives its name from the heroic Don M. Guzman, who was governor of the place when besieged by the Moors. These infidels having seized his infant son, whose nurse had strayed with him too far from the gates, thinking that the governor would surrender to save his child, summoned him to capitulate, with the option of having his son restored, or, in case of refusal, of losing the babe by the infliction of a violent death. The brave Guzman ascended the tower, and from this identical spot, with scorn, rejected the offered terms, declaring that, however distressing to his feelings as a father, he would never sacrifice his honour to save his child. To convince them of his determination, he tossed his sword over the wall, which the barbarians instantly plunged into the bosom of the young innocent, who thus gloriously, though unconsciously, died in the cause of his country.

"Having approached so close to the water's edge, and the shores of Africa appearing so temptingly near, we may as well make a trip across, and take a peep at Tangiers."

This was said to me one day by a gallant commander of one of His Majesty's gunboats. My arrangements were soon made. A few hours of fair wind sufficed to waft us across the straits, and in the evening we came to anchor in the harbour of Tangiers, alongside of a frigate which had brought Mr. A'Court, afterwards Lord Heytesbury, Ambassador from His Britannic Majesty to the Emperor of Morocco, on his way to Fez with a large assortment of presents. Early next morning I landed with my friend of the gunboat, who, having his regular pass, was permitted to enter the town; while I, having no such document to produce, was detained at the gate by a coarse-looking fellow in a brown woollen smockfrock, having a hood behind. This infidel warder swore that the *bashaw* was asleep, and that no one could enter without his permission. He showed me into a vaulted porch, with iron gratings in front, which gave it the appearance of a cage. Soon afterwards, while I was sitting on a stone bench in rather a surly mood at such usage, a fine-looking elderly Moor, in a rich Turkish dress, came in. On observing me in uniform, he saluted me in Spanish with many obeisances, and informed me that he was captain of the port—that his highness the Bashaw was a wonderfully good man—and there was no doubt but that on his being informed that an English officer had arrived, he would give orders for my being admitted. About an hour afterwards, a swarm of greedy rascals came running down, each declaring that he was the person who had obtained the favour of my being permitted to enter, and all, in a tone of demand rather than of request, prattling for remuneration. I gave them to understand that I had no intention whatever of paying each individual, and, to get clear of the hubbub, threw a piece of money amongst them. This had the desired effect, and during the scramble I beckoned to a Jew porter to take up my portmanteau. He immediately pulled off his black cap and slippers, putting both under his arm, and then, shouldering my baggage, trudged off. As this mode of proceeding was new to me, I inquired the reason. He seemed very reluctant to give an explanation which proved humiliating to himself and to his nation. The fact was, we had to pass a mosque, and on such occasions all Jews are obliged to do so uncovered and barefoot; so, to save himself the trouble of stopping on the way, or to avoid doing publicly this abhorred mark of homage, he very prudently arranged beforehand. I was conducted to a sort of hotel kept by an Italian, followed by a concourse of people, who, on the whole, behaved respectably enough, there being only an occasional salutation of *"Perro de Christiano!"* or Christian dog. Several Moors of seeming respectability came in. Some of them introduced themselves by saying they had been in England, meaning Gibraltar. The Moors in general are a fine race of men, many much fairer than their neighbours, the Spaniards, while others are of a brownish-red colour, and a few quite black; but these Othellos, I was told, were descendants of slaves who had obtained their liberty: indeed, all the rich Moors have still many black slaves. One or two persons very politely offered to show me what was most worthy of notice. I gladly accepted their offer, as a sort of protection from annoyance. Although anyone may walk about the town in safety, no Christian can venture outside the walls without a guard, which the Bashaw always grants if applied and paid for.

In my hasty departure from Tarifa, I had provided no articles of any value; and as no visit can be paid to his highness without a suitable present, I was obliged to restrain my curiosity, and refrain from soliciting an interview.

Here, as in all Moorish towns, the streets are extremely narrow and filthy, the houses in general very mean-looking, and from their having no windows towards the streets, and the shops being only dark cells, open in front, the whole had a *triste* and sombre appearance. One finds here no redeeming qualities as at Tarifa. Instead of the graceful fair ones in the black *tapada,* the only Moorish females to be seen are *outrée* figures, covered with a dirty white camel-hair cloth, hung over their heads all round—so that in order to see where to step they must walk with their arms extended, as if playing at blindman's buff, or groping in the dark; and if one might judge from their gait, they must be old and ugly before they are permitted even to enjoy this indulgence. A few of the Jewesses whom we observed sitting at their doors were, however, particularly good looking.

We visited the *zocco* or market outside the gate. This had quite an oriental appearance. Numbers of camels were lying all round, and many Arabs basking in the sun. There was an abundant display of various choice fruits, particularly oranges, which are here delicious, superior to the Spanish. Meat, poultry, game of all kinds, were surprisingly cheap; but this arbitrary government is so avaricious, that no article can be shipped without the most exorbitant duty. By a special agreement, Gibraltar and our ships of war are allowed to purchase a certain number of sheep, fowls, &c., but an individual is only permitted to carry on board one fowl, or two pigeons, each day, this being deemed a sufficient allowance. By a particular favour obtained through the consul, I was allowed to send off one dozen fowls, which had only cost two shillings. Having advanced to some distance in the *zocco,* and approached a sort of pillar or monument surrounded with wild-looking Arabs, they, on observing me, became very clamorous. One of my Moorish friends hinted that it would be prudent to retire; while he mumbled something about *un Santo.* He then conducted me to see the lions, not of the place, but real royal animals, which were waiting to be shipped for England, as a present to His Majesty. They were in a low outhouse, with a small open window placed about four feet from the ground, having only a wooden bar across. While looking in at these animals, my companion grasped hold of me, and pulled me hastily away, assuring me that if any accident should happen to me, his life would be answerable, because he would be the last person in whose company I should have been seen. I ridiculed the idea of danger, but, to convince me that there were sufficient grounds for his alarm, he told me that only a few weeks before, a respectable Jew, on one of their feast days, had brought his family to see these very lions, and that while in the act of throwing in a leg of mutton to them as a treat, one of the largest pounced up, and with one pat of his paw knocked the poor man dead in the centre of his children. Indeed, not many days after my visit, I learned that these animals broke out of the den, to the consternation and alarm of the whole town. The natives betook themselves to their houses, and, armed with their long muskets, took post on the flat roofs, while they ordered out all the Jews, on pain of being fired upon, to catch the ferocious animals. These unfortunate people managed this serious affair with some address. They killed several sheep, and laid a train of tempting *morceaux,* consisting of legs, loins, shoulders, &c., at various distances all the way to the den—no doubt taking a hint from "Jack the Giant-killer." This *ruse* succeeded, and the kings of the forest were again lodged in state.

The Jews are here treated in the most insulting and degrading manner. None are allowed to wear a round hat without paying a very handsome sum for a licence. They, however, allured by great profits—for all the trade is in their hands—bear all with the most abject servility. The most wealthy amongst them are obliged to put on the appearance of poverty, so as not to attract the attention of the lynx eyes of the *bashaws,* or the emperor; and indeed, as for that, such of the Moors as venture to show too much appearance of affluence, do not escape; for soon after my return to Tarifa, I learned that my venerable acquaintance, the captain of the port, had fled to Gibraltar. It seems the wonderful and good *bashaw* sent a very polite message to him, requesting the loan of some 20,000 *piastres.* Our friend, being well aware that if he were simple enough to send them, not one would ever return to his coffers, and that if he did not, his head would be the price of his refusal, having secretly sent off part of his treasure, hid the remainder, and accomplished his departure.

The course which political events were at this period taking in Europe created no small sensation even in this remote corner. The accounts of the French being driven over the Pyrenees, and finally out of Spain, by Lord Wellington, afforded the greatest satisfaction to the Moors. They were congratulating one another and exclaiming to me in Spanish, *"Gracias a Dios! Gracias a Dios!"* They seemed to have had great apprehensions that Napoleon, after conquering Europe, would have demolished their empire. Previously to his most astonishing success, all nations in Europe had consuls at Tangiers, who used to display their national arms and flags on their houses; but as each nation in succession was brought under the dominion of France, the French consul made each of them drop their colours; so that at one period there were only the English and French flags to be seen. But in proportion as the European States began to recover, the consuls of those nations first freed from their thraldom began to venture from their hiding-holes, and up went a Spanish flag, next a Prussian, then a Neapolitan, &c., &c., until, when I was there, all were again triumphantly displayed; while, as an instance of the mutability of human affairs, so great was the reaction, that the French flag was torn down, the arms disappeared, and the consul himself was obliged to fly from the place.

The governor of Tarifa was a good sort of man named Don Dabun, but he had no energy. His garrison was composed of a few regular, and a company or two of reserve, troops. Some jealousy having arisen between them and our troops on the island, some of our men in passing through a small square where the Spanish barracks were situated, were insulted and pursued by the Spaniards. Our people armed themselves with stones, sticks, or whatever they could first find, turned round, and beat all the Spaniards into the barracks. These fellows in cowardly manner opened a fire from the windows, and our fellows kept pelting them with stones. The Spaniards then opened the barrack gates and poured a regular fire on the defenceless men. On being informed of the circumstance I hastened to the spot, and got between the contending parties, but ere I could stop the fray a poor fellow was mortally wounded, and two others severely, by my side. I got our men drawn off, and went with them to the island. They were in a state of great excitement, and wished to turn the cannon of the fort against the town, exclaiming, *"Ces ne sont pas des soldats. Ces sont des brigands!"* The poor governor got so alarmed at our handful of men that he ordered the gates to be shut lest we should attack the town.

The English garrison consisted of nearly 200 men under my command, a party of artillery who had charge of the batteries, and a considerable depot of military stores—the whole under the command of a field-officer of the 29th Regiment.

We made excursions into various parts of the country. The fertility of the soil is remarkable. The French had destroyed all the pasture of the extensive plain adjoining, and had swept away the large herds of brood mares. Before I left the place the plain was again covered with grass, and herds of swine and horses running about in such numbers that sometimes when they were congregated together they looked like regiments of cavalry. Some of the finest horses in Andalusia are bred here. The mares do no work but trample out the corn. For this purpose a day floor is prepared in the plain, on which the sheaves of corn are placed. Five or six mares are put abreast, and a man stands in the centre, making them go round and round, which threshes out the grain, and chops the straw into small morsels at the same time. The operations of husbandry were very simple. A plough consisting of two crooked sticks drawn by two oxen scratched the ground, and a branch of a tree, dragged also by oxen, harrowed in the seed. The crops were wonderful. Still, on account of the exhaustion consequent on the war, large quantities of corn and cattle were smuggled over from Africa. We got supplies of many luxuries from Gibraltar, but the terrible malignant fever or plague having broken out, all communication was cut off.

The mountains beyond the plain being infested with wolves, which do much mischief to the sheep, and even to the horses, when a person kills a wolf he brings the skin to the town council. They pay him a certain reward, and cut a piece out of the ear. He then walks about with the skin in triumph, and receives presents from all the farmers or those that have sheep in the place. The beach abounds with most beautiful shells of every size, shape, and colour, which are manufactured into artificial flowers, &c.

The Spaniards have a great horror of consumption, believing it to be most contagious. There was a very clever young man, Dr. Ramsay, labouring under this fatal malady. He had fitted up a chimney in his lodgings. On his quitting, to return to England, no native would enter the house where he had lived. To their astonishment I took his rooms. They all assured me that I was tempting Providence, and that I assuredly would fall a victim. I, however, by having wood collected, managed to enjoy the luxury of a good fire in the wet and chilly evenings during the winter.

Here a curious reaction of principle took place. In the battalion were many native Frenchmen, while the majority were natives of Prussia, Saxony, Baden, Wirtemberg, Hanover, Nassau, &c., who had been taken from their homes as conscripts when the Confederation of the Rhine was formed. So great was the awe inspired by the French in these Germans, that they were held in the utmost respect, and it appeared from what transpired afterwards that this feeling was retained by those who promiscuously entered our service. After the tide of affairs had turned against Napoleon, from his defeat in Russia, when the Prussians and the other German powers were liberated from thraldom, the natives of these countries began to hold up their heads and bully the Frenchmen. Napoleon's reverses increased, and when he was driven over the Rhine into France, after Leipzig, the few Frenchmen in our battalion sunk into insignificance, and the others triumphed over them. They came to me to complain that they had a miserable life of it. Formerly they were looked up to, but now they were humbled.

Previous to my leaving Cadiz I had forwarded a memorial to Lord Wellington, requesting to be promoted to a company, stating my having served so long in actual service, and having been severely wounded. I had the pleasure to find by the *Gazette* that the provisional battalion had been incorporated and made permanent, being added as an eighth battalion to the 60th Rifle Regiment, and that I was promoted to a company; my commission being dated 5th November, 1813. I was made senior captain except one, who, being absent, and only a major commanding, I became from fifth lieutenant in the 29th Regiment second in command of this corps, no small step for a young man.

On the 19th March, 1814, I received orders to march for Cadiz. The first night we halted at a farmhouse. After dinner, some English cheese was produced, which created great curiosity amongst the peasant servants. I gave one a bit. He was much pleased, as he had never tasted anything like it, because in this southern clime they make no butter, and only a little goat's milk cheese. I asked him what he commonly lived upon. He shrugged his shoulders, and replied, *"*Gaspacho *et* pan *(bread), et pan et gaspacho."* This *gaspacho* is made with garlic, pods of red pepper, pounded in a mortar, to which oil is added, then vinegar, with the addition of some water; when this is well mixed, bread is sliced in. This simple mixture is the universal food of the peasantry, particularly during harvest.

We continued our journey on the 20th March. The country was still an extended plain, covered with flocks of brood mares and large herds of cattle. At some places the land was well cultivated. In the evening we arrived at Medina Sidonia. This town is singularly situated on a sugar-loaf shaped hill, rising from the plain, which surrounds it on all sides. The climate is esteemed so fine that convalescents come from all parts for the recovery of their health.

Next day we found ourselves once more in the great emporium of trade, fashion, and frivolity, although Cadiz was not now so full as formerly, as the regent, the government, the Cortes, and all public functionaries had removed to Madrid. The French having been driven out of Spain, and our armies having invaded the soil of France, Napoleon had liberated King Ferdinand the Seventh, and all were in joyous and anxious expectation for the return of their beloved king to the throne of his fathers. He did come, and never were anticipations more damped. On going as usual to visit at some of our friends' houses one evening, we found detachments of troops posted in the streets, and all the portals closed. Astonished at what could be the matter, we knocked as usual. A little wicket was opened, and through an iron grating it was inquired who we were. When they found that we were friends and English officers, we were eagerly admitted. All was sorrow and dismay. The same post which brought the intelligence of Ferdinand's entry into Madrid brought also secret warrants to seize some of the noblest and bravest of the land. Many of their friends had been arrested without a moment's warning, nor were they conscious of having been guilty of any crime, further than having wished for an ameliorated system of government, and that the Cortes should have a voice in making laws for the kingdom. For this they were termed Liberals. The *serviles*, or court and arbitrary power party, were in high spirits. All the public functionaries, generals, &c., in order to secure their places, retracted all their political sentiments which they had entertained for the six previous years. They announced a grand national *fête* to be held at the Isla. We were all invited with most pompous cards of invitation.

A kind of orchestra was erected in the *plaça*. All the young ladies of quality and of the best families who could sing, were made to exhibit their vocal powers on the occasion, and amongst them was our fair Tarifenian, Alphonsita. This was followed by fireworks, and the evening concluded with a good ball at the theatre, which was handsomely decorated for the occasion. A temporary saloon was fitted up of framework and canvas, decorated with flags and ancient arms, and devices of every description. The supper, under the superintendence of an Italian artist, was truly magnificent. In the midst of this festive scene, by some accident the canvas caught fire, which spread with great rapidity. A scene of confusion and terror ensued. All the ladies took to flight, crowding and trampling on each other.

At another grand ceremony the Constitution was publicly annulled, and the statue of the Constitution was torn from its place and broken to pieces.

While these rejoicings were going on, great dissatisfaction reigned amongst the people, and particularly amongst the lower orders. Having tasted the blessings of freedom, they had no inclination to return to their old thraldom. The gallant Valdez, who had fought against us at Trafalgar, was still governor and captain-general of the province. One evening at the theatre a demagogue shoemaker got up in the pit, and calling for the manager, handed him a Liberal song, and desired him to bring forward all the professionals to make them sing it. On his persisting, the whole house insisted on its being done. A counter revolution took place that night, but the military were in possession of the high works and fortifications on the laud side which command the town, and we were in the same barracks, in rather an awkward predicament. The populace were outrageous below, while the military on the roof above our heads were pointing the guns at them. After a great deal of talk, nothing was done, and things subsided into sullen submission. A few days afterwards it was announced that Don Villa Vicezico had been appointed governor in place of Valdez. On the day of the new governor's entry the streets were lined with military, and a grand gala day was ordered by the public functionaries. Valdez walked out on foot to meet his successor. I saw them enter together apparently on the most friendly terms. The new governor had an order in his pocket for the arrest of Valdez, who within ten days afterwards was in a solitary dungeon in the Castle of Segovia.

Cadiz was no longer the gay place it had been. All the English wealthy that were not prisoners of state left the town. The English troops had been gradually leaving this quarter. We were the only regiment that remained, and on the 14th August we embarked, with orders to proceed to Gibraltar. On our departure Cadiz was finally evacuated by the English.

On arriving in the Bay of Gibraltar we learned that the malignant pestilent fever had again made its appearance in the garrison. We were ordered to disembark, which we did on the 20th August, and were encamped on the neutral ground, without the walls. Here we were extremely healthy. It was a melancholy sight to see the dead-carts filled with dead bodies and quicklime hourly passing us to deposit the corpses in a burial ground at some distance beyond our camp About a month afterwards the fever began to abate. The governor, however, still believed that it was not extinct; but another general, insisting that it was, urged the case, so that we were ordered into the town to decide the dispute and prove who was right. By that hour next day we had an immense number of men ill of the dreadful malady. Many taken ill in the evening were dead and buried before noon next day. And so it continued daily, thinning our numbers. Nor did the officers escape. I met Mr. Duguid in the street, who had just come from his own house, where he had left one of his friends in the black vomit, the precursor of death. Several of our officers were seized, myself among the number. The fever came on like a flash of lightning: a sudden chill down the back, a dreadful headache, soon changed into a burning fever, with absolute prostration of all strength. The military medical attendance was of the worst description, in fact little or none. The army medical officers had got permission to attend the civil inhabitants. The rich Jews and Moors paid handsomely in gold doubloons; from us they were not entitled to any such fees. The consequences were evident. We were neglected. In cases which required the utmost medical skill and attention to watch the turn of the disease no one was by. The doctor paid a hasty visit at some uncertain hour, and then handed you over to some young apothecary apprentice who had volunteered his services from home in hope of getting an appointment, or to an orderly corporal, who went his round to deliver medicine. In one of the corporal's visits to myself he said, "You are very bad, sir, but Captain Pym is worse; he will be dead in half-an-hour."

The corporal was right. Poor Pym died, and was the first buried in a new ground at the ceremony of the consecration of which he had commanded only a few days before. Thanks to God, and a good constitution, I got over the disease, but I was left in a desperately weak state. If you reach the third day, hopes may be entertained of a recovery, but in general all died on the first or second day, and the dead bodies turned a gold-colour. Major-General Sir Charles Holloway, who was second in command, had taken every precaution to cut off all communication with the town and inhabitants. They were eighteen in family, servants, &c., six of whom were carried off, including a son and a daughter. It was lamentable to see the Moors carried to the Lazaretto, they holding it an abomination to be touched by a Christian. The police sergeant searched all the houses, and obliged those who had not sufficient means of comfort to go to the public hospital. The doctors made a fine harvest of it, as the Jews handed out their gold pieces in the most liberal manner. I knew some realise two hundred guineas per week during the three months the fever prevailed.

As soon as it was possible I was moved to a healthy barrack in town. Sitting one afternoon in front of the fire, I felt my chair rise with me, and instantly down I came. A loud report followed, the whole building vibrating. I thought it was an earthquake, but it proved that in a thunderstorm a magazine on the highest pinnacle of the rock had been struck by lightning, which caused the whole to explode, sending masses of rock fourteen feet square to prodigious distances, even as far as the neutral ground. Singularly enough nobody was hurt.

The history of Captain Pym was something strange. He had been an eminent miniature painter in London, and for his health had taken a trip to Jersey, where the late General Sir J. Doyle then commanded. The general was so pleased with Pym's likenesses of some of his family, that he offered him a commission in his regiment, which was accepted. He was a subaltern doing duty at Cadiz when Lord Wellington came to consult with the regency. They wanted to present him with his picture set in diamonds, but nobody could be found to do it. Mrs. Strange, who had taken a fancy for Pym, who more or less was domesticated in her husband's house, mentioned his name. He was sent for, and Lord Wellington told him that he had no time to sit to him, and asked him if he could paint his likeness by occasionally coming to him. Pym did so by going two or three mornings to breakfast, and he certainly produced the most striking likeness of Lord Wellington I have ever seen. He was noted for a company, and got it in our new battalion.

After his death at Gibraltar, Mrs. Strange sent to claim the most of his effects, alleging that she had presented him with them. The major, who always acts as executor for deceased officers, said this could not be done. She wrote a very angry letter, ending with, "A present can be claimed. See Judge Blackstone." She sent an agent to bid for the articles she claimed at the sale of the effects, and some of the wicked youngsters made her give rather long prices for them by bidding against her out of mischief.

Having heard much of Roman antiquities to be seen at Ronda, and of the magnificent scenery of the surrounding country, rendered still more interesting by the gallant conduct of the mountaineer inhabitants of the district, who during the struggle of the Peninsular war had formed themselves into *guerrilla* bands, and with the most determined courage resisted the superior numbers of the enemy, Captain C——, *aide-de-camp* to his excellency the governor, and I availed ourselves of the opportunity of Messrs. Donino, the great contractors at Gibraltar, going there to attend the annual horse fair, to accompany them, as being well acquainted in those regions. They most obligingly offered us the use of their friend's horses on the way. On the 17th May, 1815, our party left Gibraltar at 6 o'clock a.m., and, after breakfasting at St. Roque, we proceeded at 10 o'clock a.m. on our journey, through a woodland country terminating in a forest of cork and oak trees. On emerging from this, and ascending an immense mountain, we beheld a most romantic valley of some miles in length. Having descended into it by a very craggy path, and crossed a rivulet, we soon afterwards came to the river Guadiano, which being almost dry, we followed the summer road which led up the bed of the river for about ten miles. The stream at this season is small, but it winds about so much that we crossed it at least twenty times. It has high banks on each side. The winter road runs up the right side. We now began to approach the mountains. Having halted at a miserable *venta* for a short time, we began to ascend, but the ascent was so steep that we were obliged to dismount and lead our horses over rocks and round the brinks of precipices, for two or three miles. We then got a view of Guacin, which had here a most romantic appearance, seeming to form an amphitheatre on the crest of the mountain ridge, having on the left a Franciscan convent with remarkably fine gardens, and on the right a high rock crowned with old Moorish towers which command the place, which we reached about five o'clock, and were carried by Mr. Donino to the house of an acquaintance, who provided a supper of bacon, eggs, black puddings, salad, &c., with plenty of country wine. This being a remote country town, the place itself is small, with narrow steep streets. Many of the houses and churches had been much injured by the enemy during the war, and were it not for the recollections of former scenes which had here occurred, there would be little worthy of note; and of course the inhabitants were all rural people, there being few or none of any wealth or consequence amongst them. Many friends of the family crowded in during the evening to see us strangers, and many remarks did we overhear on the differences of our costumes, uniforms, &c. As this part of the country is noted for being the rendezvous of daring *banditti*, many people who were going to the fair prepared to join our party as a protection.

The next morning being extremely stormy with wind and rain, we determined to remain. A respectable farmer having begged the pleasure of our company to dinner, we, wishing to see the style of living of that class, accepted the invitation at two o'clock. Our party consisted of the parish priest, the superior of the Franciscans, a captain of militia, who had been a commander of *guerrillas*; the surgeon, *entre nous*, the barber, a shopkeeper, and a farmer or two. On sitting down there was nothing on the table excepting a plate, napkin, and a bottle of wine to each. Plates of sliced oranges were handed round. The first dish consisted of *vermicelli* prepared with milk; then a thin rice soup, made palatable by adding a spoonful of grated cheese. The *olla* then regaled our olfactory nerves. This usually consists of a good-sized piece of beef, a black pudding, and a piece of bacon, stewed for many hours, to which is added *calabazo* or pumpkins, cabbages cut small, peas, beans, tomatoes, &c., seasoned with a few pods of pimento, black pepper, salt, &c., all well stewed together in a small quantity of water. The manner of eating it is this: The beef is cut up in slices and handed round. Each person is then helped to a portion of the *olla*, which, with the bacon and pudding, is served up in a large dish. This, with the addition of an excellent sauce made from the tomato, proves a very savoury mess. Our small tumblers, used instead of wine-glasses, were frequently filled, and as often emptied. They seemed to have no idea of taking things quietly during dinner. They must needs pledge us in bumpers, each or any individual who did you that honour touching your glass hob-and-nob with his own. Fowls, sliced, roasted, and boiled, with sauce, were then introduced, followed by a kind of hasty pudding made of maize flour, milk, and eggs, ornamented on the top with lines and figures of pounded cinnamon strewed upon it. Cheese and fruits of all kinds succeeded. During dinner the landlady, assisted by two or three pretty girls and her servants, stood around, all joining in the conversation and serving us at the same time. The superior of the Franciscans filled a bumper and handed it to one of the young persons, who finished it without a halt, he then filled again and pledged her to the bottom. Following the good example of the worthy father, I performed the same ceremony with another, who was particularly handsome, The dinner party having broken up, and the reverend gentlemen having departed, the evening was spent in singing national songs, accompanied on the guitar. One old gentleman exhibited great agility in dancing *fandangos*, *boleras*, &c., for our amusement. *Marmalada*, or cheese made of quinces and other sweetmeats, was handed round. The girls displayed great naiveté, and were extremely frank and good-humoured. The captain narrated many of his exploits against the enemy. He mentioned a very narrow escape he had made, and the singular mode of his success. Having been in advance of his party reconnoitring, attended by only a few men, he was surprised and taken. They shot his companions, but reserved him to be made a public example of. With this view they were taking him to the centre of the column. He knew the road well, and that they would have to pass a place on the mountain where the lower side of the road was very steep and sloping. He managed, on approaching this point, to get pretty near the edge of the road, and just at the proper moment he made a dash, overthrowing one or two soldiers, flung himself over the low parapet, and rolled, as he expected, headlong down. They fired many shots after him, but he fortunately escaped unhurt except a few superficial bruises from the stones and brushwood, and rejoined his *guerrillas*.

We left our friends next morning amidst many *"vivas"* and wishes *"ad mil annos."* We found our party very much increased by persons who did us the honour to imagine that their purses and persons were secure when under the protection of an English uniform. The road lay generally over hills, or along the side of mountains, showing deep and verdant rich valleys, highly cultivated, and laid out in gardens round the villages here and there to be seen. The lower slopes of the mountains were generally covered with vineyards and the upper parts with wood, whose dark green foliage contrasted well with the bleak summits and frowning peaks, the regions of eternal snow, and gave a varied and picturesque appearance to the scene. On these mountains the wild goat or chamois and the wild boar range with the utmost freedom.

We passed Benoli, a small town, near which there is an old Moorish square-looking castle, with towers at each corner. As we advanced the country became more wild. We saw a *venta,* which had been burnt by the enemy. The road became very steep. We passed along a ridge, bleak and desolate, with high rocks and crags on our left hand. Our friends exhibited great symptoms of apprehension, lest they should become the prey of *banditti,* which, although perhaps not without foundation, proved visionary with regard to us. Amongst those who had joined our party was the merchant who had formed one of the dinner party on the previous day. He pointed out the several points on the road where skirmishes between his countrymen and the French had taken place. After the enemy, by the cruel examples they made of many of the inhabitants, had in some measure subdued this part of the district, they began to be less apprehensive of danger, and appeared to have confidence in the inhabitants. On their leaving Guacin one day on some expedition, a French captain had forgot something in his lodgings, and rode back alone into the town. In the act of dismounting at the door of his former lodgings, he was surrounded by several people, when one of them drew his *cuchello,* or stiletto, and stabbed him dead; and this person was the very individual merchant himself. He coolly added that he cut open the captain's cash waist-belt, and took out twenty doubloons. We looked with horror at our travelling companion, and on saying, "How could you commit so murderous a deed in cold blood? Why did you not make him prisoner and take his money if it pleased you?" He merely replied that he was a Frenchman, who had invaded and ruined his country.

On turning the angle of a high peak, several voices called out, "There is Ronda!" On looking out we beheld Ronda, this ancient stronghold of the Moors, like a white spot situated on a small sunny plain in the midst of wild majestic mountains. But as we descended, Ronda seemed to rise, until, on near approach, we discovered that it stands on a high plain of table-land, or flat rock, united to the mountains on one side, but on two other sides encircled by a valley from which the rock rises perpendicularly. On the third side, the one by which we entered, it is separated from the country by a deep, narrow chasm, which has the appearance of the rock having been rent asunder by some convulsion of nature. Through this gap dashes the river Guadiano, and over it there is a most picturesque Roman bridge of one arch of stupendous height.

The town is rather a neat place; some of the streets are pretty regular, with good houses. The few miserable *posadas* being all full on account of the fair, we had to hire lodgings, and engage a cook. The Alamaida, which is situated on the perpendicular rock, is laid out with good taste, and affords a healthy and agreeable public walk for the natives. There was from this a most splendid view of the distant mountains, and of the valley immediately at your feet, through which the river is seen meandering. The Plaça de Toros, or amphitheatre for bull-fights, is tolerably good. In the mountain valleys the finest breed of bulls is reared.

The horse-fair was well worth seeing. There were some thousands of Andalusian horses, but they made only a poor show, being all young, or very old weakly animals, owing to the French having taken all the best. They even maimed those that remained, putting out an eye, or laming them, so that they might not be of service to the *guerrillas*. Here the gipsies were in great display.

Having seen all things worthy of notice, we were greedy to see more, and desirous of verifying the truth of the Spanish proverb, "*Qui no ha vista Sevilla no ha vista maraviglia,*" we determined on seeing this wonderful place. On waiting on the magistrate to have our passports *viséd*, he strongly urged us to take a guard, as from accounts he had received the roads were by no means safe. We accordingly agreed to take two grenadiers with us. We left Ronda on the morning of the 22nd May, 1815. Passing through gardens, descending and ascending hills, in some places covered with wood, we came to a valley, down which runs a river, with sloping' hills on each side and mountains peeping over them in their rear. It came on to rain very hard, and we stopped at a *venta*. We found the stable filled with people, and amongst them was the *alcalde* of the next town, Algonzales. They informed us that a band of *ladrones* had been seen close to the place, and that for this reason they had taken refuge there until more people coming from the fair should increase their number, so as to make a formidable party, and they entreated us to remain to give them our countenance and protection. We, however, as soon as the shower passed over, mounted our horses and proceeded. The *alcalde* very civilly gave us a note to his deputy to provide us with good billets, and we continued our journey without meeting any *ladrones*. On arriving at Algonzales and presenting the order we had for lodgings, the *scrivano*, armed with a little brief authority, plumply refused to oblige us, alleging his surprise that the *alcalde* had given what he had no right to give—strangers military billets in the time of peace. Our gallant grenadiers were very indignant at this conduct, and seemed to be thoroughly ashamed of their countryman. Indeed they seemed to feel as if a gross insult had been offered to themselves. We, however, got into a *posada* kept by a smuggler, a jolly fellow, where there was, as usual, only one table and a chair or two, with nothing in the world in the shape of eatables. But the soldiers, on giving them a little money to lay out in provisions, seemed to be good foragers, for, with the assistance of our servant, they provided a capital dinner.

The road continued down the valley, along the right bank of the river. At some distance from the left bank we observed the small town of Zara, singularly situated on the rocky ridge of a hill. We were told that the roads leading up to it, and several of the streets, and many of the houses, were excavated out of the solid rock. This place in times of chivalry had been a strong fortress, as the remains of the walls and the castle, now in ruins, prove. It commands one of the strongest passes at the entrance of the *sierras*. The extraordinary manner in which this place was surprised and taken by Muley Aben Hassan, the last of the Moorish kings, in 1481, has given a celebrity to its remains. The country hereabout is bleak and wild, with only a few patches of cultivation near springs or rivulets.

In the evening, the *alcalde* and his friends, having arrived in safety, called upon us, and congratulated us on our escape. He informed us that *banditti* were seen riding on our flank for some distance on the hill above us, watching our movements. On recollection, there could not have been a more favourable place for an attack. The river, swollen with rain, was on our left hand; the road was narrow and bad, flanked on the right by a steep hill, so that it was a defile in the proper sense of the word, which would have well answered the usual mode of attack: which is, while one party advances in front, another closes in from the rear, and a few lying in ambush on the flank render escape almost impossible. They, I suppose, seeing us and our servant well mounted and armed, and having an escort of King Ferdinand's troops, did not think it prudent to attack us.

The country, although still very hilly in the neighbourhood of Algonzales, is tolerably well cultivated, and in the immediate vicinity of the place there are many olive-groves and beautiful gardens. A dreadful butchery took place at this town during the war. A French battalion marched in, and occupied the church as a barrack, without any regard for the sacredness of the place. While the men were engaged in taking off their accoutrements, and arranging themselves, a deadly volley was poured in upon them by the outraged inhabitants and a body of *guerrillas*, who had secretly approached the place. The French, thus taken by surprise, and the smoke increasing the confusion, were nearly all destroyed, and the few remaining were secured as prisoners. But diabolic revenge was taken by the French, who determined on the destruction of the place, and made a simultaneous attack on it from different points, so that very few had an opportunity of escaping. The people resolved to sell their lives as dearly as possible. They barricaded their houses, and defended themselves to the last extremity. They showed us two front rooms where a citizen, with several of his sons, all excellent shots, kept up a most deadly fire from the windows, while others loaded and handed them the firearms. The father himself brought down twenty-two of the enemy. The house was forced, and its brave defenders perished. The place was now slowly recovering from the effects of this horrible massacre.

On the 23rd May we proceeded up the mountain pass and defile to "*Puerto Serrana*" "the gate of the mountain," where we halted during some showers of cold rain. On leaving this we reached

Montellano, and, as the name indicates, the country became more level. Here a fine church had been destroyed by the enemy. The country continued open, with corn and pasture lands. We halted for the night at Coronel, a large open village, at a miserable *posada*, with empty rooms—as usual, only a table, a chair or cork seat or two, with nothing in the world in the shape of eatables; but our escort assisted us in providing fowls, sausages, vegetables, and fruit for our entertainment. On the 24th we travelled through a remarkably fine cultivated country to Utrera, which is a neat town, being on the high road from Seville to Cadiz. On leaving this we passed through fir-woods, the road being very sandy. We halted at the village of Las dos Hermanas, round which the country is rather barren, and covered with brushwood. But on approaching Seville the country becomes one field of wheat. The plain extends far beyond what human eye could reach, in the middle of which we discerned the steeple of the cathedral rearing its lofty pinnacle to the skies. On nearing the capital of Andalusia, the villas, orange-groves, and gardens have a gay appearance.

Hotel being a word almost unknown in the Spanish language, we, after roving about in quest of one for some time, were recommended to the Posada del Turco; and a most unchristian place it was, being more a rendezvous for carriers than a place for travellers.

Having letters of introduction to His Excellency Genera Count de G——, and to Don M. Saavedra, whose wife was of the blood royal, and whom I had the honour of knowing some years previously at Cadiz, we experienced the most polite and friendly attentions from both these eminent personages. Count de G——, being aware of our anxiety to behold the wonders of a place of which so much had been said, kindly insisted on becoming our cicerone. He daily drove us in his own carriage to all the most remarkable places worthy of notice. The first object of our research was the Alcazar, the old Moorish palace, noted for its beautiful Arabesque style, and its charming gardens, refreshed with fountains sportively playing in the balmy air, heightening the odoriferous fragrance of the sweet orange blossoms strewed on the ground in snow-like purity; whilst the walks are cooled by water-works so constructed, that on touching a spring near the main fountain, hundreds of jets, artfully dispersed, fall in gentle showers, allaying the dust of the heated gravel. Amongst the numerous wonders visited, none pleased me more than the superb archives of the Indies, and the museum containing specimens of all the ancient splendours of Montezuma, from Mexico, and the various costumes, &c., of Peru and Chili. On visiting the mint, I had the honour to stamp the impression of the royal countenance on a piece of silver. In fact, I made a dollar. His Excellency, who was a person of a cheerful disposition and pleasing manners, invited us to dinner; but as few people even of rank in this country keep establishments for festive dinners, he requested us to meet him at an Italian restaurateur's. He informed us that his family was originally Flemish, as his title denoted; that he had married a Miss O'Reilly, a lady of Irish extraction, but who was now dead, leaving him a daughter, who expected that we would do her the pleasure of accompanying her to ride out in the evening. During the repast an incident occurred which serves to illustrate the state of politics and society at this time in Spain. Some letters were delivered to him, one of which was marked *"Al servicio del Rey."* On observing this he threw it down in seeming agitation. Making the sign of the cross, he exclaimed, "God knows whether this is to make me captain-general of the province or to send me prisoner to Ceuta!" On venturing to open the dreaded epistle, he found it to contain many interrogations concerning the *"Coxo de Malaga,"* a cripple shoemaker who had cut no small figure as a leader in the Liberal ranks, and who was then a state prisoner. He seemed much relieved. We afterwards adjourned to his house, and were introduced to the youthful *condessa*. She was a most lovely and interesting girl, perfectly English in her appearance, language, and manners. During the French occupation and the Peninsular War she had taken refuge in Gibraltar, where, from her rank and amiable qualities, she had become an inmate in the governor's family. Having spent some time in agreeable conversation, the general gave her a hint to prepare, saying the horses would shortly be at the door. After some little delay she reappeared, but, to our amazement, now metamorphosed! *She was absolutely in white tights, booted and spurred, with a riding habit like our frock-coats, open, in front and rear.* She mounted her beautiful Andalusian palfrey *en hussar,* and away we ambled. However interesting she had previously appeared in our eyes, I must confess this Amazon dress and attitude on horseback tended much to cool the ardour of our former admiration, and dispelled that charm which a delicate and elegant woman inspires when beheld in that sphere and costume properly her own; but such was the custom of the country. She seemed perfectly unconscious that there was anything indecorous in her attire or manner of being mounted. We proceeded out at one of the gates, and rode quite round the city, along the excellent road which runs at the foot of the old Moorish walls and antique towers. This we accomplished in about an hour and a half, riding leisurely, so that this renowned town is not of the great extent generally supposed. Indeed, exclusive of the magnificent cathedral, the Alcazar, and some other remarkably line public buildings, the city in general has a very antiquated appearance, the streets being irregular and narrow. In the course of our ride we observed hundreds of urchins collecting the dust of the road into heaps. On inquiring the reason, we were informed that this was for the purpose of making saltpetre. The dust is lixiviated at the royal manufactory, and after the solution is condensed, the nitre crystallizes. Strolling one evening in the gardens of the Alcazar with my companion the *aide-de-camp*, who was in uniform, we overheard many of the *donnas* loudly grumbling and making bitter complaints that only one gate was now open for admission, through which they were obliged to force their way with the vulgar plebeian, while in the days of the king all the gates were thrown open to the public, and free ingress permitted. All were exclaiming, "What a shame!" while many a scornful glance was cast up to what appeared to us a thick wall running from the palace to a turret in the centre of the gardens. This we discovered was the royal walk, having open arches at each side, and a vaulted roof. Here his majesty and the royal family, during their occasional visits, were wont to promenade, while the gardens below were usually filled with the *grandees*, assembled to greet their majesties. No royalty or courtly dames now graced this elevated princely lounge. We there observed a tall, wan looking person, dressed in Spanish uniform, with a lady or two attended by some plain-looking men, peeping at the crowd below. Soon afterwards, this military personage came hastening towards us, and introduced himself to the *aide-de-camp*. After almost shaking his hand off, he got him by the arm, and led him towards the royal turreted summer-house. I followed to see what was to be done with my friend. On reaching the foot of the wall, he called up to a stout, rosy-cheeked fair one, not in the sonorous noble Castilian, but, to my amazement, in guid broad Scotch, "Maggie! Maggie! this is his excellency's Eddy Cang, tak' care o' him, tak' care o' him!" at the same time making many apologies for being obliged to absent himself on urgent business. The fair one who was playing the *role* of majesty invited the *aide-de-camp* to mount by a stair which led up to the private walk. I afterwards learned that his new friend, who held some situation under the *alcalde* or keeper of the Alcazar, was a British subject who had this post of honour conferred upon him for distinguished services during the Peninsular War. On the Alameida, which is beautifully situated on the banks of the Guadalquiver, shaded and divided into collateral groves by rows of trees in luxuriant foliage, we met myriads of the fair Sevillanas enjoying their favourite walk. Although not so richly decorated and adorned as the wealthy Gaditanas, they fully equalled them in the fine symmetry of their persons and elegance of costume. They informed us that when Marshal Soult held his headquarters here, however much they detested the enemies of their country, and however much they shunned all intercourse with them, this gallant commander made them gay in spite of themselves. He ordered a ball at his pleasure as he would do a parade, with commands for the noblest ladies to attend, and to be ready at such an hour, when his carriages would call for them, so that they might have no excuse. This was doing the agreeable by a *coup de main*. Had they dared to absent themselves, their families would probably have been proscribed and their properties confiscated. But it was likewise a *coup d'état*, as it led the other provincial towns to believe that he was on the best terms with the higher circles in the city, which had no small influence in keeping them quiet.

After a stay of four days in Seville, on the 28th May, 1813, we set out on our return, paying a visit on our way to Xeres and Cadiz, and arrived at Gibraltar on the 5th June.

There being nothing particular to do at Gibraltar, I got leave of absence to return home. Being intimate with the Honourable John Rous, who was a lieutenant on board the *Meander* frigate, and the other officers, they kindly offered me a passage. I had got leave on condition of taking charge of about sixty of our men, who, being of respectable parents in the different States of Germany had managed, through their different ambassadors, to obtain their discharge from our government. Captain Barton, M.P. for Dartmouth, had the kindness to accommodate them.

We embarked on the 10th November, 1815, and made the Scilly Islands after an excellent passage of nine days. Here we encountered a violent contrary gale, which kept us beating on and off for a week. We, however, got into Falmouth on the 26th, and on the gale abating we proceeded to Portsmouth, but were nearly lost in endeavouring to pass the Needles at the Isle of Wight in misty weather. We did not reach Portsmouth until the 4th December. I there received a discretionary order to march the men for Harwich. I chose the route through Godalming and Guildford by London. The frost was so intense that water left in a tumbler overnight was a lump of ice in the morning. The men having no arms or stores, I put their knapsacks into a wagon, so that they marched with perfect ease, and made long marches every day. On the 12th December we marched through London, to the surprise of the natives seeing so many men in green rifle uniform, not one of whom could speak a word of English. When the order was made known at Gibraltar, many of the men entitled to go wished to remain, and others who were anxious to return home paid them a handsome sum to allow them to take their places.

I had a most amusing scene at Chelmsford. While sitting in the coffee-room reading a newspaper, I heard a person talking very fast and loud in the broadest Scotch dialect it was possible to imagine. I soon recognised him as a person I had seen in my school days at Aberdeen, he was abusing, in the most opprobrious terms, some native of Colchester who, he alleged, had overcharged him for his passage in one of the Aberdeen smacks, of which he was proprietor, and which had been stranded coming down the Thames. He had offered his bill for half the sum demanded, which was refused. This had nettled his pride, and roused his indignation. He appeared to have been drinking, and was publishing every few minutes who he was, always repeating, *"I'm great John Catto from Aberdeen!"* No creature, I believe, understood what he was saying but myself. All crowded round to stare and listen to him. Some said he was a Jew, others a Dutchman, so little did they know the great John Catto. I kept looking at the paper, with my ears open. Finally, his antagonist came into the room, where, after a long dispute, my Northern friend proposed that they should stand on each side of a seam in the floorcloth, and take hold of each other's hands, and whoever should pull the other over should decide the sum to be paid. Some friends settled the matter, I believe, by arbitration, but the great John Catto's pride was much humbled that his credit had been doubted. He took a turn round the room to assure everybody at the different tables that *he was the great John Catto.* Amongst others he attacked me.

I said, "My dear sir, I do not doubt it. I know your bill is as good as an Aberdeen bank note signed by J. Brand."

He looked at me with astonishment, and said, "D'ye ken me, man?"

"O yes, Mr. Catto," I replied; "I know who you are very well."

This had such an effect on him that he seemed to be instantly sobered.

"O dear!" he exclaimed, "I didna think ony buddie kent me here. This sud mak fouk wary hoo they taak afore strengers."

On the 15th December I dined with the officers of the 47th Regiment at the Colchester barracks. On the next day I left the men at Harwich, and returned to London the following morning. On the 21st I left London by way of Oxford. There was much snow on the ground, and the two leaders of the coach broke loose on the road. I spent the 22nd at Birmingham, inspecting the various branches of manufactures. On the 23rd I arrived at Liverpool, and on the 26th at Kendal, where there was a deep snow-storm, and all the coaches were stopped. As I was anxious to get on, I prevailed on the postman and guard to try a post-chaise and four. They agreed, and we started. We stuck fast on the long and dreary hill of Shap. After much labour, and trampling with our feet a path for the wheels, we at last got on to Penrith about three o'clock in the morning. We continued our way through Carlisle, and reached Dumfries on the 28th.

Here I was arrested by a party of many old friends of my mother's family. They described to me a plot which had been formed against my liberty. There lived with the Dowager Lady Carnwath and her niece, Lady Elizabeth Dalzell, a young lady, representative of an ancient noble family, and heiress in possession of the patrimony of her father, but being a female she could not inherit the title, which went to the male heir of line. Things went on satisfactorily for a time, when one evening an old tabby got her!

One day I received an invitation to dine with a grand climacteric club. I found seated at dinner a party of ladies and gentlemen to the number of about twenty-four. The youngest member of the club present was sixty-three years of age, and he was called the *boy*; many of the others were from that age to nearly ninety. All were merry and hearty. I was admitted only for the day, being a stranger. The evening was spent in whist, and capital good players they were, having had years of experience.

On the 3rd January, 1810, I went by Castle Douglas to Kenmure Castle on a visit to my mother's cousin, Viscount Kenmure. This is a most interesting, fine old place, standing on a round high mound, which you ascend by a corkscrew road. Loch Ken is at a short distance from the foot of the mound. The grounds and gardens are quite in the old style, and well wooded with fine timber. There is excellent shooting, especially large quantities of black game. Nothing can exceed the trout-fishing in the river and the numerous lakes in the vicinity, particularly Lochinvar, from which Lord Kenmure derives one of his titles. New Galloway is a small burgh quite under his lordship's control. I was elected a burgess, and a ball was given in the Town House in the evening, when my ticket was presented to me.

On the 6th January, 1816, I proceeded by Dumfries and Moffat to Edinburgh, and from thence by Laurencekirk to Aberdeen. At Laurencekirk I paid a visit to a famous manufacturer of snuffboxes. I inquired if he had any for sale. He was quite indignant, and replied that the demand was so great that he never had one in his shop for sale, nor could I see one anywhere. However, on passing near something like a plate-warmer standing in front of the fireplace, I by some accident gave it a jog, and out popped some half-dozen boxes. He got over his former assertion by stating that they were all bespoken, and that he had placed them there to dry the last coat of varnish before sending them off. I arrived at my father's house on the 16th January. Here I received a letter from the secretary at war, enclosing an order for £120, "blood-money" for my wound, which after all he was obliged to grant, as I had made my case appear so clear before the medical board.

Having always a passion for travelling, and never having been in France, I resolved to take a trip to that country, which was then particularly interesting to a military man, as our army of occupation had at the moment taken up a position on the frontier after the campaign of Paris. I sailed from Aberdeen on the 3rd April 1816 The following day was very stormy. We observed a sloop running down upon us. It appeared they were in distress, and were endeavouring to run aboard of us to save themselves. Our captain, on observing this, put up his helm and stood off, to avoid them. As soon as the sloop passed, he bore up and lay to. Five or six men on board the sloop were screaming for assistance. We tied a buoy to a rope and it drifted under the bow. While some men endeavoured with a boat-hook to catch hold of it, others stripped off their jackets, preparing to swim. The sloop gave a lurch, and, melancholy to relate, in an instant down she went with every soul on board. We moved about over the place, but all in vain; we could see no one, and it was blowing so hard that no boat could have lived.

On the 9th we reached London, and I was recommended by Dr. Guthrie to go to a lodging-house kept by Miss Inverarity in Sackville Street. I left London with a French passport on the 18th April, crossed from Dover on the following day, and in three hours reached Calais. It appeared to me that the loyalty manifested was in general assumed, and that there was a strong and general, though smothered, feeling in favour of the late government. The general feeling of a people may be estimated from small incidents as well as from public demonstrations. On paying my bill on the 21st at Abbeville, I handed two *louis d'ors* to the landlady. On receiving them she said, *"Mais, Monsieur, est ce que vous n'avez pas des Napoleons?"*

I said, "Why! is not your king a very good one?"

She shrugged her shoulders, saying, *"Qu'il est bon! qu'il est grand! qu'il est gros!"*

At Amiens on the paper of the wall of the public room where we waited until the horses were changed were views of Paris, amongst others the triumphal arch of the Tuilleries and the Place du Carousel, in which were represented the Venetian horses. Some English person had written opposite to them with a pencil, *"Ils sont partis."* A Frenchman no sooner read this than he wrote under it, *"Pour retourner sans doute."* I was much tempted to add *"J'en doute."*

Paris was at this moment like the lull in a storm. Although the winds which had put the waves in motion had ceased, the troubled waters were still in agitation. The king was restored; but the revolution only slumbered, ready to break out, as it has done ever since. I stayed a fortnight in Paris, after which, on the 6th May, 1816, I set out for Cambrai. Cambrai, the headquarters of the Duke of Wellington, which I reached next day. At the *table d'hôte* there were several French gentlemen, some French officers in coloured clothes, and one or two of the National Guard. Of course there was great diversity of opinions. Some of the civilians said the English were a stupid, dull set, possessing no gaiety or life. The merchants complained that the English had all their luxuries supplied by their own suttlers from England, and that they took their French additional pay, but spent scarcely a *franc* in the place. The officers maintained a mortified silence, while the National Guards, being royalists, talked highly of the English strength and power. This so enraged one of the civilians that he exclaimed: *"Nôtre seul province de Picardie les égorgerait tous dans un moment!"*

I passed through an encampment of Cossacks, and arrived at Valenciennes, where I met a fine young man—a French officer—who had been dreadfully wounded at Waterloo. I also met a lady who was charged with the important mission of carrying a little cur pet dog from Bernadotte to Louis XVIII. On the 8th May I passed over the field of Gemappes, and entered Mons. I arrived at Brussels the same evening. On the 14th I visited the field of Waterloo.

Even in those early days of the union of Belgium and Holland, great discontent prevailed. I talked with the driver of the cabriolet going to Waterloo. He grumbled sadly at the disgrace suffered by Belgium in not being made an independent State. He said that when they were united to France, they had only one frontier and only one customhouse duty to pay, but now they were hemmed in between two fires. The Dutch, although supposed to be now of the same nation, would not allow them to have an article without passing their line of customhouses and paying duty, while France had also established her customhouses all along her frontier.

On the 21st May I passed through Malines to Antwerp. Next day I crossed the Scheldt, and proceeding through the Tete de Flandre, arrived at Ghent in the afternoon. On the 25th I went by canal to Bruges. My mother, my aunts, and my own sisters having been educated at the English convent at Bruges, and being aware the altar of the convent church was composed of curious marble work, I went to pay a visit to the convent. On mentioning to the lay-sister showing the chapel the circumstance of my family having been educated in the house, she informed the nuns. The lady abbess very politely invited me into the parlour, and mentioned that Sir Richard Bedingfeld was going to dine there, and she begged me that I would come to meet him. I, of course, accepted the invitation. The party consisted of Sir Richard, the chaplain, and myself; while one of the nuns, *a member of one of the oldest noble families in England,* stood by to see that the elderly lay-sister treated us with due hospitality. We afterwards retired to the parlour, where the lady abbess, a few nuns, and some young lady boarders received us, and where coffee and sweetmeats were served.

On the 26th May I proceeded to Ostend by canal, and on the 28th set out for Dunkerque, passing through Neuport. At Furnes, it being high water, I was delayed until the tide fell to allow us to pass along the sands. I took luncheon at the *table d'hote*. The company was composed principally of Belgians and refugee French officers. From my not joining at first in conversation, they did not know I was British. They were carrying on a curious discussion on the merits of English cavalry. We proceeded on our journey, and on an imaginary line forming the frontier of France, on the sea beach, we were stopped by one or two French customhouse officers, who came down from the benty heights, but a few civil words and a few *sous* put matters right, and we were allowed to proceed. We arrived at Dunkerque at night, and next day, the 29th May, we passed through Gravelines, and reached Calais in the afternoon.

I had been recommended to go to the Lion d'Or Hotel at Calais, kept by Mr. Oakshott, an Englishman. I found there Major Rogers of the artillery, Captain Christie, who had been *aide-de-*

camp to General Ponsonby, who was killed at Waterloo, and Captain Kerr, formerly of the 15th Hussars. After dinner they were talking about the Honourable Mr. Stanhope of the 12th Dragoons, who, having had a gambling transaction at Paris with young Lord Beauchamp of not a very creditable nature, had disappeared from the army without leave. In the midst of the conversation, to the surprise of all, the honourable gentleman appeared, entering the porch of the inn yard accompanied by a dashing-looking female and a young miss about sixteen years of age, who was leading a little child by the hand. On the following day we observed this young female sauntering about the passages and corridors, apparently playing with the youngster.

About two o'clock in the morning of the 30th May I awoke, hearing somebody quitting my room. I called out, "Who is there?" but got no answer. I heard footsteps descending the stairs, and a door bang as if in the basement story. I kept listening. Soon afterwards I heard someone stepping upstairs again. I then heard much conversation carried on in the room immediately beneath my bedroom. All at once an alarm was given. The house-bells began to ring in the most violent manner, and shouts of "Waiter!" resounded in the passages. I jumped out of bed and ran to the staircase, where I beheld the honourable gentleman's fair companion *en dishabille,* with her hair hanging about her face, in seeming distress, calling out, "I am robbed! I am robbed of all my jewels and money!"

Ere I had time to understand what she meant, other doors flew open, and people hastened with surprise from all quarters, screaming, "What is the matter? What is the matter?"

On our demanding *what was* the matter, the lady said that while she was lying in bed, and the young girl and child in another bed, a man had entered her chamber, taken her keys from the table, and opened her trunk; but not finding what he expected there, he also opened her portmanteau and took all her jewels, with fifty sovereigns in gold. That although she was awake, she was too frightened to speak, but that the instant he left the room she gave the alarm by ringing the bell. We were much astonished, but not less so on beholding one another, for, being midsummer, there was light enough for us to discern that some were only in their shirts, some with loose cassocks, some with drawers, some in petticoats, all bare-legged, and heads adorned with nightcaps; but the honourable gentleman came *completely dressed,* saying *he* had also been robbed of some crowns and five-*franc* pieces.

After sympathising with the unfortunate fair one, I began to have some misgivings lest I might possibly be a fellow-sufferer, remembering the circumstance of someone slipping out of my room, and I hurried back to my room. I remembered previously to going to bed putting my purse with about thirty Napoleons on the dressing-table, over which I laid a Russian leather pocket-book, containing my passport, both covered by a handkerchief, and on the top I had placed a beautiful, fine cairngorm brooch, set in gold. This and the pocket-book were gone, but the purse remained, while a large portmanteau was also carried off. I lost no time in descending to find out the landlord. I found the Swiss porter asleep. On awakening him and relating the circumstances, he said nobody could have gone out, and he produced the key of the outer door, which was concealed under his bedclothes. He opened the kitchen door, and to our astonishment there was my portmanteau and that of the lady, both lying empty, and all their contents strewed about the floor. The kitchen window was raised about a foot. Mr. Oakshott made his appearance by another door. We agreed before anything was touched that the commissary of police should be sent for, as suspicions began to arise that all was not right regarding our honourable countryman, who, being the only one of us dressed, proposed himself to go for the police. Some objections were made; however, he insisted on going. Suspicions were increased by the young girl declaring that the lady had not lost so much as she had declared. She said, "Oh, no! she has not. I know better than she. She has not lost so much."

I also recollected having heard a long conversation in her room before the bell rang, which was contrary to the statement she had made, and also that the little miss had been exploring all about the rooms on the previous day. The manservant also stated that she had been very inquisitive.

On the arrival of the police officer he paraded all the persons in the hotel. The lady and I set to work in his presence, each taking what belonged to us respectively. I found that not an article of my clothes had been taken. The only thing missing out of the portmanteau was a silver breastplate of the 29th Regiment, which I had worn in all the actions in which that corps had been engaged during the Peninsular war. The lady still insisted that her valuables were gone. It seemed that the object of the thieves was cash and valuables; and as notes of the Bank of England were then common in France, they had taken my pocket-book, thinking it contained banknotes. We not seeing Captain Kerr, someone said, "Let us go and tell him."

On entering his room we found it in great disorder, while he was still asleep. On awakening him, he found that his gold watch and valuable chain, his purse, and his pocket-book were gone. The drawer of the dressing-glass, containing many trinkets and his Waterloo medal, was also carried off. While we were condoling with him, the landlord entered with a handkerchief containing one hundred Napoleons, which he had fortunately given him the previous day to keep for him. The commissary, on learning all the particulars, also entertained suspicions of these personages, and he placed spies to watch their motions. We all resolved not to quit the house until some solution of this mysterious robbery transpired. The honourable gentleman, however, and his female friends made preparations to start for Boulogne, and the police sent off their agents also; and just as they were driving out of the yard they were stopped. The police carried all their baggage into the hotel again and searched it. They found the lady in possession of the valuables which she declared she had lost, but as they found none of the stolen articles upon them, they allowed them to proceed, sending a police agent to watch them.

Part 5

1816–1832

I arrived at Dover after a passage of five hours on the 1st June, 1816. The tide not being sufficiently high to admit of the packet entering the harbour, we landed in an open boat, without seeing a Custom-house or Revenue officer of any kind. We might have smuggled to any amount. Next morning, as we were getting on the coach, I observed a smart, active, ladylike little woman busily engaged in superintending the stowing away of baggage in a travelling carriage. The same carriage, with four horses, overtook us before we reached Canterbury. The lady put her head out of the window, and nodded, saying, "I'll give you the go-by, and will be in London before you." This was the Countess of Clare.

On arriving in London I learned that the eighth battalion of the 60th Rifles was to be reduced, but by my seniority in the list of captains in the regiment it would only have the effect of removing me to another battalion. I waited on our Colonel, Sir James Kempt, who very kindly arranged at the Horse Guards that my leave of absence should be extended until the reduction took place, as the men were to be drafted to the fifth, or rifle battalion, which had then gone out to Gibraltar.

On the 13th June I sailed from London on board a smack, arrived at Aberdeen on the 20th, and found my brother James home from Jamaica.

I got notice to repair to London early in July. On the 6th July I sailed from Aberdeen, and arrived in London on the 13th. On going to the Horse Guards, the Adjutant-General was kind enough to give me the choice of any of the seven battalions of the 60th Regiment. I chose the second battalion, then in Canada; but afterwards meeting a friend of mine intimate with the Earl of Dalhousie, who was appointed governor of Nova Scotia, he urged me to go there, saying he was sure his lordship would show me every attention, as he would get the Marquis of H—— to give me letters of introduction. I accordingly got permission at the Horse Guards to exchange with a captain who wished to go to Canada.

On the 12th August, 1816, I proceeded with another captain to Gravesend, where the *Royal Charlotte*, his majesty's ship, was lying. She not being ready to sail as reported, we were obliged to remain at the Inn. We embarked on the 19th, and sailed for the Isle of Wight. On the 23rd, we arrived at Cowes. The same afternoon the detachment, consisting of a few men and a number of officers and their families, embarked, a large part of the hold being fitted up for their accommodation. A number of officers and myself, having a choice of quarters, agreed to mess with the captain, and we had a magnificent cabin and a jolly party.

We arrived at Halifax, North America, on the 26th September, 1816. I reported myself to Lieutenant-Colonel Bouvere, an old Frenchman, commanding the second battalion, which had arrived a short time before from the West Indies. Never in the annals of military records or arms was such a battalion seen. From the regiment having been raised to serve exclusively in America, they were termed the Royal Americans; and an act having been passed declaring the West Indian Islands in that continent, it became, from there being no chance of ever serving in England, to all intents and purposes a condemned corps. Hence there was no difficulty in anyone getting a commission in it. Young men of money or interest on getting a commission in the regiment, or obtaining promotion in it, were always certain that they could effect an exchange into some other more select corps which wished to get quietly rid of a black sheep. The number of battalions also increased the evil. When an officer committed a misdemeanour, he was permitted to try his luck by exchanging with an officer of another battalion, who, perhaps, was obliged to do so under similar circumstances. If one might judge of the subaltern officers of the second battalion when I joined it, the majority seemed the concentration of all the worst from the others, and the men were old drunkards who had spent their best days in the West Indies. There were several officers under arrest for every crime in the calendar of Newgate. These officers dared their commanding officer B—— to bring them to trial, alleging that they would produce charges of embezzlement against himself.

This was a pretty prospect for me. I could have got transferred to the seventh battalion, which had been raised on the same principle as the eighth, fine, steady, men, and all the officers either persons who had distinguished themselves in the Peninsular War, or of the best families in England. Sir George Murray was the colonel of this battalion of Rifles, and a better appointed regiment was not to be found in any service, but they were under orders to be reduced, as their predecessors the eighth had been. This was a great mistake. Had these two battalions been kept up, by merely changing their numbers to first and second, and the ill-organised battalions disbanded, an immense improvement would have been made, and a decidedly more effective force preserved. The light company of the second battalion was a rifle company, and the colonel, fortunately for me, and without any solicitation on my part, put me in orders as its commanding officer, as the duty and exercise were different from those of the battalion. Being aware that in a few months the contemplated reduction would sweep away the seventh battalion, I became more reconciled to my situation, particularly as the Earl of Dalhousie, the governor, had been pleased to show me particular attention.

The first province which I had the good fortune to visit was Nova Scotia: the very name at once endeared it to me as an old friend reminding me of my native land. Nor was I disappointed on further acquaintance with my transatlantic country, having the gratification of finding that this infant state was making rapid strides in improvement, under the benevolent sway of an excellent nobleman, the Earl of Dalhousie. Trade was rapidly reviving: agriculture, long neglected, received a new impetus, and started into vigorous activity by the wisdom of his lordship's measures and the energy of his administration; while, under the influence of his amiable and intelligent countess, society took a higher and more polished tone, and many institutions for charitable purposes or feminine instruction were founded, promoted, or improved.

I reached these western shores after the intense heats of summer had subsided, succeeded by bright sunshine and serene cloudless skies. This period is aptly termed the Indian summer; because during this benignant season these wild hunters roam their native forests and more distant prairies, in search of those fierce animals which afford the richest peltries. By this trade these children of nature supply their wants for the long winter, procure objects of luxury for the nobles of Europe, and comfortable trappings for the natives of all ranks, against the severity of the inclement season. The appearance of the country during this period is remarkably beautiful. The sharp nocturnal frosts, changing the verdant foliage of the extensive forests, produce the richest and most variegated tints, in which orange and red predominate. Winter now advances apace; the transition is most rapid: to the surprise of the stranger, he finds some night in October that the snow has fallen, covering fields and forests to an immense depth. After a few days the sky becomes again serene—the sun recovers his wonted brilliancy; and with the exception of some occasional interruptions, and some additional falls of snow at times, so continues until the month of April.

A general metamorphosis in the appearance of dress, costumes, and equipages now takes place; but the Canadian cold, although very intense, is in reality but little felt, so excellent are the arrangements within doors and without for obviating its effects. Furs in the shape of caps, car-covers, cloaks, and gloves, in addition to those articles of the material usually worn by European *belles*, come into universal requisition; with snow-boots made of carpet stuff of the gayest colours, for driving, or moccasins and creepers for walking. These moccasins are made of a sort of chamois leather, prepared in a particular manner by the Indians, and neatly embroidered in fancy figures, with porcupine quills of brilliant colours. These have the advantage of being light, and at the same time of keeping the feet remarkably warm; and being in some degree impervious to water, one may walk in the snow without the risk of getting damp feet. The creepers are flat pieces of iron, with sharp prongs under each end, and are fastened on with straps, like a spur, which enables one to walk with ease on the most slippery paths. All wheeled carriages are now abandoned. Sleighs of elegant forms are introduced, single and double, handsomely and comfortably fitted up with hanging robes of bear, tiger, or lynx skins, having a large buffalo hide or cover over all. The whole of these are neatly ornamented with scarlet borders, fringes, &c., with the heads and claws of the ferocious animals dangling around; so that the lover or his rival may literally have a lynx-eyed monster constantly staring him in the face, as if watching his diversions. These sleighs, filled with *élégantes* and driven by monstrous-looking exquisites, muffled up to the eyes, are seen dashing along at a wonderful pace, some drawn by one horse, others by two, either abreast or tandem. They glide along so smoothly, that, in order to give warning of their approach, bells are attached to the horses' heads, the tinkling of which has a lively and pleasant effect. Invalids and families going to evening parties have their close carriages removed from the wheels and placed on runners.

Many of the best houses, being built entirely of wood, might be imagined to be cold and comfortless; but, extraordinary as it may appear, they are much drier and warmer in winter and cooler in summer than those built of stone, which is accounted for by the stratum of air which occupies the vacant spaces between the outside clap-boards on the frame and the inside lining of lath and plaster. This prevents the great heat in summer from entering, and the warmth created inside in winter from escaping. The plan adopted to counteract the effects of the intense frost is very effective, and is accomplished by having a large stove in the entrance-hall, the flues of which are conducted by the staircase to the top of the house. One never feels chilled in going along passages or from one chamber to another.

The brilliant winter had now seriously commenced; society began its merry sway; feasting and amusements became the only possible occupations. The labours of agriculture were at a stand—all military exercises had ceased—the course of busy trade and commerce was frozen up, but the stream of warm-hearted hospitality, in seeming inverse ratio to the intensity of the weather, began to overflow. Many of the inhabitants who were very wealthy, kept up a constant round of entertainments, dinners, balls, &c., in continued succession. The festivities at the government house were on the most liberal and extended scale. His excellency held *levees* on certain public days, and gave two public dinners each week, to which the civil authorities were invited in rotation; while her ladyship had generally a public night once a week, exclusive of grand balls and suppers on particular occasions. Nor did these public festivities interrupt their own private society: they saw a numerous circle of friends in a constant succession of dinners, musical soirees, quadrille parties, &c. These were very select, including various young noblemen, who happened to be doing duty with their corps, or in vessels of war on the station. Admiral G——, with Lady W——, the commissioner, the bishop, the secretary of the province, and numerous heads of departments, gave frequent and most agreeable parties. Nor did the judges of the land fail to contribute to the general harmony, as everyone well knows who has enjoyed the acquaintance of the Honourable Judge Haliburton, whose flow of wit enlivened every society. The military and navy, resolved not to be deemed ungrateful, gave occasional *fêtes de bal,* exclusive of frequent entertainments during the winter. The harbour being frozen over, the ships of war were prepared accordingly for the rigour of the season, being brought close to the wharfs, and covered in by wooden sheds erected over them, with stoves placed in various parts, so as not only to render them comfortable habitations, but also scenes of gaiety, by occasional performances of amateur plays and fancy balls.

All these parties were graced and enlivened by the presence of many of our fair countrywomen and their American sisters. The latter proved as amiable as they are famed for personal charms. They are endowed with great natural abilities and lively dispositions. Many are extremely well-informed—all are eager in search of information; and though absorbed too much in local ideas and provincial habits, they are, in general, by no means deficient in polite feeling and gentle manners. Many, on returning from visits to England or France, had attained the elegant acquirements and easy good-breeding of the most refined sphere of life. Halifax may justly pride itself on the beauty of its daughters. They have fine complexions, lit up by soft blue eyes. Their peculiar charms of countenance have been attributed to the humidity of the climate, which is liable to frequent fogs during summer; and it certainly would appear that this dampness of atmosphere does impart a softness and clearness of complexion to the female features, as may be observed under similar circumstances in the sweet faces of our own Devonshire and Lancashire witches. But, however much the peculiarity of this transatlantic climate may tend to improve the features, it is, unfortunately, not attended with the same permanent effects as in England. It seems rather to have a fatal influence: a premature decay of teeth and youthful bloom indicates that beauty here too often proves, indeed, a fading flower.

Intellectual amusements were not wanting during the prolonged and dreary season. Amongst others, an excellent amateur theatre under the patronage of the Countess of Dalhousie was established for weekly performances. It was admirably conducted under the skilful management of Colonel C——. It boasted of many artists, whose superior dramatic powers would have enabled them to shine as first-rate actors on any stage. Amongst the many were the distinguished Sir E. Parry, Captain Beechy, and, alas! poor Joe Bowers. He, merry soul! a middy in vessel commanded by Lord J. H——, possessed talents of the most humorous, comical cast. It was said that he was foster-brother to the Princess Charlotte, and—a coincidence indeed—he was cut off by a fit of apoplexy on the very day that closed upon all that was earthly of that lamented princess.

The morning amusements generally consisted in large assemblages of fashionables uniting in sleighing parties and driving through various parts of the city. Lady Dalhousie used to patronise this sport very much—frequently making up parties to visit some of the romantic lakes in the vicinity, where the ice is generally smooth as glass. These excursions afford such health and pleasure, that, although the rigour of the season may pinch the toes or freeze a finger—though even a nose may be frost-bitten—there are no cold hearts.

Many a matrimonial union has commenced on these icy expeditions; and one case which had taken an untoward turn was brought to a successful conclusion in an extraordinary manner. A gallant major had been very attentive in offering a place in his elegant cariole to the beautiful Miss B——: the offer was always accepted. This daily attention went on for a great part of the season: however, rumours reached the family that the gay Lothario was about to take his departure for England. The mamma became alarmed; the young lady was in despair. The major was called to an account by the sons, who demanded, of course, what his intentions were. He declared that his only motive had been common politeness in return for the many friendly civilities he had experienced from the family. The major was denounced as a false man, abused and cut by the ladies, who unanimously took part with the disappointed fair one. It happened one day, he having occasion to pass the house, that his horse must needs bring up at the door, according to the established custom. The major whipped, swore, pulled, and tugged, but all without effect. The obstinate brute was determined not to budge; he could not be flogged out of his sense of the fact that there he was to stop. This ludicrous difference of opinion between the horse and his master brought the ladies to the windows, the servants to the door, and the old gentleman at last to offer assistance. This awkward dilemma and a pitiless snowstorm induced the major to take the proffered shelter. So much kindness awakened his slumbering and tender sympathies. The former friendly intercourse was renewed, and he soon afterwards became a Benedict, blest with a lovely wife. *Match-makers may take a lesson from the instinct of a horse.*

The ladies in the transatlantic provinces, but more especially amongst their neighbours in the United States, have decidedly the advantage of the gentlemen in personal appearance and manners. The lords and masters of these charming fair ones, however acute their understandings, however sharp-witted they may be in driving a bargain, are not endowed in general with any very particular personal attributes. Mistaking familiarity for easy address, they assume, without, I believe, meaning to be offensive, an abrupt, blunt style of independence; and, having had little or no experience in the great world, they are often conceited and opinionative. It is needless to remark that they are proverbially inquisitive and curious in prying into the affairs of others, constantly thinking, not only for themselves, but also for you—by eternally *guessing* or *expecting* that you are this or that, or going hither or thither. All these blemishes arise from their secluded situation. Local habits and the democratic state of society are consequently their misfortune rather than their fault, for they possess many sterling John Bull qualities—high patriotism, undaunted bravery, enterprising dispositions, and determined perseverance in overcoming difficulties; they are most ingenious in contrivances, handy at all work, and frequently hospitable and kind-hearted to strangers. Numbers, however, who have visited Europe have acquired more extended notions, and attained the polished manners and address of well-bred gentlemen. Many of the British-born inhabitants are no exceptions to some of the above observations: having left the mother country in search of fortune, they began the world with but small means, and, by industry and enterprise, particularly during the war, as prize agents, accumulated considerable wealth. But while some retain their former simplicity of manners, others, not a little purse-proud, endeavour to ape those of more refined attainments; their original ideas and habits, however, and their *parvenu* style are but too evident. The members of the house of parliament, who are principally returned from the different settlements, are of all classes. Many are shrewd, well-meaning men, while others are of a very original cast. As an illustration of the manners and habits of the latter, the following may suffice:

At one of the entertainments usually given by the governor to the members, one of these representatives was disappointed at not getting "sling"—cold water and rum—to drink at dinner in place of wine, according to Yankee usage. On the finger-basins being placed on the table, he, immediately imagining that this was his favourite beverage, hastily seized the glass and gulped down the pure contents. Horror-stricken to find that it was an entirely aqueous element, and mortified at his mistake, he, with a strong expression of surprise, looked round to the servant, and, handing back the empty vessel, said: "My friend, when you bring me that again, do not forget to put a little rum into it."

In no country does there exist a greater degree of nationality maintained with more fervour than in these our colonies. This is especially the case with the Scotch and Irish, or their descendants. The Scotch, imbued with an innate love of country, never forget their native land and its social recollections. They cherish these with the fondest affection; and the festival day of their patron, St. Andrew, is commemorated with all due honour. The Scotch Society, instituted for benevolent purposes, and of infinite benefit to thousands of poor emigrants, celebrates this occasion with a festive dinner, at which his excellency the governor and all the authorities assist. None of the essentials requisite to constitute a true *Auld Lang Syne* feast are omitted; nor is St. Patrick's Day less splendidly commemorated by the warm-hearted Irish: indeed the enthusiasm displayed on this anniversary is not exceeded in old Ireland itself.

Notwithstanding the rigour of the winter, the *munition de bouche* and all the requisites for good living are in no part of the world more plentifully found, more varied in kind, more excellent in quality, or more reasonable in price, than in this province at all seasons of the year. Halifax being a free port, one may command, in addition to the necessaries the country affords and the good things imported from England, the choicest fruits and wines of France, Portugal, Madeira, &c., which are the common beverage; while the West Indies supply numerous luxuries, such as turtle, pineapples, preserves, &c., sufficient to satiate the palate of the most distinguished *gourmand*.

The gaieties of the merry season are unfortunately at times attended with gravities. Many of the houses, being of wood, are liable to accidents from fire. How often after a ball, perhaps at the dead hour of night, have our peaceful slumbers been disturbed by the bugle sounding the alarm, accompanied by piercing cries of fire from the inhabitants. On such distressing occasions the military must instantly turn out, which is done with surprising alacrity; and were it not for their timely and skilful assistance most serious damage to the town but too often might accrue, as not only single houses but even the whole side of a street may be in flames; and the heat is frequently so intense, that even the opposite side will suddenly burst into flames. The great misery is that these calamities almost always occur in winter, owing to the number of stoves and flues required in that season. It becomes a most severe duty to the soldiers to hand the water along, often from a great distance, while the thermometer is usually far below zero. I have seen a bucket of water dashed at an idle looker-on who refused to work. He was instantly covered with a crust or coat of icy armour, and appeared glittering in the silvery light of the moon, like an ancient chivalrous knight in his midnight watchings.

About April the welcome spring bounds in at a leap. To the frigid cold a genial warmth suddenly supervenes, succeeded by a rapid thaw. This transition and the pleasing change in the face of nature are most extraordinary: dormant vegetation revives, the ground is quickly covered with luxuriant herbage of the richest verdure, trees bud and blossom in an incredibly short space of time, and are in full foliage ere the snow has disappeared from the valleys or places shaded from the sun, which has now a most powerful influence, and before another month has passed over summer has commenced. Sportsmen lose no time in resuming their rural diversions. Picnics and fishing parties to the beautiful sequestered lakes, where the finest red trout imaginable afford excellent sport, become frequent, and were so much the fashion that a regular club was established, under the patronage of the Earl of Dalhousie and the gallant Admiral Sir D. Milne. Many scions of noble blood, valiant knights and baronets, were amongst its members, including Lords R——, M——, John H——, Frederick Lennox, Henry The——, Schomberg Kerr, &c., the gallant Sir J. G——, Sir J. L——, &c. This agreeable reunion continued for several seasons. Never was there a more harmonious or a better regulated social meeting. A bivouac was erected or a marquee pitched in some romantic spot; dinners and choice beverages were provided, and so much were the vocal powers of the members in requisition that the cognomen of the "Tol de Rol" club was unanimously adopted. One member, the worthy and witty Mr. Lawson, who had in his youth spent much of his time when engaged in the for trade with the wild tribes of Indians in the forest, used to entertain us with a representation of the terrific war-song and dance of death as practised by those savages previous to their scalping a victim. So entirely did he enter into the spirit of the exhibition that, in imitating their wild caperings, ferocious gestures, low gruntings and yells, he worked himself apparently into a frenzy, and, when sufficiently excited to consummate the tragedy, would conclude, at the expense of some of the new members or strangers, by suddenly seizing one by the hair of the head and running his finger round the scalp, much to their horror and astonishment. A most ludicrous scene of this kind occurred with a Scotch piper, who had attended to play after dinner. He was exhibiting the musical powers of his noisy chanter, and strutting about with much national pride, when Mr. Lawson commenced his savage display. The child of the mountains was at first much delighted, and seemed flattered, thinking the dancing was inspired by his sonorous strains; but when he himself became the object of the practical part of the scalping operation, the poor piper, surprised and horror-struck, uttered a piercing shriek, came to the ground as if he had actually been felled by a murderous tomahawk, and had he not been overcome with faintness through fright, he no doubt would have fled, abandoning his dear pipes, bonnet, and all, to the mercy of the good-humoured member who had so unceremoniously assailed him.

As a consequence of the reduction of the 60th Regiment from eight battalions to two, I came within the sphere of reduction. Being about to be placed on half-pay, my name disappeared from the Army List in December, 1819; and my gallant friend, Sir James Gordon (Wardhouse), who was about to proceed to England, had been kind enough to offer me a passage in his cabin, which I gladly accepted; but Lord Dalhousie said, with his usual kindness, that as the officer had not arrived to replace me, and there were so few captains to do duty, he would take the responsibility of delaying my departure, as something might turn up in the meantime to my advantage. He had already sent to the Horse Guards my memorial and statement of services, with a strong recommendation for their favourable consideration, and he accordingly put me in general orders to remain.

However, in a few months afterwards, in June, 1820, the Earl of Dalhousie was appointed governor-general of Canada; and on his being relieved of the command in Halifax by Sir James Kempt, he was kind enough to ask me what I wished to do, or what he could do for me. I then begged to be allowed to go home in the first packet, which was readily granted.

We sailed in the *Cambden,* Captain Tilly, and although my companions were not numerous, they were rather extraordinary. One was Ramee Samee, the famous Indian juggler; another was a squat, stout, Irish friar, who had been stationed as a missionary in Newfoundland, but as he had shown a great propensity to hoard up the mammon of iniquity, and had realised a large sum contrary to the rules of his order, the bishop had suspended him, and ordered him to refund a due proportion to the poor fishermen from whose earnings he had acquired his ill-gotten wealth.

He was on his way to some convent in Europe to do penance for his offence. Ramee was very particular in inquiring at the steward every day before he touched any meat, to know whether it was beef or not, that being prohibited food for him. The steward, aware of his religious prejudices, invariably swore that every bullock was a lamb, but Ramee, in case of accidents, had laid in a private stock of pickled salmon, fruit, &c.

After a pleasant enough voyage, as we were approaching the land, I observed that all our common ware was changed into sets of the very richest real china, and that the captain's wife, who was on board, was daily getting stouter and stouter. She seemed to be rapidly getting on in a most thriving way. We at length arrived at Falmouth, on the 16th July, 1820. Previous to my departure, I called at the captain's house to thank him for his civilities while on board. I found his wife amazingly altered. All her *en bon point* had disappeared. The mystery was explained by looking round the room. There lay about Indian muslins, &c., and the superb china was displayed. She had managed to pass £500 worth of valuables without any inquisitive customhouse officer offering to inquire for his majesty's duty.

We proceeded to Plymouth, through Penryn and Truro. The heath and stone walls of Cornwall put me in mind of old Caledonia. Being acquainted with some of the engineer officers in the garrison, I had been viewing the works, and it being warm, they requested me to enter the mess-room and take a glass of wine and water. On handing me a newspaper, the very first article which I looked at was my own name in the *Gazette,* as having been brought in on full pay into my corps again, in exchange with another captain. This was an unexpected good fortune for me, particularly as it was without my giving a difference. The captain next above me had a short time before given £500 to come in again on full pay.

On the 20th July, I went to London. On waiting on the military secretary, the amiable Sir H. Taylor, to thank him for my reappointment, he said that he was happy in having had it in his power to serve me, but that he was not entitled to all the merit, and that I must wait on H.R.H. the Duke of York, as the person to whom I owed my good fortune. Accordingly, the next levee day I did myself that honour. His royal highness was most gracious, giving me a very flattering reception, and he said that the report of my services and the recommendations of the generals under whom I had served had entitled me to his favourable notice. He was also pleased to give me six months' leave of absence.

Having it in my choice either to return to the second battalion of the 60th Regiment at Halifax or to join the first battalion in Canada, I preferred the latter, being most anxious to visit that part of America. On the 12th May I sailed for London, and arrived there on the 18th; I then proceeded to the Isle of Wight. On the 9th June, a troopship being prepared, I got the command of 200 men, principally Germans, for our battalion, and about the same number for the other regiments in Canada, and embarked at Cowes.

We sailed from Cowes on the 11th dune, 1821, and entered the Gulf of St. Lawrence on the 30th. After entering the Gulf of St. Lawrence, and passing the barren Isle of Anticosti, the dark mountains above Gaspe are discerned on the left, the first original settlement of the French in these northern regions. As one continues to ascend, the shores become perceptible on either hand, indicating that we are now on the magnificent river St. Lawrence. At intervals we pass numerous rich, fertile, and verdant islands, while the country on the left hand, being cleared of wood, and dotted with white villages glittering in the noonday sun, from the roofs of the buildings and the steeples of the churches being covered with tin, presents a smiling and lively appearance, particularly Ramaraska, which is a fashionable resort as a bathing quarter. On rounding the upper point of the Island of Orleans, a perfect garden in itself, one beholds one of the finest views that the world affords. On the right is the stupendous fall of Montmorenci, the immense volume of water dropping like a curtain two hundred feet perpendicular. In front Quebec is seen gradually rising from the water in the form of an amphitheatre, with its cathedral, churches spires, convents, the castle of St. Louis, and the commanding citadel on its rocky site, frowning defiance. The town is situated on a point of land formed by the junction of the river St. Charles with the St. Lawrence. From the low marshy bed of the former the land rapidly recedes until it reaches the citadel posted on an elevated rocky summit, which on the other side is almost perpendicular down to the St. Lawrence, which washes its base. The grand river is here much narrowed by

Point Levi, which juts out, so that it is scarcely one mile broad. On landing at the commodious wharf in the lower town, the curious traveller threads his way up the declivities and steep streets to the higher regions, where the seat of government is, and wealth and fashion hold their sway.

On gaining the citadel, which is constructed on the most approved principle of fortification, the stranger is amply gratified by a most extensive view of splendid scenery. Looking to the north-east, he beholds the city lying at his feet: on the right hand, far below, he looks down on the grand river covered with vessels, and Point Levi, on the opposite shore, covered with villas and gardens. On the left hand he surveys in the distance the blue mountains beyond the river St. Charles, covered with elevated forests, while from their base to the environs of the town he contemplates a finely cultivated country adorned with pleasant seats. On turning round and looking west, the scene of Wolfe's triumph lies before him. There are the plains of Abraham, now under cultivation, and at some distance beyond is a capital race-course. In short, the surrounding romantic scenery may be equalled, but certainly not exceeded either by Naples or Edinburgh. The town is also worthy of notice. The fortifications, as far as nature and art can make them, are most imposing, and almost impregnable. The streets are regular, the houses chiefly of stone, and painted, which gives a lively appearance to the place. Quebec being the seat of government, the presence of the governor-general gives a tone and greater brilliancy to the society than what is usually expected to be met with in the colonies.

I proceeded up the river St. Lawrence in a steamer, and joined the first battalion, 60th Regiment, on the 19th July, 1821, at Montreal.

Montreal is situated on an extensive island formed by the St. Lawrence and a branch of the Ottawa, but in its appearance there is nothing very remarkable. Hospitality has here, as in all parts of America, unbounded sway during the winter. But society is on a different footing, as it is in Canada in general, than in any other part of the New World. It is divided: there are two distinct races—Canadian French, and English or Anglo-American. The former, who are descendants of the original French, and many of them connected with some of the oldest nobility in France, still love to retain the feudal system. These *seigneurs*, with their numerous vassals, cling with extraordinary pertinacity to all the notions, habits, and opinions of the old *régime*. As lords of the soil, they cannot brook the idea of becoming traders; nor will they in general over condescend to mix with the sons of commerce; while the latter, being active, adventurous, and enterprising, are accumulating wealth, acquiring prosperity, and living extravagantly. In all mercantile communities wealth constitutes a patent of nobility: hence all here who are rich, or by a profuse style of living appear to he so, are deemed fashionables and *haut ton,* and eclipse the old *noblesse*—however inferior in lineage, manners, and address; consequently, heart-burnings, bickerings, and jealousy exist to a serious degree between the two races.

To us, who were birds of passage, it was fun to hear both sides; we enjoyed alternately their good fare, without mixing in the embitterment of party feelings. But from this jarring of interests, I regretted to find that the same benevolent nobleman who had done so much good in Nova Scotia, by whom contentment and prosperity were established and ensured in that province, had been less successful in Canada. His enlightened views were frustrated and counteracted, and measures which would have proved of incalculable advantage to both parties were thwarted by their mutual petty jealousies and unyielding dispositions.

The cold, after the winter is fairly set in, is most intense. I have been out when the temperature was upwards of fifty degrees under zero, but without experiencing any great inconvenience, because the air was perfectly still; but the horses were completely enveloped in a white frosted coating, with long icicles dangling from their nostrils. The beauty of the Canadian sky during this season has been often remarked—a pure, clear, cloudless blue, yet tinged with a golden hue in the afternoon; its richness and softness almost rival the charms and lustre of exquisite Italy. As usual, in these climates, sledging parties constituted one of the principal amusements, and to heighten the enjoyment, dinners and balls were combined with the diversion, under the patronage of the heads of families; the married ladies having the privilege—no doubt in imitation of the lady patronesses at Almack's—to admit the bachelors by vouchers; all vying with each other who should furnish the most savoury viands, the choicest fruits, and the most eligible young men. These, termed country parties, were usually held at a hotel in some of the villages within a few miles of the city; so that we were always certain of a good dinner, a merry dance, and a fair companion in the cariole, during a chilly midnight drive home.

As spring advances, these assemblies are continued in the shape of shad-fishing parties. The proper time is indicated by the appearance of myriads of large brown flies which fill the air; but this plague is of short duration; after a few days they begin to die, and the streets are strewed with them. Parties drive out to the branch of the Ottawa; and there, on the brink of a rapid, the ladies stand to behold the gentlemen with bag-nets attached to a hook, having a long pole for a handle, scooping out at random one or two of these delicate fishes at a time, each perhaps weighing four or five pounds. Dinner, and dancing in a mill, in some sequestered grove in the forest, conclude the sports of the day.

The great *dons* of the place in those days were the "Nor'-Westers," that is, gentlemen who had realised fortunes in the fur trade, or North-West Company. To commemorate the scenes of their youth, they had established a society denominated the "Beaver Club," and, exclusive of all the luxuries money could procure, they treated their friends to a variety of sylvan dainties in the shape of beaver tails, beaver hams, buffalo tongues, &c. After dinner, individuals dressed as Indians enter, holding the *calumet* or pipe of peace, with other symbols of friendship; one addressed the company with a speech, or "talk," in the Indian language, while another went round presenting the pipe to each guest, who had to take a whiff, to demonstrate his good fellowship. Alter this, all the members stand up, in a row on either side of the table, each having a canoe-paddle in his hand, and all join in singing the beautiful Canadian *voyageur* boat-songs in French, keeping time by the motion of the paddle to the varied strains of the tune, as the hardy venturous voyagers are wont to do when descending a rapid, stemming a current, or skimming the still bosom of a romantic lake. On one of these occasions, when the governor-general, the Earl of Dalhousie, was dining at the club, a member, representing an Indian chief, after a complimentary speech, threw down at his lordship's feet a rich full Indian costume, saying, "Father, take that." This magnificent dress was made of whole skins, exquisitely embroidered with stained porcupine quills, and ornamented with the claws, teeth, and nails of the rarest and most ferocious animals, only found in the far interior of this vast continent, while the head-dress was composed of most beautiful feathers, of birds I believe, still unknown to us. The whole, including the arms and weapons, was valued at five hundred pounds; and, what is more remarkable, the tribe from whom it had been procured were so far removed from the haunts of civilised men that they had never seen a European, nor communicated with one, until a few adventurous traders had stumbled upon them in exploring those remote regions.

As nothing can demonstrate more clearly the general feelings of a people than the internal state of society in a country at large, it may be mentioned, to prove how diametrically opposed parties are to each other, that the French Canadians complain that they are kept in the background; that all situations in every department are grasped at by the British, to the prejudice of their rights and liberties; while the British assert that the Canadians want to be independent, and that they hold the British who conquered the country as mere intruders. Which party is right or wrong, it is to determine; but from all I have observed, there is reason to believe that there are faults on both sides, like all other domestic quarrels; and, if remedies are not applied, the consequences may prove fatal to the prosperity of the country. This, however, is certain. So exclusive was the best French society, and so shy of associating with the English, that we seldom met any of them at the houses of the British residents—not even at the select parties of the accomplished Mrs. B——, the lady of a gallant general who fell at the head of his brigade in the Peninsula, and the daughter of the brave veteran Sir W—— J——, so famed in all the wars in America, from General Bradock's affair in 1757, down to the last rupture with the United States, as a leader having great influence over the Indian nations, of whom he was superintendent, and who consequently had done much for Canada—with the exception of a limited number of individuals, including the beautiful Madam P——, and Judge F——, a lively *chevalier* of the old French school, who entertained sumptuously persons of all parties. Many of the ladies, both English and French, are in this climate particularly handsome. The latter retain all their native vivacity of manner peculiar to French women; but they seldom study the English language even as an elegant accomplishment, much less do they acquire it as a necessary means of intercourse. Hence all the *beaux* who speak French are preferred, and become peculiar favourites; but intermarriages with British are almost unknown. The only instances of any note are the Baroness of L'Isle, who married a Scotch gentleman, and the charming young Marquise de T———, who gave her heart and hand to Mr. B——— B———, a person of great wealth, having large stake in the English funds, and princely possessions in the United States, which perhaps occasioned an exception in his favour.

The only point of resemblance in manners between the two parties is adopted from the French. It is the custom on New Year's Day for the gentlemen to visit all their acquaintances, and the omission of this observance would be considered a decided insult. The routine is as follows:

The ladies of a family remain at home to receive visits; the gentlemen are actively engaged paying them, driving in superb sleighs from house to house. You enter, shake hands, and after giving and receiving the usual felicitations of the season, talk for a minute or two, and then hurry off as fast as you can. Wine and cake are on the table, and each guest is invited to partake. The influence of this ceremony on the social intercourse of families is very salutary. The first day of the year is considered a day of kindness and reconciliation, on which petty differences are forgotten, and trifling injuries forgiven.

The Canadians were much captivated by a certain Scotch chieftain, whose declining fortune at home induced him to endeavour to establish his ancient name, family renown, and clansmen in the new world. They were impressed with a degree of respect for the ancestry which he claimed. The very buttons on his tartan jacket were, as he asserted, heirlooms of some centuries old, descending from father to son. The imposing pomposity of his manners, which, however haughty to his inferiors, were to them all polite blandishment and condescension, won them entirely, as the Irish say. The Mac became a pet lion. It was amusing to observe their eagerness in listening to his many extraordinary stories detailed to them in his Scotticised French. One of his stories may be worth recording.

He hinted that he was employed by Lord Castlereagh in some confidential transactions during the Congress at Aix-la-Chapelle. Returning one morning from walking, absorbed in thought, and ruminating on this important affair, he, in hastily turning the corner of a street, ran against a gentleman with such force as to knock him down. To his horror and dismay, he discovered that this was no less a personage than the czar of all the Russias, the Emperor Nicholas himself, who was in the act of recovering himself, and was actually on his knees, bareheaded, before him. Our great Mac, looking most penitent for such an outrage against the sacred person of his majesty, exclaimed: *"Je vous demande mille pardons!"*

The emperor asked: *"Qui êtes vous?"*

"Moi," replied he, *"je suis chef de Montaguards sauvages Eccossais."*

"Je le crois bien," said the emperor, at the same time picking up his hat from the mud, *"vraiment bien sauvage!"*

However hospitable society in Canada may be, and however agreeable the amusements, there still lacks much of that intellectual refinement to be found prevailing in the enjoyments of life in Europe. Here are no monuments of olden times; no remains of antiquity to be explored and admired; no galleries of paintings, or museums of arts, displaying and recording the genius of man, to lounge away a morning in; no opera to attract the lovers of music to beguile an evening. Here the reflecting stranger can only contemplate the wonders of nature in magnificent waterfalls, dangerous and terrific rapids, and majestic scenery. Although Canada cannot boast of famed memorials of former ages to attract the antiquarian, there is much to interest the curious traveller in the wildness of its scenery. To satisfy his taste, however, in beholding this, or to acquire a knowledge of the country, he must frequently retire from the haunts of men, and forego the pleasures of society. He must in some measure become for a time a recluse in the wilderness. This is termed going into the bush. Nay, so great are the attractive charms of this solitary existence to some persons, that many have permanently remained there, and some are now to be found cultivating their lots of ground, having abandoned gay life, rank and station, friends, country, and home, to gratify their propensity for the life of a settler in the forest. Indeed, with numbers it becomes quite a passion, although to many, who are not calculated to encounter difficulties, it may prove an infatuation. A short excursion in these localities soon proves, alas! that there are contrasts in rural felicity.

The French *seigneuries* seldom extended to any distance from the banks of the St. Lawrence, or other large rivers; consequently, on the separation of the United States, a tract of forest wilderness intervened between the French locations and the new frontier of America. In course of time this began to be settled, and the inhabitants to increase. It likewise became a kind of neutral ground, the rendezvous of evildoers, smugglers, &c., from both sides of the frontier. Being in the vicinity of the boundary-line, these characters could easily evade the officers of justice. The peaceable inhabitants were much annoyed by these refugees, and the eastern townships becoming of importance from the rapid improvements in progress, the governor-general determined to enforce the laws. A commission, consisting of two judges from the supreme court at Quebec, was deputed to hold courts of justice, and in order to give due solemnity and protection to their proceedings, a detachment of troops was ordered to occupy the principal villages of the district. I having been entrusted with the command in this duty, we proceeded by steam down the St. Lawrence to Sorel, a neat small town, where his excellency the Earl and the Countess of Dalhousie were residing at their charming summer retreat, on the 22nd August, 1822. There having received final instructions from his lordship, we continued our route through a well cultivated country to Yamaska. On enquiring for the captain of militia, who likewise acted as justice of peace and billet-master, we easily found his residence, which was denoted by a lofty flagstaff, which likewise served the purpose of displaying his loyalty by having the British ensign flying upon it on his majesty's birthday, and other *jours de fête*. But this military magistrate was absent, and there being no other public authority to provide quarters, I had recourse to the *curé*, requesting him to use his influence with some of his parishioners to accommodate the men. He kindly did so, and on my thanking him for his courtesy, he said, "You have not dined! You must partake of my *petit menagé*."

The old housekeeper looked aghast, either thinking that the promised fare was very indifferent, or that, if particularly dainty, it would prove scanty for an additional guest. The *curé* good-humouredly quieted her alarms, exclaiming that I was a soldier, and had been accustomed to short allowances, and perhaps worse than he could give me. So down we sat. The first dish was a basin of soup each, which certainly appeared little better than thin barley water. As I vacantly stirred this liquid about, doubtful whether I should venture to prove its quality, I discovered two morsels of meat which kept chasing one another about. Ere I had ventured to cast a glance at the hospitable *curé*, he had stuffed his porringer with slices of bread, so as to bring the contents to a proper consistency. This was succeeded by a delicate *fricasseé*, but whether of the legs of chickens or of frogs I have not yet been able to determine. It was, however, accompanied with excellent bacon. Then followed apples stewed, and strewed with maple sugar. The repast closed by the thrifty housekeeper producing a double portion of her *fromage rafiné*, a favourite *bonne bouche* with the Canadians of all classes. This is neither more nor less than a sort of cream cheese preserved until almost putrid, so that the odour might be discerned across the St. Lawrence. Only imagine what the effect must be on the olfactory nerves when placed under your nose, and pressingly urged to devour it. This was too much. I pleaded the necessity of attending to duty, and notwithstanding the temptation of a cool bottle of claret, I left the *curé* to enjoy the luxury of the cheese himself.

These quiet country *curés* are much respected by all ranks, and beloved by the *habitants*. They seem to follow the even tenor of their way, attending to their duty without, as far as I could learn, mixing in political strife. Indeed, the advantage of religious freedom is proved in Canada. No religious discord envenoms the relations of life, however much they may differ on other points.

We next day reached the river St. Francis, which we crossed in boats. Here was a tolerably neat Indian village, which certainly did credit to the superintendent in charge of it. The following morning we moved up the banks of the river. We began to leave cultivation behind us, and to dive into the forest, through which a track had been cut. That is to say, the trees had been felled about three feet from the ground. As the stumps remained, we had to wind our way between them. In crossing a marshy valley, we passed over what they term a "corduroy" road, which is made with round trees placed close together. Nothing can be imagined more horrid than driving over such a substitute for a turnpike. The noisy rolling and continued jolting is insufferable. The good-humoured *habitants* sang and chatted to their small horses to urge them on. It was really surprising how these creatures dragged such loads over these bad roads; but they are invaluable animals, truly adapted to the particular climate by nature, being a stout sort of punch or cob. However beautiful and sleek their skins are in summer, they become like large bears in winter, getting on a shaggy, rough coating to protect them against the rigour of the season. They are strong, active, and extremely handy, capable of performing with sleighs incredibly long journeys.

The *habitants* retain much politeness of manner when addressing people. One fine morning I heard one of the commonest-looking fellows ask his neighbour—a ditto of himself: *"Comment va votre santé!"* to which the other replied: *"Superbe! comme le temps."*

The succeeding day brought us to a location which had been settled under the patronage of a distinguished general (after whom it was named), under the superintendence of a gallant colonel, who had had an active share in the last war with the United States. This gentleman, when the toils of war were concluded, established himself at once in the wilderness, carrying with him many of his old comrades, officers and men. The colonel had a capital mansion, romantically situated on a lawn near a fine cascade on the river. The embryo of a town had been formed, and churches had been built. For some time matters went on in a prosperous manner, but, unfortunately, the very means taken to ensure the success of the enterprise proved the proximate cause of its near ultimate ruin. government had generously allowed to the discharged warriors a certain proportion of agricultural implements and rations for a year or two. Hence the men, not being entirely dependent on their own resources, did not exert themselves in speedily getting their lots under cultivation; consequently, when the rations were withdrawn, they were unprepared to exist on their own resources. Many of them abandoned the place. The colonel, however, and the other officers persevered, and success had crowned their exertions. All seemed highly pleased with their situation and mode of life. After two more days fagging through the bush, we reached our destination. We found a tolerable inn in a tolerable village. The innkeeper (a captain of militia) messed us for a mere trifle, including "sling," if we chose to drink it. The judges were received with all due honour, and opened the assizes in a half-finished church. It was, however, with some difficulty that "respectable" enough could be found to form a grand jury. Nay, so scarce were they that absolutely none of the prisoners, who was out on bail, was included in the number.

A fellow was tried for stealing a cow from Mr. I——, which he had killed and sold. The evidence was clear and strongly against him. No doubt seemed to be entertained of his being convicted, when, unexpectedly, in answer to a cross-question, one of the last witnesses, a servant of the proprietor, said the cow was one of the best cows "we" had. When asked what he meant by the word "we," it came out that instead of paying wages in money, in order to make servants take more care of the stock, it is customary here to allow the servants a certain share of the produce; and the calf which the cow was expected to produce was to have been the property of the witness. This co-partnership proved fatal to the indictment, and saved the culprit from an ignominious end—as he would most certainly have been made an example of, as a warning to the evil spirits infesting the frontier.

I was waited upon by the Honourable Mr. F——, who politely invited me to pay him a visit at his domicile in the woods. The learned and accomplished Judge B—— was also of the party. It was with no small surprise that we beheld a charming villa in the Italian style, with saloons *en suite,* adorned with many objects of *vertu,* furnished with everything comfort could require or a refined taste could imagine. The ladies were most accomplished, of elegant manners, and finished musicians. All this was accounted for. Mr. F—— had been employed in a public situation in Italy, where he realised a certain independence; but, having a numerous family, he determined on retiring to the far shores of America. Being a person of great taste and a collector of antiquities, he had bought a large and splendid collection of rare articles to decorate his mansion, such as marble chimney-pieces, pillars, statues, vases, pictures, &c., all which he had placed in a temporary wooden house until the villa was prepared to receive them. Most unfortunately the house was enveloped in flames, and the whole of the fine marbles were reduced to lime powder. A few of the pictures and small ornaments alone were saved. He had proceeded in his improvements on a large scale and with great judgment. On surveying the domain from a commanding height, it appeared chequered with clumps of forest, like a chess-board. This was owing, he informed us, to the crown and clergy reserves, every seventh lot being retained for these purposes, which proved detrimental to him as interrupting his system of farming, and prevented his having a compact property, while these lots were at present worthless. government, however, expected they would become valuable, as the settlers were obliged to improve and make roads round them. The system seemed to be regarded as a great hardship, and undoubtedly it tended to retard the rapid improvement of the country.

The assizes moved on to a small town on the frontier. The judges, whom I accompanied, were escorted by a corps of volunteer cavalry, who, although the fashion of their various uniforms was more of the marquis of Granby's time than those of the present day, were well mounted on excellent steeds, and everyone had a good broadsword in his hand. We tried their horses' mettle by going at a dashing pace.

On the termination of the assizes, we, judges and all, made a trip across the line. In justice to the Americans, it must be allowed that they are a most diligent and thriving people. Immediately on crossing a brook it was observable. Here the people are "at home"—not refugee emigrants driven from their country to seek a chance asylum in a distant land. They seemed as permanently settled and surrounded with all the domestic conveniences and comforts of life as in the most nourishing county in England; indeed, in a general sense, perhaps more so, as every individual seemed to be in easy circumstances. They not being fettered with the reserves above alluded to, the country had a tine open appearance and the roads were capital.

The object of our expedition being accomplished, the troops were ordered to be withdrawn. We consequently retraced our steps to Montreal. One day during the march, in passing a cottage in the forest, round which a partial clearance had been made, a person, apparently not much above thirty years of age, introduced himself to me, saying he had been in the army; but the miserable plight of his garb would sorely have belied his assertion, had not his manners and address bespoken the gentleman, and one who evidently had seen better days. On entering the cottage, I was introduced to a lady surrounded by a numerous progeny. They informed me that he had been an officer of hussars. Indeed, they both appeared to have moved in the gayest spheres of life; but pecuniary circumstances, and a rising generation rapidly increasing, had induced him to quit his profession and to emigrate, entertaining the vain prospect of easily finding a comfortable independence in the land of their choice, without reflecting that to people in such circumstances nothing but prudence, exertion, and industry can realise these blessings in any part of the world, much less in a wilderness. Here they came as strangers, and remained unknown; by the world forgotten, without they themselves being able to forget the world. Both were totally unsuited for this mode of life, he having no experience or turn for agricultural pursuits, and she no knowledge of the management of, or taste for, rural affairs. They were, to say the truth, in a deplorable situation of misery. This case I deemed infatuation.

In order to induce such of the scattered tribes of Indians as might choose to locate themselves and reside in domiciles, and to deter them from wandering about or starving in their own now cultivated country, government had established villages for these people in various parts of the colony. These Indian villages consist of neat wooden houses, laid out in regular wide streets. Here the squaws with the children always remain, while their barbarous husbands, during the proper hunting season, roam the forests and distant wilderness, returning from thence with their canoes loaded with peltries, on the produce of which they exist during the rigorous winter, loitering away their time in idleness, or at times in fishing, which they accomplished by making a hole in the ice, erecting a *wigwam* over it, and there, sitting at their ease, catch fish at their leisure. This race of beings are as lazy and indolent when their means permit them to remain in repose, as they are active and enterprising when necessity compels them to exertion, whether for subsistence or in war. All these settlements are under the direction and management of the general superintendent, and in each village there is a resident deputy to preserve order and regularity in its affairs. It is also the custom of the government to give the Indians presents every year. This is a grand affair, and a kind of holiday time with them. They never fail to assemble at the appointed places of rendezvous to receive the donations there distributed. These generally consist of red and blue cloths, fowling-pieces, rifles, blankets, &c., for the chiefs, black cloth and silver trinkets for the ladies, and blankets, hatchets, &c., for the common herd of wild ones.

In gratitude for favours of this kind, which had been bestowed a few days previously, a band of about fifty of these warriors from the Indian village of Cocknawaga, situated on the right bank of the St. Lawrence some miles above Montreal, came to the latter place in order to do honour to the superintendent. They made their appearance in the city, not decked in full costume for a ball, but absolutely in *puris naturalibus,* as far as decency would permit. This afforded us an opportunity of witnessing the extraordinary sight of the savage exhibition of an Indian dance in the public streets. These wild sons of the woods had striped to the buff. They entered the city as devoid of covering as when they entered the world, except that each had a kind of scarf fastened about his loins, so arranged as to seem like a pair of inexpressibles reduced to the smallest dimensions, tucked short up. Their faces and naked bodies were painted, or rather daubed in a hideous manner. Some had spots, others stripes, generally of black, red, or yellow, each according to his own taste or fancy, agreeable to their wonted usage previous to preparing to attack their enemies in battle. Their breasts were decorated with large trinkets, such as moon crescents, chains of silver, or plated ornaments, and claws of ferocious animals. Many had superb head-dresses of rare and various coloured feathers, while others had their long, shaggy, black hair hanging dishevelled about their shoulders in all their native savage wildness. All were armed with sabres, tomahawks, or other implements of war. And finely formed men they were as ever stepped, displaying great muscular power, seeming to combine great agility with strength. They hurried along at a quick pace, capering and leaping at times, uttering, occasionally, wild hurrahs and shrieks, mingled with the monotonous sound of a dull sort of drum. In this manner they proceeded to the house of the general superintendent, in front of which they commenced their fantastic exhibition, by dancing and capering through fanciful evolutions in an odd style. Their principal movement consisted of a kind of measured stamping with both feet, and at the same time turning their bodies to and fro, to right and left, and all brandishing their weapons, and flourishing their sabres in the air, accompanied with a grunting guttural, *"Heu uch, heu uch,"* with bursts of shrill yells. They afterwards adjourned to the residence of the commandant at government house, and to those of the other heads of departments, whom they honoured with a repetition of the same compliments. Yet, notwithstanding this ferocious display, the Indians have now become a harmless set, only noxious to themselves, many of them being addicted to intemperance, an evil which their French Catholic *curés*, with all their zeal and influence over them, have not been able entirely to repress.

I once met a most respectable-looking chief, of a portly figure, near the Falls of Niagara, who was particularly well-dressed—that is to say, his habiliments were clean and neat. He sported a kind of blue frock-coat, having the seams and edges inlaid with red or white cloth; a leather belt round the body, superbly worked over in curious devices of various coloured porcupine quills, to which was attached a small pouch adorned in the same manner; with scarlet pantaloons. He was accompanied by a handsome squaw, whose face, although dark, still displayed sufficient tints of the rose and lily, while her dark brown eyes gave her general appearance a soft and dignified effect. She was smartly dressed in richly-worked *moggans*, black stockings, blue under garments, which did not reach lower than mid-leg, with a gown of the same stuff and colour, the train of which was turned over her head so as to form a mantle, which was fastened in front by a variety of silver brooches, large-headed pins, &c. Her fingers were adorned with rings. They had in their train some Indians, whose clothing was of the same make and form as their chief's, except that the stuff was made up of blankets. On showing some surprise when I observed that the rims of the ears of these grim warriors were cut, and left hanging pendent at the lower point like a ring, and silver ornaments attached to them, the chief stopped and addressed us. "Yes, gentlemen," said he, in French, at the same time pointing to his ears, "you have your fashion; this is ours. I trust you admire it." He informed us that he had had a command as a leading chief amongst his wild brethren during the last war with the United States, and he produced certificates from several generals of his faithful and gallant conduct. He added that he now had settled on his allotment of land, which he was cultivating, and that his people also were raising good crops of Indian corn, with fruits and vegetables of all kinds.

On the 21st July I sailed from Quebec, and reached England on the 15th August. In 1826 I commanded some troops during the riots at Manchester; and from March, 1828, to December, 1832, I served in Ireland; after which I retired from the army.

******

There seems no bounds to British enterprise. The globe itself appears almost too limited a sphere of action to display the courage of Englishmen. Not content with the deeds of valour performed in the Peninsula, many officers who had distinguished themselves on various occasions by gallant conduct in the field during that arduous struggle, disregarding the ease and indolence of retired life, availed themselves of the advantages held out in the New World by the South American states, then in arms to assert their rights and free themselves from the oppressions and exactions to which they had so long been subjected while under the dominion of Spain.

Amongst the many who volunteered their services to aid these oppressed people in the recovery of their freedom were three who had served in the corps to which I belonged: Captain Rafler, Lieutenant Acton, and Lieutenant Boss of the 60th Rifles. The latter, who possessed a very determined courage, with cool judgment, had, by his bravery, particularly distinguished himself at the sieges of Cuidad Rodrigo and Badajos; and it was principally owing to his talents on the occasion I am now alluding to that the expedition to which these three officers were attached succeeded in the capture (afterwards reversed) of Porto Bello in the states of Columbia, on the Isthmus of Panama, although this operation was carried on under the nominal command of Sir Gregor M'Gregor, under the high-sounding title of Cacique of Poyais. The said *cacique*, deeming this a place of some security, established here his headquarters, dubbed himself governor, and in that capacity took possession of an excellent house, lived in luxurious indolence, and had a sloop of war in the offing at his command. His force, although principally consisting of British, being all new levies, required much drilling and exercise to make them effective, their numbers not being sufficient to admit of a proper distribution for defence and instruction separately. The advanced piquets were posted every night in the principal roads, at some little distance from the town; and as no movement of the enemy to attack the place was apprehended, they were withdrawn every morning after sunrise for the purpose of being drilled. They went quietly on in this manner until lulled into a fatal security.

One beautiful, balmy spring morning the luxurious shrubs ornamenting the neighbouring heights were yielding their fragrance to the gentle breeze, which playfully waved their tops to and fro, while the clear waters of the adjacent river, shaded by the verdant foliage of the acacia and the weeping willow, seemed by their delightful coolness to invite those who had been on the midnight watch to refresh their wearied limbs. The piquets had been withdrawn as usual; the men had piled arms, and, along with those off duty, were at drill in squads in front of the government house in the Grand Plaça, when, before a sound was heard or any alarm given, many of the best and bravest were by a murderous volley laid low. This most unexpected vicissitude staggered the whole for a moment, but they soon recovered themselves; the former piquet seized their arms, and, being joined by the governor's guard, a stand was made to enable the others to retreat to a fort at no great distance. This was effected after considerable loss. During this disastrous attack the vainglorious Cacique of Poyais, instead of gallantly heading his troops and sharing their fortunes, on the first alarm jumped out of bed, leaped out of a back window, plunged into the sea, swam on board his ship of war, got under weigh, and thus saved himself by an ignominious flight, to the horror and mortification of his brave people in the fort, who beheld him making his escape to sea in a vessel which was their only effectual means of defence. They were thus abandoned to the mercy of a relentless enemy; whereas, if he had brought the broadside of the ship to bear on the town, so as to give a cross-fire to that of the fort, the enemy would probably have been driven out again without much difficulty.

The fort, which had been constructed more to protect the harbour and lower part of the town than to form any defence against an attack from the interior of the country, was surrounded by some houses, which the Spanish army got possession of, and picked the men off who were working the guns. Ross cleverly got some guns turned round and dislodged them. But the place not having been provisioned, any further defence was only maintained with a view of getting terms. They, therefore, offered to capitulate, on being provided with shipping to quit the country and return to England. The Spaniards readily acceded to the proposition, and further promised to treat them with respect, but the instant the men laid down their arms, upon marching out of the fort, they were surrounded by an armed force, the officers separated from the men, and all divided into small parties, and marched in different directions far up the country.

The officers were treated in the most degrading manner, being obliged to perform menial offices, and literally to become hewers of wood and carriers of water. Under a pretence that it had been discovered that they were forming a plan to make their escape, their legs were put into stocks every night, so that they could get but little rest after their daily labours. Ross complained of this to the Spanish commander, stating that such usage was ungenerous after the service he had performed for them in Spain. But all the redress he got was a grin, with the repetition of *"tan peor,"* "so much the worse," to every particular action he mentioned. It was thus implied that if he had fought for the king of Spain *then,* he had no business to fight against him *now.*

One morning, before they were relieved from the stocks, a corporal and a file of men marched up and began leading their firelocks in front of the officers. On being asked what they meant by this, they pointed to Captain Rafler, and said to him, "We are going to shoot you!" He earnestly insisted that there must be some mistake. They replied that there was no mistake, adding that he was the person who was plotting to escape, and that, in order to frighten the others, he must be made an example of. They accordingly released him, and made him proceed in front of them to some short distance, when they deliberately fired and shot him dead!

The fate of poor Acton was particularly melancholy, and so, in its proportion, was that of his favourite poodle dog, Leo. This fine animal had been for years his most attached and faithful companion.

Leo had been sheared and trimmed up into the shape and appearance of a most ferocious lion; but this was only in outward resemblance, for Leo had a kind and playful spirit. He possessed wonderful instinct and sagacity, and performed many amusing pranks and tricks, such as fetching anything from his master's room which he desired him to bring. His *forte*, however, was in aquatic displays, particularly in diving or leaping overboard, and then scrambling up again by a rope thrown over the side. And Leo was the constant attendant on his master on all occasions of bathing. Acton had been an out-picket on the night preceding the surprise, and, on returning, had remained to bathe. While enjoying this luxury after the fatigue of the night, being helpless and defenceless, the enemy came rapidly on—escape was impossible—and these cruel agents of oppression bayoneted him in cold blood. His faithful Leo made a vigorous attack on the barbarous miscreants, and likewise fell covered with wounds, in the vain endeavour to defend his master.

The successful surprise of this place by the Spaniards was owing to information of the manner in which the liberating forces carried on the duty, given by spies and those within the town friendly to the old *regime*. The Spaniards had with the utmost secrecy moved a large force on the fortress, and had concealed them behind the heights, covered with brushwood, as above described; and it is supposed that on a signal from some traitor to his country within, and at the fitting moment, they dashed on and obtained their success.

Lieutenant Ross continued for fifteen months under the control of his hard taskmasters; when, reduced by ill-health and despair, he was fortunately relieved in exchange for some Spanish officers, on whom retaliation was about to be made.

Appendices

Notes For Portugal

Junot, seeing the rapid spread of the popular movement, and that the communication between the different corps of his army was interrupted by the hostile population, determined to concentrate his forces in the vicinity of Lisbon, leaving garrisons at Elvas, Almeida, Peniche, and Setubal.

Loison, who was at Guarda, received orders to assume the command of Oporto. He left a garrison at Almeida, and, on the 16th June, 1808, he set out with two regiments of Infantry, and a brigade of artillery. But after crossing the Douro at Regora, on finding that the armed population occupied the strong country in his front, he determined to retreat. During his retreat, on the 23rd June, he had an affair with the peasantry at Castro d'Airo, and inflicted considerable loss on them. He then continued his retreat to Guarda, where he received orders from Junot to return to Lisbon. He proceeded by Pinhel to Almeida, where he left his sick and a garrison of 1200 men; and having destroyed the fort, he continued his march to Lisbon. On approaching Guarda again, on the 3rd July, he was opposed by the peasantry, whom he attacked and routed, and a terrible scene of massacre and pillage ensued. Next day he resumed his march, and on the 5th July he defeated the patriots at Alpedrinham (?). After this he continued his march, and reached Abrantes on the 11th July without molestation.

The province of Alentejo was now also in arms. The people attacked the French at Villa Vicosa on the 23rd June, and compelled them to retire to the castle. General Kellerman, who commanded the district, hastened to relieve the troops driven into the castle, and he took a cruel revenge on the people by butchering many of the inhabitants. The people, however, were not dismayed. They attacked and took the fort of Juramenha, which commanded the passage of the Guadiana.

On the 24th June an outbreak took place at Beja. On the 26th General Maransin defeated the people, and then entered the town, which was pillaged and burned, and many of the inhabitants put to the sword.

About the same time a large body of patriots assembled at Leiria. Junot endeavoured to induce them to submit by means of promises, but without effect. General Margaron, with 4000 men and a battery of artillery, was then sent against them. On the 4th July he dispersed the patriots without difficulty, and then entered the city, when a deliberate massacre of the unoffending inhabitants took place, attended with the greatest atrocity.

At Evora the standard of freedom was raised by General Leite, and on the 16th July a *junta* was formed to regulate the patriotic movements south of the Tagus. A body of troops was collected in the vicinity of the town, but before they were fully prepared intelligence was received that Loison had crossed the Tagus and was rapidly advancing with a column of 5000 men. On the 28th July, Loison appeared in front of Montemor Novo, where a body of patriots was posted. These hastily retired on Evora. A cry of treason arose, and the people became much excited. Suspicion fell upon the *corregidor*, who was supposed to be playing false. He, to escape popular resentment, fled from the city. Order was restored on the arrival of a reinforcement of Spanish troops. On the 29th July, General Leite, with nearly 2000 men, took up a position in front of the town. Loison attacked him with great energy, and ordered General Solignac to turn the right, while Margaron's brigade, divided into two bodies, assailed the front and left flank. The Portuguese infantry made a gallant defence, but were overpowered. The cavalry abandoned the field in shameful flight.

The infantry retired on the town, where an attempt at resistance was again made, but unsuccessfully, General Solignac succeeded in forcing the place, after meeting a desperate resistance in the streets. The Spanish and Portuguese troops escaped as best they could.

Then commenced a series of the most sanguinary and atrocious cruelties that ever disgraced the annals of war. An indiscriminate slaughter of the inhabitants took place; no age or sex was spared, no sanctuary was respected; the convents were broken into, the churches were pillaged, even the Blessed Sacrament was taken from the tabernacles and trampled under foot. All who attempted to escape from the town were cut down by the cavalry placed outside; 8000 Portuguese were killed or wounded.

From Evora, Loison marched to Elvas, to drive off the Spanish troops on that frontier, and to throw in a supply of provisions for the garrison. He then proceeded to Portalegre, in which town he levied heavy contributions, but found some difficulty in collecting them. He ordered five or six of the principal inhabitants to remain at the palace where his headquarters were, to see that the money was duly paid according to lists he had procured. While they were in the act of counting the money already received, a despatch arrived announcing to him that the English had landed. This unwelcome news came upon him like a thunder-clap. The drums were instantly ordered to beat to arms, and the troops to march immediately. The money still untold was hurriedly crammed into bags, and the principal inhabitants, who had been detained in the palace, were carried off as hostages that the remaining part of the contribution should he paid. He then left the town, and proceeded with his troops by forced marches to cross the Tagus to Abrantes.

When Junot learned that the English had landed, he detached General de Laborde with two brigades of infantry, a regiment of cavalry, and a brigade of artillery, by Villa Franca to Condieiros, to watch the British forces and to watch the prevent Loison's column from being cut off. Laborde, finding that Loison's corps was safe across the Tagus, and that the English army was taking the coast road, proceeded to Alcobaca, so as to get between them and Loison, and then to form a junction at Leiria with Loison, who with eight thousand men was coming by forced marches from Abrantes. But the heat of the weather, the haste of the march, the want of provisions, and the hostility of the country caused such numbers of his men to become exhausted that he was detained on the road. Time was lost, and Sir Arthur Wellesley had got possession of Leiria.

Therefore Loison was obliged to change his route to the southward, in order to endeavour to form a junction with Laborde.

Junot concentrated his remaining forces at Lisbon, having withdrawn all his posts to the south of the Tagus, except Palmela.

Letter from Colonel Charles Leslie, K.H.
To the Editor of the *United Service Journal*
The 29th Regiment at Rolica
Mr. Editor,
In justice to a gallant old corps, I have to request that you will give the following statement a place in your most impartial and excellent journal.

I observe with much regret, in Colonel Napier's work on the Peninsular War, several inaccuracies in the account which he gives of the operations of the 29th Regiment in the action of Rolica. To a regiment jealous of its reputation, it is at all times a matter of great interest that its deeds in arms should be fairly recorded, but infinitely more so that no misstatements, even by mistake, should be made tending to its prejudice and disadvantage. I feel confident Colonel Napier would not willingly hurt the feelings, much less tarnish the fame and blight the laurels, of a corps which during several arduous campaigns distinguished, itself in every action that was fought, as testified by his grace the Duke of Wellington's general orders, when that regiment was sent a skeleton from the field, in consequence of the severe losses it had sustained in the numerous actions in which it had been engaged.

I have long wished that somebody more capable than myself would have undertaken the task of correcting these mistakes. However, as no abler advocate has yet appeared, and as the colonel has since, in a reply to General Brennier, called upon the officers of the 29th to confirm or deny the general's statement, wherein he affirms that he with only two companies broke the 29th Regiment, I shall, by simply stating matters of fact as they occurred, endeavour to show that both are mistaken. I may add that, however inadequate to the task, I am entitled to do this without much presumption, having had the honour and good fortune to serve in that gallant corps during the whole period of their service in the Peninsula.

I have the honour to remain, sir,
Your obedient servant,
An officer late of the 29th Regiment
Cork
21st August, 1830

Colonel Napier states that the 29th and 9th Regiments forced the two strongest passes.

That the 29th Regiment arrived first in disorder at the top.

That ere they could form, a French battalion broke through the midst of them, slaying the colonel and many others, and making one major and fifty or sixty men prisoners.

I flatter myself that I shall satisfactorily prove, by the following extract from a journal kept at the time, that the colonel has been misinformed when he makes the above assertions.

Notes For Spain

Charles IV. succeeded his father, and joined the European confederacy against the French Revolution, but his efforts were unsuccessful. The army of the Republic passed the Pyrenees, defeated the Spanish army, took St. Sebastian, and occupied Biscay and Navarre. Charles sued for peace, and by the Treaty of Basle in July, 1795, he regained the lost provinces on giving up to France the Spanish portion of St. Domingo. He neglected, however, to maintain his army on a proper footing, to repair and strengthen his fortresses, and to improve the military resources of the country; whilst from the weakness of his position he was soon afterwards compelled by France to engage with her in the war against England, in which he lost Minorca and Trinidad; Spanish trade was destroyed, and great part of her fleet taken.

Napoleon, on seizing the throne in France, imposed upon Spain by appearance of friendship, in which he was supported by an unworthy minion, Don Manuel Godoy, then minister and arbiter of the destinies of Spain. This fellow, raised from the rank of a *guard du corps* in 1788, at the instigation of the queen, whose favourite he was, to the highest posts in the state, acquired an unbounded influence over the imbecile Charles. He was invested with the Golden Fleece, made Principe de Paz in 1795, after the Treaty of Basle, and the weak king gave him his niece, the Princess Maria Theresa do Bourbon, in marriage. Under Godoy the honour and interests of Spain were swamped, the court became degraded and dissolute. In 1802 Godoy became *generalissimo* by sea and land, and in 1807 *high admiral* of Spain and the Indies.

The war with France seemed to have paralysed Spain—her spirit seemed subdued; and although she took no decidedly active part in the war which commenced between England and France in 1803, after the Peace of Amiens, she only acquired permission to remain neutral by paying large subsidies to Napoleon. The British government, aware that she had thus broken her neutrality, and that the Spanish government only waited the arrival of a large amount of treasure from South America to declare war, Mr. Pitt decided on intercepting these vessels, and accordingly a squadron under Sir Graham Moore went to Cape St. Marys, 4th October, 1804. Spain immediately declared war openly against England, and Nelson at Trafalgar, October, 1805, defeated the Spaniards.

The Spanish nobility were indignant at Godoy's elevation and jealous of his power. Ferdinand, the heir to the throne, beheld this scene with terror and disgust, and a large party was formed under him in opposition to the favourite. Godoy, dreading the hostility of such a strong party and the indignation of an injured people, saw the necessity of endeavouring to adopt some measures in accord with the general feeling of the country. Finding Napoleon deeply engaged in German wars, he entered into some negotiations with the Russian and Portuguese ambassadors at Madrid, that in concert with England a plan should be formed to attack France; but before matters were arranged in any favourable state, he most perniciously issued a manifesto calling the country to arms.

Napoleon suppressed his resentment until he had completed his triumphs in the north of Germany by the Treaty of Tilsit, August, 1807. He now determined to persevere in ambitious projects, and to wreak his vengeance on the Spaniards by the subjugation of the Peninsula. He had contingents of her best troops out of the country; 16,000, under the Marquis of Romana, were left in the north of Germany, and he assembled a large army at Bayonne. Under fallacious pretexts he induced Charles to become a party to the Treaty of Fontainebleau, by which the partition of Portugal was agreed on, for which purpose a French army should enter Spain and proceed, in combination with certain portions of the Spanish army, to Portugal.

In August, 1807, the first part of the drama commenced by the French and Spanish ambassadors at Lisbon demanding that Portugal should close her ports against England, and all English ships and property confiscated; threatening on refusal that a declaration of war would take place.

After some ineffectual remonstrance, the prince regent of Portugal, overawed by threats and the seizure of Portuguese vessels in the ports of France, was at last obliged to acquiesce. The property of English subjects was seized, and a proclamation issued prohibiting all commerce whatever between the countries; but these unjust sacrifices, extorted from the prince regent, did not retard the execution of Napoleon's projects against Portugal. Under the pretence of emancipating her from the yoke of England, a French army under Marshal Junot, who had formerly been ambassador at Lisbon, crossed the Pyrenees early in November, and advanced by Salamanca towards Portugal.

The British government saw that Portugal had been coerced to take proceedings against her, but intimated that any further act of aggression would be considered a declaration of war. A squadron under Sir Sidney Smith was sent to cruise off the Tagus, and another proclamation appeared ordering the confiscation of English property, Lord Strangford quitted Lisbon and retired on board the admiral's ship, Lisbon being declared under blockade.

On 17th November Junot issued a proclamation at Alcantara, stating that his only object in entering Portugal was to emancipate the government from the yoke of England, and called upon the people to receive the invader as friends.

On the 19th November the French army and Spaniards crossed the frontier and marched on Lisbon by Castello Branco. On the 23rd their advanced guard reached Abrantes. This rapid advance took the regent by surprise. Deceived by the hope that hostilities might be avoided by compliance with Napoleon's wishes, all defensive precautions had been neglected, and it was only when the French were but four days' march from Lisbon that the regent became aware of the danger. He at length yielded to the counsel of Lord Strangford, and determined to quit the kingdom for Brazil; and having nominated a council of regency, of which the Marquis of Abrantes was named president, he embarked with all the royal family on 24th November, 1807.

The French entered Lisbon without opposition. The suddenness of events by which the independence of the country had been sacrificed seemed to have east a stupor on the nation. Had the smallest energy on the part of the government been exerted to resist the enemy and organise the people to oppose the invader, they might have been effectively resisted with undoubted success, because from the haste Junot was in to accomplish Napoleon's intentions, and to seize upon his prey, his army was pushed on by forced marches. The season was particularly inclement, and the roads almost impassable. No magazines for supply had been formed. These circumstances introduced disorder into their ranks. The men quitted their corps in search of food and plunder. The number of stragglers and sick or weakly men left along the line of march was immense. Every regiment was more or less disorganised, so that had any military force opposed their passage in the difficult parts of the country, or had even the peasantry attacked them in such places, they must have been cut up in detail.

When they arrived at Punhete, situated on a point of land at the junction of the Zezare and the Tagus, both rivers were so swollen, and not sufficient boats, the French were detained two days cooped up in this corner, where they might have been attacked and compelled to surrender without any difficulty. They arrived at Lisbon in detached parties, in wretched condition, emaciated and in rags, many without shoes, and most of the officers without a change of linen.

Junot affected to conciliate the inhabitants by professions of friendly intentions, and the usual system of government was continued; but when he had reorganised his army and secured the principal fortresses, he threw off the mask, and, in accordance with Napoleon's desire, publicly announced that the house of Braganza had ceased to reign; that the regent by leaving the country had forfeited all right to the allegiance of the nation. He assumed the chief authority, governing in the name of Napoleon, and exacted enormous contributions.

Although the French had partisans amongst the nobility, such as the Marquis d'Alorna and others, still the mass of the people were full of noble spirit, and felt indignant at the degradation of their country, and the oppression endured from a foreign invader. Junot, in order to render ineffectual all opposition, marched off the flower of the Portuguese army to France, consisting of 10,000 men, under the Marquis d'Alorna. All the officers who went voluntarily were promised a step of promotion; but many of them, and the greater part of the men, contrived to escape during the march, and returned home. Many nobility were, under various pretexts, sent on missions to France; amongst others the Marquis de Mon——, who was much regretted by his countrymen. A deputation, consisting of the Bishop of Coimbra, the Marquis d'Abrana, Don Nuno Caetano de Melle, &c., was sent to congratulate the emperor. These, under his influence, addressed a letter in April, 1808, to their countrymen, puffing off the emperor's generous policy towards Portugal, and urging submission to their great deliverer.

But the people were not to be deceived by such false advice from treacherous friends. The exorbitant contributions and exactions of horses, wagons, &c., levied with great severity; the extensive confiscation of property and goods of all descriptions, under pretence that they were of English manufacture; the churches pillaged of the sacred vessels; the palaces of the nobility plundered; the violence and robberies committed by the soldiery on the poor peasants, too clearly proved they were under the iron sway of a foreign despot. Smothered feelings of indignation and revenge reigned in every breast against foreign intruders who had insulted their religion, and carried rapine and oppression into every home.

Intelligence of the massacre at Madrid, and the general insurrection in Spain against their common foe, soon reached Lisbon. Junot, in vain endeavoured to deceive the people by publishing false accounts of a contrary nature.

On the 6th June, 1808, General B——, commanding the corps at Oporto, having received directions from the *junta* of Gallicia to return to Spain, arrested the French General —— and his staff, and immediately marched off for Spain, carrying them prisoners along with him! On this news reaching Junot he immediately adopted measures to secure the whole of the Spanish division then at Lisbon under General Cariffa, and took strong measures to overawe the people. All persons were ordered to give their arms, and every householder was declared responsible for all persons in the family.

On the 18th of June the feast of Corpus Christi was celebrated with the usual magnificence. The procession was most numerously attended by all ranks. Several French generals and a strong body of French troops were also there, for the purpose of imposing on the people. Scarcely had the solemn procession begun to move, when in a moment the crowd became agitated. Cries of "The English are landed!" resounded in all directions. Many in the confusion, not knowing whence the commotion originated, were seized with terror, and apprehended that a massacre was going to occur. Lamentations were heard on every side, and they overthrew one another in their endeavours to escape. General disorder prevailed, and the ground remained strewed with wax tapers. The French soldiers remained firm. Their officers formed the men, who were leaving the streets, into close order, ready to act as required. Junot, seeing the necessity for the procession going on, in order to show his determination to preserve order, assured the principal clergy and nobles that he would offer every protection. All was again arranged and carried through without disturbance. We were told this was a trick of some people to annoy the French.

Although matters were thus lulled for the time at Lisbon, not so at Oporto, for on the very same day the flame of patriotism burst forth. The people, encouraged by the appearance of an English ship of war in the offing, rose and declared against the French authority. The governor, Don Luiz de Olivera, who attempted to repress their proceedings, was seized and committed to prison. The arsenal was broken open, and the people helped themselves. The bishop approved of the movement, and a *junta* was appointed, of which he was president, for provisional government. The rising in the Algarves took place about the same time, whilst it spread from Oporto in all directions—from Braga in the north to Coimbra, Lerida, &c., in the south. The *junta* acted with great vigour. Military leaders of good position were appointed, the disembodied military organised in regiments, and artillery trains equipped.

Viscount B—— was sent ambassador to England, and communication opened with the *juntas* in Spain.

Partial encounters took place in various places between the patriots and detached portions of the enemy, so that the French lost all possession of the country, except the actual military positions they held.

Junot, on learning the outbreak at Oporto, adopted the most

severe measures to prevent such occurring at Lisbon, and, to intimidate the people, fulminated the most cruel decrees, threatening to destroy the towns and villages with fire and sword.

By the Treaty of Fontainebleau Portugal was to be divided. Entre Minho et Douro was to be given to the King of Etruria, whose Italian possessions were ceded to France. The Alentejo and Algarve to be erected into a principality for Godoy. That the other provinces should be disposed of as might be agreed upon afterwards. That a French army should be hurried immediately to Portugal, that a corps of 12,000 Spaniards should take possession of Entre Minho et Douro and the city of Oporto, and that a large French army of reserve should be assembled at Bayonne.

Ferdinand, indignant at the favour Godoy enjoyed with his father and mother, came to an open quarrel with his father, and, having joined the party opposed to that minister, measures were begun for his overthrow.

In October, 1807, Ferdinand wrote a secret letter to Napoleon, soliciting to be united to one of his family, and begging that he would interfere to remedy the disorders of Godoy's government. Godoy, having found this out, had Ferdinand arrested at the Escurial, on the 28th October, and accused of high treason in having formed a conspiracy to dethrone the king, his father. The people showed demonstrations of favour to Ferdinand and of hatred to Godoy, who got alarmed, and effected a reconciliation between father and son. Charles wrote to Napoleon expressing surprise that the emperor had not consulted him about the marriage of his son with one of his family, to which he received no answer. Godoy afterwards prevailed upon the imbecile king to write another letter to the emperor, soliciting that his son Ferdinand might have the honour of forming an alliance with a member of his imperial family. He, however, got no reply for some time; at length the emperor wrote from Italy denying that he had ever received any proposal from Ferdinand, and that the first intelligence he had of it was from the king's own letter, but expressed his approbation of the proposed arrangement.

No sooner had the French army destined to attack Portugal in November, under Junot, passed the frontiers of Spain than 24,000 men of the army of reserve, under Dupont, were speedily pushed after them, and directed its march to Valladolid in December, thus commanding both roads either to Madrid or Lisbon. A third army of nearly 20,000 men, under Marshal Morney, crossed the Bidassoa, 9th January, and took possession of Biscay and Navarre, whilst another army was collected to invade Catalonia in the eastern side of Spain. Junot attempted to justify his pouring such large forces into Spain on the plea of rescuing Portugal; but the forces assembled on the north-east frontier offered no such excuse, and evidently showed hostile intentions; still no measures were taken to prevent the entrance of such invaders.

In March an army of 80,000 under Murat entered Spain and occupied Vittoria, ready to advance on Madrid, while the fortresses of St. Sebastian, Pampeluna, Terzieras, and Barcelona fell into the hands of these dreadful *friends* by fraud or treachery.

In the meanwhile Napoleon kept flattering Charles, expressing his anxious wish for the completion of a family alliance, and stated his intention to visit Madrid to settle by personal arrangement all points of difference. He however evaded the promised visit, but sent proposals that he would give the sovereignty of Portugal, which he claimed, to Spain, and get in exchange Galicia, Biscay, and Navarre, and participate in the trade of her colonies, and that the succession to the Spanish throne should be finally settled. Godoy became sensible by these transactions that his hopes of the principality in Portugal, promised him by the Treaty of Fontainebleau, were at an end, that all his plans of acquiring wealth and honour were thwarted; and he became anxious to escape from impending dangers. He proposed to Charles to remove his seat of government to his South American states. Charles, despairing of settling the affairs of Spain with Napoleon, agreed to this arrangement, and secret preparations were made for the departure of the court; but the plan being denounced, the people made violent demonstrations of discontent. Ferdinand also declared his objection to the project, as he considered that Napoleon would favour his views.

On the 17th March the populace at Aranjuez, finding that there were preparations for the departure of the royal family, rose, shouting, "Death to Godoy!" attacked and destroyed his house. The troops not only refused to fire on the people, but resisted with them. The same scenes were enacted next day at Madrid. The palace there was destroyed. Godoy made his escape, and on the 19th March was found concealed at Ocana, when he would have fallen a victim to popular fury, if Ferdinand had not interfered and saved his life. Tranquillity was only restored by a proclamation from the king announcing the departure of Godoy.

On the 20th March, Charles IV., by a public decree, abdicated in favour of Ferdinand, as he said, by a spontaneous act of his free-will, because from infirmities he found the burden of government too much for him. The joy of the nation was unbounded. Ferdinand was in high favour. The people looked to him for deliverance from all their oppressions. He published an order for the confiscation of Godoy's property, and deprived him of his honours, and filled up all public situations with his own adherents. Ferdinand then despatched a letter to Napoleon announcing his accession to the throne, with assurances that the recent changes should not affect the relations with France.

Murat, who was already marching on Madrid when these events occurred, continued his advance, and, entering the capital on 23rd March, took military possession of the city.

Ferdinand entered next day, but the French ambassador and Murat excused themselves from acknowledging him until they had the emperor's decision. Charles had likewise written to Napoleon announcing his abdication, solicited protection, and hoped that the alliance between the countries would continue.

Napoleon availed himself of these communications from both father and son, as giving him a right to interfere in the affairs of Spain. His ministers and generals assumed and exercised the direction of all public affairs. The command of the capital was seized upon by the intruder, cannon placed in the most favourable positions for commanding the palace and other public places, so as to overawe the people, and no effort was made by Ferdinand to counteract their encroachments or to resent them.

Napoleon came in March to Bayonne, so as to be at hand to carry out his project of dethroning the reigning family. He was led to this no doubt by finding that Ferdinand, though weak and destitute of abilities, still possessed the affections of the Spanish people, and that he raised the nation against his father successfully. He gave Charles to understand that he considered his abdication had been forced upon him, that he would therefore support his cause, and arranged that the place of exile for the dethroned king should be Badajos. Pleased with this, Charles sent a letter to Napoleon through Murat declaring that his abdication was compulsory, and that he relied on the emperor to be re-established. These transactions were kept secret from Ferdinand.

A report was spread that the emperor intended coming to Madrid, and it was hinted to Ferdinand that if he would advance to meet the emperor, it would be considered a mark of respect. In the meantime Savary arrived with a message from Napoleon assuring him that if his sentiments towards France were similar to those of his father, the emperor would look over the proceedings of his acquiring the throne, and would acknowledge him as king of Spain. He likewise informed him that the emperor had entered Spain on 2nd April on his way to Madrid, and that it would be taken as a compliment if he would go as far as Burgos to meet him. Ferdinand therefore set out on 10th April, and was persuaded to go as far as Vittoria, a journey of over 200 miles, and on arriving there found not the emperor, but a letter from him in which he did not acknowledge him as king; hinted his surprise at the manner in which he had attained the throne; desired that the prosecution of Godoy should cease, as any investigation might cast doubts on Ferdinand's own legitimacy; and warned him against popular commotions.

Ferdinand would fain have returned to Madrid; but dreading to offend Napoleon, and urged by Savary, who assured him that on his arrival at Bayonne he would be fully acknowledged as king of Spain, he continued his journey.

On 20th April Ferdinand arrived at Bayonne. Napoleon received him with the greatest respect, invited him to dinner, and treated him as a royal personage; but, on returning to his residence, Savary informed him of the emperor's decision to expel the Bourbons, and urged him to sign an abdication. This base proposal Ferdinand furiously refused, and expressed a wish to return to Spain. The only reply he got was that his guards were doubled.

In the meantime Murat assumed the chief authority at Madrid. He demanded the release of Godoy, and stated that Charles IV. alone would be recognised by Napoleon as king of Spain. The council of government, induced by their fears, readily complied: Godoy was sent off under escort to Bayonne, and Charles with his unworthy consort followed, by directions of Napoleon, on 24th April.

On these people reaching Bayonne, 30th April, they became willing instruments in the hands of Napoleon for the enslavement of Spain, and deprived their son Ferdinand of the crown. He was no longer treated with the honours of sovereignty, and was denounced as a rebel by his father. Ferdinand attempted to vindicate his conduct, and expressed his readiness to resign the crown in presence of the *cortes*, or to govern the kingdom as his father's deputy.

On 6th May Napoleon had a conference with Charles and his queen, to which Ferdinand was summoned and treated as a culprit. His father asserted his usurpation and his mother denied his legitimacy, and Napoleon, by threats and promises, endeavoured to obtain his abdication, to which he at length yielded.

It afterwards appeared that on the previous day, May 5th, Charles IV. had already conveyed his rights to Napoleon, who, by an edict to the supreme *junta* at Madrid, had appointed Murat to act as lieutenant of the kingdom and president of the council of government. He likewise issued a proclamation to the people assuring them that he was concerting with his allies measures to promote the interest of Spain. Charles retired to Compiégne, supported by a pension from Napoleon. Ferdinand and his brother Don Carlos were sent off under safe keeping as prisoners to the Chateau of Valenciennes.

The departure of Ferdinand spread alarm through the nation. The French hitherto had been regarded as allies. The progress of their armies had been silent but sure. At length, however, the burden of their armies pressed upon the people. The French were haughty and overbearing. Castilian pride was wounded by the military arrogance A spirit of national animation began to spread, to which the abdication of their monarch gave additional strength. There was indignation in every heart and defiance on every lip.

The French took the strictest precautions to provide for their own security and designs. In various places popular tumults and encounters with the French took place, who regarded the partisans of Ferdinand as enemies, and were oven anxious for a conflict.

On the 30th April Murat presented a letter from Charles IV. to the Infante Don Antonio, directing him to send the Queen of Etruria and Don Francisco di Paula, brother to Ferdinand, to Bayonne.

On May 1st, no intelligence having arrived from Bayonne, and the next day, May 2nd, being fixed for the departure of the royal personages, great multitudes assembled early that morning at the Puerta del Sol, waiting in a state of great excitement the arrival of the expected courier, while the square in front of the palace was crowded with women, who watched the preparations for the journey of the royal party. The *cortege* departed at 9 o'clock; but two heavy carriages having still remained at the palace, it was reported that Don Antonio was also going off to Bayonne. The populace became much excited. The cry arose: "They are all forsaking us! The last of the royal family are to be torn from us!" A violent commotion ensued, and the carriages were broken to pieces. One of Murat's staff, having been sent to ascertain the cause of the tumult, was attacked, and would have been massacred, had not a party of the Imperial Guard arrived in time to rescue him. Murat ordered out a battalion, which fired on the people. This only increased the numerous cries of vengeance. "Death to the French!" *"Viva Ferdinando!"* rent the air, and masses rushed in armed with whatever weapons they could procure.

Resume of Spanish Notes

Bonaparte having subdued the Austrians, Russians, and Prussians, and concluded a peace at Tilsit, 1807, determined on subjugating Spain and placing one of his own family on the throne. By various intrigues he created dissensions between Charles IV. and his son Ferdinand, intending to get them into his power by pretending to act as mediator between them.

Meanwhile Bonaparte had, in October, 1807, made a treaty with the king of Spain, to whom he guaranteed his domain, but by a secret article added the division of the kingdom of Portugal; and it was resolved that a French army under General Junot, who had formerly been ambassador at Lisbon, should enter Spain and thence proceed to Portugal, and in a proclamation declare that the House of Braganza had ceased to reign.

Having determined to seize upon Portugal, he demanded, early in 1807, that the Portuguese should shut their ports against England, to detain all English and confiscate all English property, threatening war if these terms were not agreed to. The prince regent of Portugal strongly remonstrated against these unjust measures, but finding it fruitless, he at length, on 8th November, very reluctantly signed the order, and announced his intention of retiring from Portugal to the Brazils. Our ambassador at Lisbon, Lord Strangford, protested against the decree, and on 17th November retired on board our fleet, under Sir Sydney Smith. He shortly afterwards succeeded in persuading the prince regent to embark for Brazil, leaving a regent to act during his absence; and on the 29th November the royal family sailed under an escort of four English men-of-war.

No sooner had the Portuguese fleet departed than Junot appeared close to Lisbon with 28,000 French and a body of Spaniards, and entered the city without opposition, as he made great professions of friendship.

French armies were poured into Spain, and succeeded by various artifices in getting possession of all the principal fortresses. On the abdication of Charles IV. by French intrigues in favour of Ferdinand VII., Murat rapidly pushed on and entered Madrid on 24th March.

Bonaparte requires the royal family to come to Bayonne, where he forced them to resign the Spanish crown, 5th May, 1808. Napoleon artfully succeeded in getting a contingent of 7000 Spanish troops, which he marched into France.

Joseph appointed King of Spain; entered Madrid 20th July.

The supreme command at Seville assumed independent powers, proclaimed Ferdinand king, and declared war with France. This *junta* was acknowledged as superior by the others in various district. Peace was instantly proclaimed with England, and six deputies sent to London, who received liberal assistance in money, arms, and munitions of war.

General Certanas, Spanish commander at St. Roque, immediately opened friendly communications with Sir H. Dalrymple, governor of Gibraltar.

General Morla succeeded Solano at Cadiz.

Admiral Rossilly surrendered French fleet 14th June.

English Admiral Purvis at Cadiz.

Sir Charles Cotton off Lisbon.

Notes For Halifax

There are few places so wretched as to be without some attractions of climate. In tropical countries the night is the sweet season; in colder climes the day, though not exclusively. Of all the varieties of temperature which I have seen, and of all the places where the air breathes health and life, commend me to the "Indian Summer" of North America, and the picturesque drive round the basin of Halifax harbour. The Indian summer is the "latter autumn" of Europe. The frosts have set in, sharp and keen, in the morning and evening—a clear blue sky, without a cloud, pervades all space, and overhead the resplendent sun tempers the atmosphere. The face of nature is then invested with supernatural beauty; the brilliant hues which dye the bright foliage can be likened only to the high transparent colour which tints the check of those—the "favourites of heaven"—whom death prematurely claims; it is also the precursor of the mortality of nature. Yet a few weeks she wears this gorgeous garb, and, lo! the night-winds come, the heavens descend, and the earth is wrapped in a shroud of snow!

But the death of nature in this climate is the life of man. During the glowing autumn his enjoyment is of a contemplative kind; but when once the winter has set in his energies are excited, and he leads a life of activity. Of this the sledge-driving, which is called *sleighing,* is the principal feature. Everyone, however limited his means, contrives to establish some vehicle on runners, whether it be an ordinary truck for wood, casks sawn in two, the bodies of old gigs, indeed anything in which a man may sit. But the fashionable sleighs are carriages of no ordinary pretensions, and rejoice in all the splendour that arctic invention can bestow upon them. The winter of 1816 was remarkable for gaiety: the sleighing of Halifax assumed a new character; the "sleigh club" was established. Originating with the naval and military officers, the "Arcadian Union Club" included all the civilians who chose to become honorary members. The judges and other grave functionaries of the law, his honour the president, the official dignitaries of all degrees, the wealthiest merchants, and of course the whole of the garrison, composed a numerous and striking assemblage. The laws of the club were simple. A president and vice-president were elected every week, whose duty it was—the first, to lead; the latter, to bring up the *cortege*. Another duty, no less pleasing, devolved upon the former: on the days of meeting at the general place of rendezvous, in front of "the province building," after driving in procession through the town, the club drew up at the president's house, or, at a noted pastry-cook's, where he, the president, stood the brunt of "gingerbread and cherry-brandy" for the whole party. This was the luncheon *de rigueur* provided on the occasion; but if the roads were firm away all started for "the nine-mile house," at the extremity of the Halifax basin. Then might be seen the caracoling of steeds, the waving of plumes, the glancing of bright eyes, and the gorgeous display of gaudy trappings; then might be heard the silver tinkling of the collar bells, the laughter of the ladies, the merry cry of the charioteers, and the mellow notes of the bugle as they rang through the frosty air. It was a sight to warm the frozen, to arouse the torpid, to enliven the dullest. First led the way, with four bright bays, the sleigh named "The Aurora Borealis, or *Northern Light* Conveyance." Each carriage bore some appropriate designation, the body of the carriage, open to the sky, with an enormous bearskin for an apron; and, wrapped in shawls and sables, the beauties of Halifax were seen, dispensing smiles to all within their view. In the rumble behind were places for two more—one, whose delight was to blow the bugle; the other leaned beside him, and talked to the ladies.

Next, gaily decked in scarlet housings and embroidered collars, and scarcely to be restrained by their no less impetuous driver, came the "Reindeer," with two gallant steeds, in Indian file, or tandem fashion. Then followed a troop of charioteers, in tandem, curricle, unicorn, and single harness; first, the "Arctic Ranger," then the "Iceberg," and, close following, the "Esquimaux," the "Chebucto," the "Meteor," the "Walrus," and the "Mic-Mac;" some twenty or thirty sleighs formed the general cavalcade, and another four-in-hand, the "Avalanche"—which Mrs. A—— did not disdain to drive—brought up the rear of the procession. All was mirth and glee. The signal-bugle sounded, and *via!* we were off at twelve miles an hour on our track through the snow, with no sound to indicate our rapid flight but the quick harmony of the sleigh bells. Here was every motive for high spirits; youth, health, no care (save for an upset, and that not cared about), dear friends, and dearer objects still! There was also another end besides driving, which Lord Byron says is "the great *end* of travel"—there was the nine-mile house in perspective, a well known place of resort for the newly-wed; in fact, the Salt-hill of Halifax, where Arcadian honeymoons are passed. We soon drew near the haven of our wishes, where a famous luncheon was ready. Hot turkeys, smoking caribou steaks, reindeer tongues, pickled herrings from Digby, bear-hams from Armopolis, cherry-brandy, *noyeau*, and Prince Edward's Island whiskey. Here was enough to satisfy all tastes and appetites; a rapid drive and a thermometer 40 degrees below freezing-point were sufficient excuse for a *tuck-in*.

Accordingly all ate, drank, and made merry; we filled a health to the ladies, and coupled it with a speedy return to the nine-mile house, at which some blushed, others *tried* to look cross, and the "princess royal" laughed outright.

Returning, we reversed the order of driving, the lady led; and soon the word was passed for an impromptu party at the E—— Barracks.

Anecdotes of Colonel Leslie

The colonel used to relate the following, which seems to prove he was one of the strongest officers in the British army. It was considered a great feat of strength if, after considerable practice, a man could take the heavy Brown Bess of that day by the muzzle and hold it out at arm's length. One day when the subject was being discussed, the colonel, who had never done such a thing in his life, coolly took up a musket and held it out at arm's length, to the astonishment of everybody. The reputation of this feat reached the ears of the then Lord Kintore, who was a great patron of athletics; and when Colonel Leslie next came to Scotland, Lord Kintore happened to have one of the famous prize-fighters on a visit, and sent him to call on Colonel Leslie, who lived only a few miles off. The colonel on entering the room was surprised to find his venerable mother chatting away with "the gentleman," she not having, of course, the remotest idea of his real character. On the venerable lady quitting the room, the prize-fighter stated his errand, and then examined the colonel's arm, which he declared was the most powerful one he had ever seen in his life in a non-professional.

In Ireland the horse he rode could be managed by no other person, but Colonel Leslie controlled him by sheer strength alone. The horse, a stallion, felt it had a master.

ALSO FROM LEONAUR
AVAILABLE IN SOFTCOVER OR HARDCOVER WITH DUST JACKET

A HISTORY OF THE FRENCH & INDIAN WAR *by Arthur G. Bradley*—The Seven Years War as it was fought in the New World has always fascinated students of military history—here is the story of that confrontation.

WASHINGTON'S EARLY CAMPAIGNS *by James Hadden*—The French Post Expedition, Great Meadows and Braddock's Defeat—including Braddock's Orderly Books.

BOUQUET & THE OHIO INDIAN WAR *by Cyrus Cort & William Smith*—Two Accounts of the Campaigns of 1763-1764: Bouquet's Campaigns by Cyrus Cort & The History of Bouquet's Expeditions by William Smith.

NARRATIVES OF THE FRENCH & INDIAN WAR: 2 *by David Holden, Samuel Jenks, Lemuel Lyon, Mary Cochrane Rogers & Henry T. Blake*—Contains The Diary of Sergeant David Holden, Captain Samuel Jenks' Journal, The Journal of Lemuel Lyon, Journal of a French Officer at the Siege of Quebec, A Battle Fought on Snowshoes & The Battle of Lake George.

NARRATIVES OF THE FRENCH & INDIAN WAR *by Brown, Eastburn, Hawks & Putnam*—Ranger Brown's Narrative, The Adventures of Robert Eastburn, The Journal of Rufus Putnam—Provincial Infantry & Orderly Book and Journal of Major John Hawks on the Ticonderoga-Crown Point Campaign.

THE 7TH (QUEEN'S OWN) HUSSARS: Volume 1—1688-1792 *by C. R. B. Barrett*—As Dragoons During the Flanders Campaign, War of the Austrian Succession and the Seven Years War.

INDIA'S FREE LANCES *by H. G. Keene*—European Mercenary Commanders in Hindustan 1770-1820.

THE BENGAL EUROPEAN REGIMENT *by P. R. Innes*—An Elite Regiment of the Honourable East India Company 1756-1858.

MUSKET & TOMAHAWK *by Francis Parkman*—A Military History of the French & Indian War, 1753-1760.

THE BLACK WATCH AT TICONDEROGA *by Frederick B. Richards*—Campaigns in the French & Indian War.

QUEEN'S RANGERS *by Frederick B. Richards*—John Simcoe and his Rangers During the Revolutionary War for America.

AVAILABLE ONLINE AT **www.leonaur.com**
AND FROM ALL GOOD BOOK STORES

ALSO FROM LEONAUR
AVAILABLE IN SOFTCOVER OR HARDCOVER WITH DUST JACKET

JOURNALS OF ROBERT ROGERS OF THE RANGERS *by Robert Rogers*—The exploits of Rogers & the Rangers in his own words during 1755-1761 in the French & Indian War.

GALLOPING GUNS *by James Young*—The Experiences of an Officer of the Bengal Horse Artillery During the Second Maratha War 1804-1805.

GORDON *by Demetrius Charles Boulger*—The Career of Gordon of Khartoum.

THE BATTLE OF NEW ORLEANS *by Zachary F. Smith*—The final major engagement of the War of 1812.

THE TWO WARS OF MRS DUBERLY *by Frances Isabella Duberly*—An Intrepid Victorian Lady's Experience of the Crimea and Indian Mutiny.

WITH THE GUARDS' BRIGADE DURING THE BOER WAR *by Edward P. Lowry*—On Campaign from Bloemfontein to Koomati Poort and Back.

THE REBELLIOUS DUCHESS *by Paul F. S. Dermoncourt*—The Adventures of the Duchess of Berri and Her Attempt to Overthrow French Monarchy.

MEN OF THE MUTINY *by John Tulloch Nash & Henry Metcalfe*—Two Accounts of the Great Indian Mutiny of 1857: Fighting with the Bengal Yeomanry Cavalry & Private Metcalfe at Lucknow.

CAMPAIGN IN THE CRIMEA *by George Shuldham Peard*—The Recollections of an Officer of the 20th Regiment of Foot.

WITHIN SEBASTOPOL *by K. Hodasevich*—A Narrative of the Campaign in the Crimea, and of the Events of the Siege.

WITH THE CAVALRY TO AFGHANISTAN *by William Taylor*—The Experiences of a Trooper of H. M. 4th Light Dragoons During the First Afghan War.

THE CAWNPORE MAN *by Mowbray Thompson*—A First Hand Account of the Siege and Massacre During the Indian Mutiny By One of Four Survivors.

BRIGADE COMMANDER: AFGHANISTAN *by Henry Brooke*—The Journal of the Commander of the 2nd Infantry Brigade, Kandahar Field Force During the Second Afghan War.

BANCROFT OF THE BENGAL HORSE ARTILLERY *by N. W. Bancroft*—An Account of the First Sikh War 1845-1846.

AVAILABLE ONLINE AT **www.leonaur.com**
AND FROM ALL GOOD BOOK STORES

ALSO FROM LEONAUR
AVAILABLE IN SOFTCOVER OR HARDCOVER WITH DUST JACKET

AFGHANISTAN: THE BELEAGUERED BRIGADE *by G. R. Gleig*—An Account of Sale's Brigade During the First Afghan War.

IN THE RANKS OF THE C. I. V *by Erskine Childers*—With the City Imperial Volunteer Battery (Honourable Artillery Company) in the Second Boer War.

THE BENGAL NATIVE ARMY *by F. G. Cardew*—An Invaluable Reference Resource.

THE 7TH (QUEEN'S OWN) HUSSARS: Volume 4—1688-1914 *by C. R. B. Barrett*—Uniforms, Equipment, Weapons, Traditions, the Services of Notable Officers and Men & the Appendices to All Volumes—Volume 4: 1688-1914.

THE SWORD OF THE CROWN *by Eric W. Sheppard*—A History of the British Army to 1914.

THE 7TH (QUEEN'S OWN) HUSSARS: Volume 3—1818-1914 *by C. R. B. Barrett*—On Campaign During the Canadian Rebellion, the Indian Mutiny, the Sudan, Matabeleland, Mashonaland and the Boer War Volume 3: 1818-1914.

THE KHARTOUM CAMPAIGN *by Bennet Burleigh*—A Special Correspondent's View of the Reconquest of the Sudan by British and Egyptian Forces under Kitchener—1898.

EL PUCHERO *by Richard McSherry*—The Letters of a Surgeon of Volunteers During Scott's Campaign of the American-Mexican War 1847-1848.

RIFLEMAN SAHIB *by E. Maude*—The Recollections of an Officer of the Bombay Rifles During the Southern Mahratta Campaign, Second Sikh War, Persian Campaign and Indian Mutiny.

THE KING'S HUSSAR *by Edwin Mole*—The Recollections of a 14th (King's) Hussar During the Victorian Era.

JOHN COMPANY'S CAVALRYMAN *by William Johnson*—The Experiences of a British Soldier in the Crimea, the Persian Campaign and the Indian Mutiny.

COLENSO & DURNFORD'S ZULU WAR *by Frances E. Colenso & Edward Durnford*—The first and possibly the most important history of the Zulu War.

U. S. DRAGOON *by Samuel E. Chamberlain*—Experiences in the Mexican War 1846-48 and on the South Western Frontier.

AVAILABLE ONLINE AT **www.leonaur.com**
AND FROM ALL GOOD BOOK STORES

ALSO FROM LEONAUR
AVAILABLE IN SOFTCOVER OR HARDCOVER WITH DUST JACKET

THE 2ND MAORI WAR: 1860-1861 *by Robert Carey*—The Second Maori War, or First Taranaki War, one more bloody instalment of the conflicts between European settlers and the indigenous Maori people.

A JOURNAL OF THE SECOND SIKH WAR *by Daniel A. Sandford*—The Experiences of an Ensign of the 2nd Bengal European Regiment During the Campaign in the Punjab, India, 1848-49.

THE LIGHT INFANTRY OFFICER *by John H. Cooke*—The Experiences of an Officer of the 43rd Light Infantry in America During the War of 1812.

BUSHVELDT CARBINEERS *by George Witton*—The War Against the Boers in South Africa and the 'Breaker' Morant Incident.

LAKE'S CAMPAIGNS IN INDIA *by Hugh Pearse*—The Second Anglo Maratha War, 1803-1807.

BRITAIN IN AFGHANISTAN 1: THE FIRST AFGHAN WAR 1839-42 *by Archibald Forbes*—From invasion to destruction-a British military disaster.

BRITAIN IN AFGHANISTAN 2: THE SECOND AFGHAN WAR 1878-80 *by Archibald Forbes*—This is the history of the Second Afghan War-another episode of British military history typified by savagery, massacre, siege and battles.

UP AMONG THE PANDIES *by Vivian Dering Majendie*—Experiences of a British Officer on Campaign During the Indian Mutiny, 1857-1858.

MUTINY: 1857 *by James Humphries*—Authentic Voices from the Indian Mutiny-First Hand Accounts of Battles, Sieges and Personal Hardships.

BLOW THE BUGLE, DRAW THE SWORD *by W. H. G. Kingston*—The Wars, Campaigns, Regiments and Soldiers of the British & Indian Armies During the Victorian Era, 1839-1898.

WAR BEYOND THE DRAGON PAGODA *by Major J. J. Snodgrass*—A Personal Narrative of the First Anglo-Burmese War 1824 - 1826.

THE HERO OF ALIWAL *by James Humphries*—The Campaigns of Sir Harry Smith in India, 1843-1846, During the Gwalior War & the First Sikh War.

ALL FOR A SHILLING A DAY *by Donald F. Featherstone*—The story of H.M. 16th, the Queen's Lancers During the first Sikh War 1845-1846.

AVAILABLE ONLINE AT **www.leonaur.com**
AND FROM ALL GOOD BOOK STORES

ALSO FROM LEONAUR
AVAILABLE IN SOFTCOVER OR HARDCOVER WITH DUST JACKET

THE FALL OF THE MOGHUL EMPIRE OF HINDUSTAN *by H. G. Keene*—By the beginning of the nineteenth century, as British and Indian armies under Lake and Wellesley dominated the scene, a little over half a century of conflict brought the Moghul Empire to its knees.

LADY SALE'S AFGHANISTAN *by Florentia Sale*—An Indomitable Victorian Lady's Account of the Retreat from Kabul During the First Afghan War.

THE CAMPAIGN OF MAGENTA AND SOLFERINO 1859 *by Harold Carmichael Wylly*—The Decisive Conflict for the Unification of Italy.

FRENCH'S CAVALRY CAMPAIGN *by J. G. Maydon*—A Special Correspondent's View of British Army Mounted Troops During the Boer War.

CAVALRY AT WATERLOO *by Sir Evelyn Wood*—British Mounted Troops During the Campaign of 1815.

THE SUBALTERN *by George Robert Gleig*—The Experiences of an Officer of the 85th Light Infantry During the Peninsular War.

NAPOLEON AT BAY, 1814 *by F. Loraine Petre*—The Campaigns to the Fall of the First Empire.

NAPOLEON AND THE CAMPAIGN OF 1806 *by Colonel Vachée*—The Napoleonic Method of Organisation and Command to the Battles of Jena & Auerstädt.

THE COMPLETE ADVENTURES IN THE CONNAUGHT RANGERS *by William Grattan*—The 88th Regiment during the Napoleonic Wars by a Serving Officer.

BUGLER AND OFFICER OF THE RIFLES *by William Green & Harry Smith*—With the 95th (Rifles) during the Peninsular & Waterloo Campaigns of the Napoleonic Wars.

NAPOLEONIC WAR STORIES *by Sir Arthur Quiller-Couch*—Tales of soldiers, spies, battles & sieges from the Peninsular & Waterloo campaigns.

CAPTAIN OF THE 95TH (RIFLES) *by Jonathan Leach*—An officer of Wellington's sharpshooters during the Peninsular, South of France and Waterloo campaigns of the Napoleonic wars.

RIFLEMAN COSTELLO *by Edward Costello*—The adventures of a soldier of the 95th (Rifles) in the Peninsular & Waterloo Campaigns of the Napoleonic wars.

AVAILABLE ONLINE AT **www.leonaur.com**
AND FROM ALL GOOD BOOK STORES

ALSO FROM LEONAUR
AVAILABLE IN SOFTCOVER OR HARDCOVER WITH DUST JACKET

AT THEM WITH THE BAYONET *by Donald F. Featherstone*—The first Anglo-Sikh War 1845-1846.

STEPHEN CRANE'S BATTLES *by Stephen Crane*—Nine Decisive Battles Recounted by the Author of 'The Red Badge of Courage'.

THE GURKHA WAR *by H. T. Prinsep*—The Anglo-Nepalese Conflict in North East India 1814-1816.

FIRE & BLOOD *by G. R. Gleig*—The burning of Washington & the battle of New Orleans, 1814, through the eyes of a young British soldier.

SOUND ADVANCE! *by Joseph Anderson*—Experiences of an officer of HM 50th regiment in Australia, Burma & the Gwalior war.

THE CAMPAIGN OF THE INDUS *by Thomas Holdsworth*—Experiences of a British Officer of the 2nd (Queen's Royal) Regiment in the Campaign to Place Shah Shuja on the Throne of Afghanistan 1838 - 1840.

WITH THE MADRAS EUROPEAN REGIMENT IN BURMA *by John Butler*—The Experiences of an Officer of the Honourable East India Company's Army During the First Anglo-Burmese War 1824 - 1826.

IN ZULULAND WITH THE BRITISH ARMY *by Charles L. Norris-Newman*—The Anglo-Zulu war of 1879 through the first-hand experiences of a special correspondent.

BESIEGED IN LUCKNOW *by Martin Richard Gubbins*—The first Anglo-Sikh War 1845-1846.

A TIGER ON HORSEBACK *by L. March Phillips*—The Experiences of a Trooper & Officer of Rimington's Guides - The Tigers - during the Anglo-Boer war 1899 - 1902.

SEPOYS, SIEGE & STORM *by Charles John Griffiths*—The Experiences of a young officer of H.M.'s 61st Regiment at Ferozepore, Delhi ridge and at the fall of Delhi during the Indian mutiny 1857.

CAMPAIGNING IN ZULULAND *by W. E. Montague*—Experiences on campaign during the Zulu war of 1879 with the 94th Regiment.

THE STORY OF THE GUIDES *by G.J. Younghusband*—The Exploits of the Soldiers of the famous Indian Army Regiment from the northwest frontier 1847 - 1900.

AVAILABLE ONLINE AT **www.leonaur.com**
AND FROM ALL GOOD BOOK STORES

ALSO FROM LEONAUR
AVAILABLE IN SOFTCOVER OR HARDCOVER WITH DUST JACKET

ZULU:1879 *by D.C.F. Moodie & the Leonaur Editors*—The Anglo-Zulu War of 1879 from contemporary sources: First Hand Accounts, Interviews, Dispatches, Official Documents & Newspaper Reports.

THE RED DRAGOON *by W.J. Adams*—With the 7th Dragoon Guards in the Cape of Good Hope against the Boers & the Kaffir tribes during the 'war of the axe' 1843-48'.

THE RECOLLECTIONS OF SKINNER OF SKINNER'S HORSE *by James Skinner*—James Skinner and his 'Yellow Boys' Irregular cavalry in the wars of India between the British, Mahratta, Rajput, Mogul, Sikh & Pindarree Forces.

A CAVALRY OFFICER DURING THE SEPOY REVOLT *by A. R. D. Mackenzie*—Experiences with the 3rd Bengal Light Cavalry, the Guides and Sikh Irregular Cavalry from the outbreak to Delhi and Lucknow.

A NORFOLK SOLDIER IN THE FIRST SIKH WAR *by J W Baldwin*—Experiences of a private of H.M. 9th Regiment of Foot in the battles for the Punjab, India 1845-6.

TOMMY ATKINS' WAR STORIES: 14 FIRST HAND ACCOUNTS—Fourteen first hand accounts from the ranks of the British Army during Queen Victoria's Empire.

THE WATERLOO LETTERS *by H. T. Siborne*—Accounts of the Battle by British Officers for its Foremost Historian.

NEY: GENERAL OF CAVALRY VOLUME 1—1769-1799 *by Antoine Bulos*—The Early Career of a Marshal of the First Empire.

NEY: MARSHAL OF FRANCE VOLUME 2—1799-1805 *by Antoine Bulos*—The Early Career of a Marshal of the First Empire.

AIDE-DE-CAMP TO NAPOLEON *by Philippe-Paul de Ségur*—For anyone interested in the Napoleonic Wars this book, written by one who was intimate with the strategies and machinations of the Emperor, will be essential reading.

TWILIGHT OF EMPIRE *by Sir Thomas Ussher & Sir George Cockburn*—Two accounts of Napoleon's Journeys in Exile to Elba and St. Helena: Narrative of Events by Sir Thomas Ussher & Napoleon's Last Voyage: Extract of a diary by Sir George Cockburn.

PRIVATE WHEELER *by William Wheeler*—The letters of a soldier of the 51st Light Infantry during the Peninsular War & at Waterloo.

AVAILABLE ONLINE AT **www.leonaur.com**
AND FROM ALL GOOD BOOK STORES

ALSO FROM LEONAUR
AVAILABLE IN SOFTCOVER OR HARDCOVER WITH DUST JACKET

OFFICERS & GENTLEMEN *by Peter Hawker & William Graham*—Two Accounts of British Officers During the Peninsula War: Officer of Light Dragoons by Peter Hawker & Campaign in Portugal and Spain by William Graham.

THE WALCHEREN EXPEDITION *by Anonymous*—The Experiences of a British Officer of the 81st Regt. During the Campaign in the Low Countries of 1809.

LADIES OF WATERLOO *by Charlotte A. Eaton, Magdalene de Lancey & Juana Smith*—The Experiences of Three Women During the Campaign of 1815: Waterloo Days by Charlotte A. Eaton, A Week at Waterloo by Magdalene de Lancey & Juana's Story by Juana Smith.

JOURNAL OF AN OFFICER IN THE KING'S GERMAN LEGION *by John Frederick Hering*—Recollections of Campaigning During the Napoleonic Wars.

JOURNAL OF AN ARMY SURGEON IN THE PENINSULAR WAR *by Charles Boutflower*—The Recollections of a British Army Medical Man on Campaign During the Napoleonic Wars.

ON CAMPAIGN WITH MOORE AND WELLINGTON *by Anthony Hamilton*—The Experiences of a Soldier of the 43rd Regiment During the Peninsular War.

THE ROAD TO AUSTERLITZ *by R. G. Burton*—Napoleon's Campaign of 1805.

SOLDIERS OF NAPOLEON *by A. J. Doisy De Villargennes & Arthur Chuquet*—The Experiences of the Men of the French First Empire: Under the Eagles by A. J. Doisy De Villargennes & Voices of 1812 by Arthur Chuquet.

INVASION OF FRANCE, 1814 *by F. W. O. Maycock*—The Final Battles of the Napoleonic First Empire.

LEIPZIG—A CONFLICT OF TITANS *by Frederic Shoberl*—A Personal Experience of the 'Battle of the Nations' During the Napoleonic Wars, October 14th-19th, 1813.

SLASHERS *by Charles Cadell*—The Campaigns of the 28th Regiment of Foot During the Napoleonic Wars by a Serving Officer.

BATTLE IMPERIAL *by Charles William Vane*—The Campaigns in Germany & France for the Defeat of Napoleon 1813-1814.

SWIFT & BOLD *by Gibbes Rigaud*—The 60th Rifles During the Peninsula War.

AVAILABLE ONLINE AT **www.leonaur.com**
AND FROM ALL GOOD BOOK STORES

ALSO FROM LEONAUR
AVAILABLE IN SOFTCOVER OR HARDCOVER WITH DUST JACKET

ADVENTURES OF A YOUNG RIFLEMAN *by Johann Christian Maempel*—The Experiences of a Saxon in the French & British Armies During the Napoleonic Wars.

THE HUSSAR *by Norbert Landsheit & G. R. Gleig*—A German Cavalryman in British Service Throughout the Napoleonic Wars.

RECOLLECTIONS OF THE PENINSULA *by Moyle Sherer*—An Officer of the 34th Regiment of Foot—'The Cumberland Gentlemen'—on Campaign Against Napoleon's French Army in Spain.

MARINE OF REVOLUTION & CONSULATE *by Moreau de Jonnès*—The Recollections of a French Soldier of the Revolutionary Wars 1791-1804.

GENTLEMEN IN RED *by John Dobbs & Robert Knowles*—Two Accounts of British Infantry Officers During the Peninsular War Recollections of an Old 52nd Man by John Dobbs An Officer of Fusiliers by Robert Knowles.

CORPORAL BROWN'S CAMPAIGNS IN THE LOW COUNTRIES *by Robert Brown*—Recollections of a Coldstream Guard in the Early Campaigns Against Revolutionary France 1793-1795.

THE 7TH (QUEENS OWN) HUSSARS: Volume 2—1793-1815 *by C. R. B. Barrett*—During the Campaigns in the Low Countries & the Peninsula and Waterloo Campaigns of the Napoleonic Wars. Volume 2: 1793-1815.

THE MARENGO CAMPAIGN 1800 *by Herbert H. Sargent*—The Victory that Completed the Austrian Defeat in Italy.

DONALDSON OF THE 94TH—SCOTS BRIGADE *by Joseph Donaldson*—The Recollections of a Soldier During the Peninsula & South of France Campaigns of the Napoleonic Wars.

A CONSCRIPT FOR EMPIRE *by Philippe as told to Johann Christian Maempel*—The Experiences of a Young German Conscript During the Napoleonic Wars.

JOURNAL OF THE CAMPAIGN OF 1815 *by Alexander Cavalié Mercer*—The Experiences of an Officer of the Royal Horse Artillery During the Waterloo Campaign.

NAPOLEON'S CAMPAIGNS IN POLAND 1806-7 *by Robert Wilson*—The campaign in Poland from the Russian side of the conflict.

AVAILABLE ONLINE AT **www.leonaur.com**
AND FROM ALL GOOD BOOK STORES

ALSO FROM LEONAUR
AVAILABLE IN SOFTCOVER OR HARDCOVER WITH DUST JACKET

OMPTEDA OF THE KING'S GERMAN LEGION by *Christian von Ompteda*—A Hanoverian Officer on Campaign Against Napoleon.

LIEUTENANT SIMMONS OF THE 95TH (RIFLES) by *George Simmons*—Recollections of the Peninsula, South of France & Waterloo Campaigns of the Napoleonic Wars.

A HORSEMAN FOR THE EMPEROR by *Jean Baptiste Gazzola*—A Cavalryman of Napoleon's Army on Campaign Throughout the Napoleonic Wars.

SERGEANT LAWRENCE by *William Lawrence*—With the 40th Regt. of Foot in South America, the Peninsular War & at Waterloo.

CAMPAIGNS WITH THE FIELD TRAIN by *Richard D. Henegan*—Experiences of a British Officer During the Peninsula and Waterloo Campaigns of the Napoleonic Wars.

CAVALRY SURGEON by *S. D. Broughton*—On Campaign Against Napoleon in the Peninsula & South of France During the Napoleonic Wars 1812-1814.

MEN OF THE RIFLES by *Thomas Knight, Henry Curling & Jonathan Leach*—The Reminiscences of Thomas Knight of the 95th (Rifles) by Thomas Knight, Henry Curling's Anecdotes by Henry Curling & The Field Services of the Rifle Brigade from its Formation to Waterloo by Jonathan Leach.

THE ULM CAMPAIGN 1805 by *F. N. Maude*—Napoleon and the Defeat of the Austrian Army During the 'War of the Third Coalition'.

SOLDIERING WITH THE 'DIVISION' by *Thomas Garrety*—The Military Experiences of an Infantryman of the 43rd Regiment During the Napoleonic Wars.

SERGEANT MORRIS OF THE 73RD FOOT by *Thomas Morris*—The Experiences of a British Infantryman During the Napoleonic Wars-Including Campaigns in Germany and at Waterloo.

A VOICE FROM WATERLOO by *Edward Cotton*—The Personal Experiences of a British Cavalryman Who Became a Battlefield Guide and Authority on the Campaign of 1815.

NAPOLEON AND HIS MARSHALS by *J. T. Headley*—The Men of the First Empire.

AVAILABLE ONLINE AT **www.leonaur.com**
AND FROM ALL GOOD BOOK STORES

ALSO FROM LEONAUR
AVAILABLE IN SOFTCOVER OR HARDCOVER WITH DUST JACKET

COLBORNE: A SINGULAR TALENT FOR WAR by *John Colborne*—The Napoleonic Wars Career of One of Wellington's Most Highly Valued Officers in Egypt, Holland, Italy, the Peninsula and at Waterloo.

NAPOLEON'S RUSSIAN CAMPAIGN by *Philippe Henri de Segur*—The Invasion, Battles and Retreat by an Aide-de-Camp on the Emperor's Staff.

WITH THE LIGHT DIVISION by *John H. Cooke*—The Experiences of an Officer of the 43rd Light Infantry in the Peninsula and South of France During the Napoleonic Wars.

WELLINGTON AND THE PYRENEES CAMPAIGN VOLUME I: FROM VITORIA TO THE BIDASSOA by *F. C. Beatson*—The final phase of the campaign in the Iberian Peninsula.

WELLINGTON AND THE INVASION OF FRANCE VOLUME II: THE BIDASSOA TO THE BATTLE OF THE NIVELLE by *F. C. Beatson*—The final phase of the campaign in the Iberian Peninsula.

WELLINGTON AND THE FALL OF FRANCE VOLUME III: THE GAVES AND THE BATTLE OF ORTHEZ by *F. C. Beatson*—The final phase of the campaign in the Iberian Peninsula.

NAPOLEON'S IMPERIAL GUARD: FROM MARENGO TO WATERLOO by *J. T. Headley*—The story of Napoleon's Imperial Guard and the men who commanded them.

BATTLES & SIEGES OF THE PENINSULAR WAR by *W. H. Fitchett*—Corunna, Busaco, Albuera, Ciudad Rodrigo, Badajos, Salamanca, San Sebastian & Others.

SERGEANT GUILLEMARD: THE MAN WHO SHOT NELSON? by *Robert Guillemard*—A Soldier of the Infantry of the French Army of Napoleon on Campaign Throughout Europe.

WITH THE GUARDS ACROSS THE PYRENEES by *Robert Batty*—The Experiences of a British Officer of Wellington's Army During the Battles for the Fall of Napoleonic France, 1813 .

A STAFF OFFICER IN THE PENINSULA by *E. W. Buckham*—An Officer of the British Staff Corps Cavalry During the Peninsula Campaign of the Napoleonic Wars.

THE LEIPZIG CAMPAIGN: 1813—NAPOLEON AND THE "BATTLE OF THE NATIONS" by *F. N. Maude*—Colonel Maude's analysis of Napoleon's campaign of 1813 around Leipzig.

AVAILABLE ONLINE AT **www.leonaur.com**
AND FROM ALL GOOD BOOK STORES

ALSO FROM LEONAUR
AVAILABLE IN SOFTCOVER OR HARDCOVER WITH DUST JACKET

BUGEAUD: A PACK WITH A BATON *by Thomas Robert Bugeaud*—The Early Campaigns of a Soldier of Napoleon's Army Who Would Become a Marshal of France.

WATERLOO RECOLLECTIONS *by Frederick Llewellyn*—Rare First Hand Accounts, Letters, Reports and Retellings from the Campaign of 1815.

SERGEANT NICOL *by Daniel Nicol*—The Experiences of a Gordon Highlander During the Napoleonic Wars in Egypt, the Peninsula and France.

THE JENA CAMPAIGN: 1806 *by F. N. Maude*—The Twin Battles of Jena & Auerstadt Between Napoleon's French and the Prussian Army.

PRIVATE O'NEIL *by Charles O'Neil*—The recollections of an Irish Rogue of H. M. 28th Regt.—The Slashers—during the Peninsula & Waterloo campaigns of the Napoleonic war.

ROYAL HIGHLANDER *by James Anton*—A soldier of H.M 42nd (Royal) Highlanders during the Peninsular, South of France & Waterloo Campaigns of the Napoleonic Wars.

CAPTAIN BLAZE *by Elzéar Blaze*—Life in Napoleons Army.

LEJEUNE VOLUME 1 *by Louis-François Lejeune*—The Napoleonic Wars through the Experiences of an Officer on Berthier's Staff.

LEJEUNE VOLUME 2 *by Louis-François Lejeune*—The Napoleonic Wars through the Experiences of an Officer on Berthier's Staff.

CAPTAIN COIGNET *by Jean-Roch Coignet*—A Soldier of Napoleon's Imperial Guard from the Italian Campaign to Russia and Waterloo.

FUSILIER COOPER *by John S. Cooper*—Experiences in the 7th (Royal) Fusiliers During the Peninsular Campaign of the Napoleonic Wars and the American Campaign to New Orleans.

FIGHTING NAPOLEON'S EMPIRE *by Joseph Anderson*—The Campaigns of a British Infantryman in Italy, Egypt, the Peninsular & the West Indies During the Napoleonic Wars.

CHASSEUR BARRES *by Jean-Baptiste Barres*—The experiences of a French Infantryman of the Imperial Guard at Austerlitz, Jena, Eylau, Friedland, in the Peninsular, Lutzen, Bautzen, Zinnwald and Hanau during the Napoleonic Wars.

AVAILABLE ONLINE AT **www.leonaur.com**
AND FROM ALL GOOD BOOK STORES

ALSO FROM LEONAUR
AVAILABLE IN SOFTCOVER OR HARDCOVER WITH DUST JACKET

CAPTAIN COIGNET by *Jean-Roch Coignet*—A Soldier of Napoleon's Imperial Guard from the Italian Campaign to Russia and Waterloo.

HUSSAR ROCCA by *Albert Jean Michel de Rocca*—A French cavalry officer's experiences of the Napoleonic Wars and his views on the Peninsular Campaigns against the Spanish, British And Guerilla Armies.

MARINES TO 95TH (RIFLES) by *Thomas Fernyhough*—The military experiences of Robert Fernyhough during the Napoleonic Wars.

LIGHT BOB by *Robert Blakeney*—The experiences of a young officer in H.M 28th & 36th regiments of the British Infantry during the Peninsular Campaign of the Napoleonic Wars 1804 - 1814.

WITH WELLINGTON'S LIGHT CAVALRY by *William Tomkinson*—The Experiences of an officer of the 16th Light Dragoons in the Peninsular and Waterloo campaigns of the Napoleonic Wars.

SERGEANT BOURGOGNE by *Adrien Bourgogne*—With Napoleon's Imperial Guard in the Russian Campaign and on the Retreat from Moscow 1812 - 13.

SURTEES OF THE 95TH (RIFLES) by *William Surtees*—A Soldier of the 95th (Rifles) in the Peninsular campaign of the Napoleonic Wars.

SWORDS OF HONOUR by *Henry Newbolt & Stanley L. Wood*—The Careers of Six Outstanding Officers from the Napoleonic Wars, the Wars for India and the American Civil War.

ENSIGN BELL IN THE PENINSULAR WAR by *George Bell*—The Experiences of a young British Soldier of the 34th Regiment 'The Cumberland Gentlemen' in the Napoleonic wars.

HUSSAR IN WINTER by *Alexander Gordon*—A British Cavalry Officer during the retreat to Corunna in the Peninsular campaign of the Napoleonic Wars.

THE COMPLEAT RIFLEMAN HARRIS by *Benjamin Harris as told to and transcribed by Captain Henry Curling, 52nd Regt. of Foot*—The adventures of a soldier of the 95th (Rifles) during the Peninsular Campaign of the Napoleonic Wars.

THE ADVENTURES OF A LIGHT DRAGOON by *George Farmer & G.R. Gleig*—A cavalryman during the Peninsular & Waterloo Campaigns, in captivity & at the siege of Bhurtpore, India.

AVAILABLE ONLINE AT **www.leonaur.com**
AND FROM ALL GOOD BOOK STORES

ALSO FROM LEONAUR
AVAILABLE IN SOFTCOVER OR HARDCOVER WITH DUST JACKET

THE LIFE OF THE REAL BRIGADIER GERARD VOLUME 1—THE YOUNG HUSSAR 1782-1807 *by Jean-Baptiste De Marbot*—A French Cavalryman Of the Napoleonic Wars at Marengo, Austerlitz, Jena, Eylau & Friedland.

THE LIFE OF THE REAL BRIGADIER GERARD VOLUME 2—IMPERIAL AIDE-DE-CAMP 1807-1811 *by Jean-Baptiste De Marbot*—A French Cavalryman of the Napoleonic Wars at Saragossa, Landshut, Eckmuhl, Ratisbon, Aspern-Essling, Wagram, Busaco & Torres Vedras.

THE LIFE OF THE REAL BRIGADIER GERARD VOLUME 3—COLONEL OF CHASSEURS 1811-1815 *by Jean-Baptiste De Marbot*—A French Cavalryman in the retreat from Moscow, Lutzen, Bautzen, Katzbach, Leipzig, Hanau & Waterloo.

THE INDIAN WAR OF 1864 *by Eugene Ware*—The Experiences of a Young Officer of the 7th Iowa Cavalry on the Western Frontier During the Civil War.

THE MARCH OF DESTINY *by Charles E. Young & V. Devinny*—Dangers of the Trail in 1865 by Charles E. Young & The Story of a Pioneer by V. Devinny, two Accounts of Early Emigrants to Colorado.

CROSSING THE PLAINS *by William Audley Maxwell*—A First Hand Narrative of the Early Pioneer Trail to California in 1857.

CHIEF OF SCOUTS *by William F. Drannan*—A Pilot to Emigrant and Government Trains, Across the Plains of the Western Frontier.

THIRTY-ONE YEARS ON THE PLAINS AND IN THE MOUNTAINS *by William F. Drannan*—William Drannan was born to be a pioneer, hunter, trapper and wagon train guide during the momentous days of the Great American West.

THE INDIAN WARS VOLUNTEER *by William Thompson*—Recollections of the Conflict Against the Snakes, Shoshone, Bannocks, Modocs and Other Native Tribes of the American North West.

THE 4TH TENNESSEE CAVALRY *by George B. Guild*—The Services of Smith's Regiment of Confederate Cavalry by One of its Officers.

COLONEL WORTHINGTON'S SHILOH *by T. Worthington*—The Tennessee Campaign, 1862, by an Officer of the Ohio Volunteers.

FOUR YEARS IN THE SADDLE *by W. L. Curry*—The History of the First Regiment Ohio Volunteer Cavalry in the American Civil War.

AVAILABLE ONLINE AT **www.leonaur.com**
AND FROM ALL GOOD BOOK STORES

ALSO FROM LEONAUR
AVAILABLE IN SOFTCOVER OR HARDCOVER WITH DUST JACKET

LIFE IN THE ARMY OF NORTHERN VIRGINIA by *Carlton McCarthy*—The Observations of a Confederate Artilleryman of Cutshaw's Battalion During the American Civil War 1861-1865.

HISTORY OF THE CAVALRY OF THE ARMY OF THE POTOMAC by *Charles D. Rhodes*—Including Pope's Army of Virginia and the Cavalry Operations in West Virginia During the American Civil War.

CAMP-FIRE AND COTTON-FIELD by *Thomas W. Knox*—A New York Herald Correspondent's View of the American Civil War.

SERGEANT STILLWELL by *Leander Stillwell*—The Experiences of a Union Army Soldier of the 61st Illinois Infantry During the American Civil War.

STONEWALL'S CANNONEER by *Edward A. Moore*—Experiences with the Rockbridge Artillery, Confederate Army of Northern Virginia, During the American Civil War.

THE SIXTH CORPS by *George Stevens*—The Army of the Potomac, Union Army, During the American Civil War.

THE RAILROAD RAIDERS by *William Pittenger*—An Ohio Volunteers Recollections of the Andrews Raid to Disrupt the Confederate Railroad in Georgia During the American Civil War.

CITIZEN SOLDIER by *John Beatty*—An Account of the American Civil War by a Union Infantry Officer of Ohio Volunteers Who Became a Brigadier General.

COX: PERSONAL RECOLLECTIONS OF THE CIVIL WAR--VOLUME 1 by *Jacob Dolson Cox*—West Virginia, Kanawha Valley, Gauley Bridge, Cotton Mountain, South Mountain, Antietam, the Morgan Raid & the East Tennessee Campaign.

COX: PERSONAL RECOLLECTIONS OF THE CIVIL WAR--VOLUME 2 by *Jacob Dolson Cox*—Siege of Knoxville, East Tennessee, Atlanta Campaign, the Nashville Campaign & the North Carolina Campaign.

KERSHAW'S BRIGADE VOLUME 1 by *D. Augustus Dickert*—Manassas, Seven Pines, Sharpsburg (Antietam), Fredricksburg, Chancellorsville, Gettysburg, Chickamauga, Chattanooga, Fort Sanders & Bean Station.

KERSHAW'S BRIGADE VOLUME 2 by *D. Augustus Dickert*—At the wilderness, Cold Harbour, Petersburg, The Shenandoah Valley and Cedar Creek..

AVAILABLE ONLINE AT **www.leonaur.com**
AND FROM ALL GOOD BOOK STORES

ALSO FROM LEONAUR
AVAILABLE IN SOFTCOVER OR HARDCOVER WITH DUST JACKET

THE RELUCTANT REBEL by *William G. Stevenson*—A young Kentuckian's experiences in the Confederate Infantry & Cavalry during the American Civil War..

BOOTS AND SADDLES by *Elizabeth B. Custer*—The experiences of General Custer's Wife on the Western Plains.

FANNIE BEERS' CIVIL WAR by *Fannie A. Beers*—A Confederate Lady's Experiences of Nursing During the Campaigns & Battles of the American Civil War.

LADY SALE'S AFGHANISTAN by *Florentia Sale*—An Indomitable Victorian Lady's Account of the Retreat from Kabul During the First Afghan War.

THE TWO WARS OF MRS DUBERLY by *Frances Isabella Duberly*—An Intrepid Victorian Lady's Experience of the Crimea and Indian Mutiny.

THE REBELLIOUS DUCHESS by *Paul F. S. Dermoncourt*—The Adventures of the Duchess of Berri and Her Attempt to Overthrow French Monarchy.

LADIES OF WATERLOO by *Charlotte A. Eaton, Magdalene de Lancey & Juana Smith*—The Experiences of Three Women During the Campaign of 1815: Waterloo Days by Charlotte A. Eaton, A Week at Waterloo by Magdalene de Lancey & Juana's Story by Juana Smith.

TWO YEARS BEFORE THE MAST by *Richard Henry Dana. Jr.*—The account of one young man's experiences serving on board a sailing brig—the Penelope—bound for California, between the years 1834-36.

A SAILOR OF KING GEORGE by *Frederick Hoffman*—From Midshipman to Captain—Recollections of War at Sea in the Napoleonic Age 1793-1815.

LORDS OF THE SEA by *A. T. Mahan*—Great Captains of the Royal Navy During the Age of Sail.

COGGESHALL'S VOYAGES: VOLUME 1 by *George Coggeshall*—The Recollections of an American Schooner Captain.

COGGESHALL'S VOYAGES: VOLUME 2 by *George Coggeshall*—The Recollections of an American Schooner Captain.

TWILIGHT OF EMPIRE by *Sir Thomas Ussher & Sir George Cockburn*—Two accounts of Napoleon's Journeys in Exile to Elba and St. Helena: Narrative of Events by Sir Thomas Ussher & Napoleon's Last Voyage: Extract of a diary by Sir George Cockburn.

AVAILABLE ONLINE AT **www.leonaur.com**
AND FROM ALL GOOD BOOK STORES

ALSO FROM LEONAUR
AVAILABLE IN SOFTCOVER OR HARDCOVER WITH DUST JACKET

ESCAPE FROM THE FRENCH by *Edward Boys*—A Young Royal Navy Midshipman's Adventures During the Napoleonic War.

THE VOYAGE OF H.M.S. PANDORA by *Edward Edwards R. N. & George Hamilton, edited by Basil Thomson*—In Pursuit of the Mutineers of the Bounty in the South Seas—1790-1791.

MEDUSA by *J. B. Henry Savigny and Alexander Correard and Charlotte-Adélaïde Dard*—Narrative of a Voyage to Senegal in 1816 & The Sufferings of the Picard Family After the Shipwreck of the Medusa.

THE SEA WAR OF 1812 VOLUME 1 by *A. T. Mahan*—A History of the Maritime Conflict.

THE SEA WAR OF 1812 VOLUME 2 by *A. T. Mahan*—A History of the Maritime Conflict.

WETHERELL OF H. M. S. HUSSAR by *John Wetherell*—The Recollections of an Ordinary Seaman of the Royal Navy During the Napoleonic Wars.

THE NAVAL BRIGADE IN NATAL by *C. R. N. Burne*—With the Guns of H. M. S. Terrible & H. M. S. Tartar during the Boer War 1899-1900.

THE VOYAGE OF H. M. S. BOUNTY by *William Bligh*—The True Story of an 18th Century Voyage of Exploration and Mutiny.

SHIPWRECK! by *William Gilly*—The Royal Navy's Disasters at Sea 1793-1849.

KING'S CUTTERS AND SMUGGLERS: 1700-1855 by *E. Keble Chatterton*—A unique period of maritime history-from the beginning of the eighteenth to the middle of the nineteenth century when British seamen risked all to smuggle valuable goods from wool to tea and spirits from and to the Continent.

CONFEDERATE BLOCKADE RUNNER by *John Wilkinson*—The Personal Recollections of an Officer of the Confederate Navy.

NAVAL BATTLES OF THE NAPOLEONIC WARS by *W. H. Fitchett*—Cape St.Vincent, the Nile, Cadiz, Copenhagen, Trafalgar & Others.

PRISONERS OF THE RED DESERT by *R. S. Gwatkin-Williams*—The Adventures of the Crew of the Tara During the First World War.

U-BOAT WAR 1914-1918 by *James B. Connolly/Karl von Schenk*—Two Contrasting Accounts from Both Sides of the Conflict at Sea D uring the Great War.

AVAILABLE ONLINE AT **www.leonaur.com**
AND FROM ALL GOOD BOOK STORES

www.ingramcontent.com/pod-product-compliance
Lightning Source LLC
Chambersburg PA
CBHW030229170426
43201CB00006B/163